Dictionary of Developmental Psychology

revised edition

Ian Stuart-Hamilton

Jessica Kingsley Publishers
London and Bristol, Pennsylvania

Acknowledgements

As usual, my greatest thanks are to my wife for the nigh-impossible feat of proof reading my work whilst remaining sane. My gratitude also to Dr Carol Holland for reading a late draft of the work, and for the very useful comments. I would also like to thank the Librarian and staff of the library of the Department of Educational Studies, University of Oxford, for their very generous assistance.

The right of Ian Stuart-Hamilton to be identified as author of this work has been asserted by him in accordance with the Copyright, Designs and Patents Act 1988.

First published in hardback in the United Kingdom in 1995 (ISBN 1-85302-200-4) by
Jessica Kingsley Publishers Ltd
116 Pentonville Road
London N1 9JB, England
and
1900 Frost Road, Suite 101
Bristol, PA 19007, U S A

Copyright © 1995 Ian Stuart-Hamilton
Revised edition copyright © 1996 Ian Stuart-Hamilton

Library of Congress Cataloging in Publication Data
Available from the Library of Congress on request

British Library Cataloguing in Publication Data (Hardback)
Stuart-Hamilton, Ian
Dictionary of Developmental Psychology
I. Title
155

ISBN 1-85302-146-6 PB
ISBN 1-85302-427-9 HB

Printed and Bound in Great Britain by
Cromwell Press, Melksham, Wiltshire

Dictionary of Developmental Psychology

of related interest

Dictionary of Cognitive Psychology
Ian Stuart-Hamilton
ISBN 1 85302 148 2 PB
ISBN 1 85302 202 0 HB

Dictionary of Psychological Testing, Assessment and Treatment
Ian Stuart-Hamilton
ISBN 1 85302 147 4 PB
ISBN 1 85302 201 2 HB

To my parents

L'accent du pays ou l'on est né demeure dans
l'esprit et dans le coeur comme dans le langage.

Duc de la Rochefoucauld (1678) *Maxims*

Introduction

Mme du Deffand, on being told the legend that St Denis, after his beheading, picked up his head and walked two leagues, remarked that 'the distance is nothing; it is only the first step that is difficult'. The aphorism is useful advice in many situations other than the malaise which presumably creeps over one post-martyrdom. However, it is singularly useless in writing a dictionary – it is not a matter of how one starts, but rather, how and where one stops. Because developmental psychology, by definition, covers the development of every psychological skill or trait, it is tempting to add definitions of technical terms for all of these as well. However, such an approach would result in a full dictionary of psychology, which would defeat the object of the exercise. Equally, some 'non-developmental' definitions are necessary, because they are in very common currency within the subject. Hence, specialist terms, such as *phoneme*, are included, as well as brief sketches of some influential theories which are in frequent use in the subject (e.g. working memory, Freudian theory, etc.). The 'pure' developmental psychological terms have been chosen to guide the reader through the key areas of the subject. I do not claim to have included every piece of jargon produced by researchers (every new issue of a journal is likely to produce a neologism or contrived acronym, but most fade from sight without ever becoming common currency). In general, I have chosen insertions based upon the frequency with which they occurred in general textbooks, as well as more esoteric journal articles. If I have overlooked a key term which a reader feels ought to be in, then I will be delighted to consider the said term(s) for any future edition of this dictionary.

Many of the dictionary entries are cross-referenced. This has the advantage that by judiciously using this facility, the reader should be able to gain at least an overview of the appropriate subject area. However, a caveat to this is needed. Dictionary definitions, no matter how lengthy, are intended solely as guides and primers – they are not a substitute for reading a textbook or journal article, which can provide a deeper, if less immediately accessible level of understanding than a dictionary can ever hope to do.

Dr Ian Stuart-Hamilton
Principal Lecturer in Psychology,
Worcester College of Higher Education

Introduction to Revised Edition

This revised edition gives me an opportunity to spruce up a few of the existing definitions and to add a few entries which slipped through the net. It also gives me the chance to respond to a couple of enquiries I received about the hardback edition of this text. First, it will not have escaped the reader's notice that there is no Bibliography in this book. Why is this so? This can be best explained in the following way: Q: why will someone be looking up a term or the name of a test in a dictionary? A: because they have read about the term or test in a book or article – *which will have a bibliography*. Not only would a list of references be superfluous, but it would also at least double the length of the book. The second point is that descriptions of some of the tests in this book are very brief. There are two reasons for this. The first is that usually all the information someone wants is what the test is assessing – details can be burdensome and will militate against understanding. The second reason is that this dictionary and its companion volumes are textbooks which are going to be readily available, inter alia, to the general public and undergraduates – in other words, not fully trained psychologists. Without being pompous about this, I feel a certain moral responsibility not to divulge lots of details of tests to the occasional reader who may be looking up a definition to see what sort of test they are about to be given or have been given during, for example, a clinical examination or selection procedure. Where tests are described in greater depth, it is because the details are already widely available in textbooks. If people want to know lots of details of tests, then they are welcome to consult the *Mental Measurements Yearbooks* – that is their purpose. However, if people want to understand the terms used in books such as the MMYs, then they may well need a dictionary such as this one – that is *its* purpose.

I would like to take this opportunity once again to thank the staff of Jessica Kingsley Publishers for their invaluable support in the preparation of these dictionaries, and to my wife for putting up with my behaviour whilst writing them.

Ian Stuart-Hamilton
Worcester College of Higher Education

Guide to use

Cross-references are in italics. Three caveats are required, arising from a desire to avoid unnecessary repetition or superfluous entries and definitions.

(1) Very occasionally, italicized words' entries are in a slightly different grammatical inflexion (e.g. *feral children* may actually be entered as **feral child**).

(2) Within a definition, an italicized word in bold (e.g. ***definition*** rather than *definition*) indicates that the term is fully defined within the entry being read. The word's own entry will simply refer the reader back to this definition.

(3) An entry followed only by a word or phrase in italics indicates a synonym, which should be consulted for the full definition.

(4) Words linked by a hyphen are treated as if there is a space between them.

There are relatively few inverted headings – entries are usually given the word order they have in normal text. Therefore, if the reader looks up 'deep play', he or she finds **deep play,** not an irritating note to see *play, deep*. Where an inverted heading has been used, it is for clear logical reasons.

There are entries for a number of key studies and experiments. These have been entered by their popular nickname (e.g. **naughty teddy experiment**). There are also potted biographies of key historical figures (e.g. Baldwin). These simply give the key findings or topics which they were famous for in their lifetimes. There is no bibliography, since this book is intended as a quick guide, not a textbook manqué.

A

A level thought See *Rp level thought*.

A not B error See *object concept*.

A-68 Protein found in abnormally high concentration in patients with *dementia of the Alzheimer type*.

AAMD *American Association for Mental Deficiency*.

AAMD Adaptive Behaviour Scale *Adaptive Behaviour Scale*.

AAT *Achievement Anxiety Test*.

AB error *A not B error*.

ABC *Movement Assessment Battery for Children*.

abecedarians (1) Teachers of the *alphabetic method*. (2) Pupils of the same method.

ability grouping Group of subjects united by having a similar level of ability on a particular measure.

ABS *Adaptive Behaviour Scale*.

ABS-SE *Adaptive Behaviour Scale – School Edition (ABS-SE)*.

abstract control structures See *sensorimotor control structures*.

abstract counting Counting sequentially: such a process could theoretically proceed until death. In children beginning to learn about number, there is an upper limit. See *object counting*.

abstract modelling *Observational learning* of an abstract rule or principle.

abused child Child suffering *child abuse*. Compare with *neglected child*.

academic education Secondary or tertiary education aimed at other than vocational or technical matters.

accelerated education Education course (usually for brighter pupils) which progresses through the curriculum at a faster and more intensive pace than usual.

acceptance of prospect of dying stage See *denial of dying stage*.

accepting-rejecting dimension T e r m devised by Baumrind to denote the level of parent–child affection.

accommodation (1) In *Piagetian* theory, changing a mental *schema* to take account of (accommodate) new information. There is a complementary skill of *assimilation*, which is the attempt to understand an event/item/person using an existing schema. The mind thus has the task of deciding which aspects of a situation are novel, and hence need accommodating, and which are already familiar, and therefore can be assimilated. There is a danger that if the individual accommodates too much, then s/he is creating spurious and unnecessary schemas, whilst too much assimilation means that new information is being overlooked. *Piaget* argues that children become more adept at balancing the two processes as they get older (this is linked with his concept of *equilibrium*). When assimilation and accommodation are in equilibrium, *adaptation* to the situation is said to have occurred. (2) In vision, the ability to focus.

accrediting agency American term for agency which regulates professional standards (e.g. in education).

accretion See *complex learning*.

acculturation Learning to adapt to the strictures of the culture in which one finds oneself – hence, the child's learning of social and cultural skills.

ACER Tests Set of tests of basic skills pertinent to engineering.

achievement age *education(al) age.*

Achievement Anxiety Test (AAT) Measure of the degree to which anxiety enhances an individual's performance (the 'facilitation scale') and hinders it (the 'debilitating scale').

achievement motivation The desire to do well (especially towards some socially approved goal, such as scholastic tests).

achievement test A measure of what the subject is currently capable of (e.g. a child's scholastic attainment). Compare with *aptitude test.*

acommunicative speech Speech whose primary purpose is not communication (e.g. 'talking to oneself').

acquired aphasia See *aphasia.*

acquired dysgraphia A profound difficulty in writing (particularly spelling) resulting from brain damage.

acquired dyslexia A profound difficulty in reading resulting from brain damage. This takes various forms, some of which resemble *developmental dyslexia* or children learning to read (see *phonological dyslexia* and *surface dyslexia*); one form (*demented dyslexia*) is usually associated with *dementia.*

ACS (1) *acute confusional state.* (2) *Analysis of Coping Style.*

action reversibility *practical reversibility.*

active life expectancy The average number of years remaining in which members of an *age cohort* can expect to lead an active life.

active reading Nebulous term for any reading teaching scheme which emphasizes the use of *contextual cues* over *grapheme-phoneme conversion.* Such schemes stress that the child must be made to feel involved in reading (e.g. by making stories more relevant to the child's experiences).

active vocabulary The vocabulary used by a person when communicating. See *passive vocabulary.*

activity theory The counter-argument to *disengagement theory,* which argues that older people should be kept involved and active in the community.

acuity (vision) Ability to focus clearly.

acute brain disfunction *acute confusional state.*

acute brain disorder *acute confusional state.*

acute confusional state (ACS) A major disturbance (usually temporary) in intellect and perception resulting from a general deleterious change in the metabolism of the central nervous system (e.g. through fever, intoxication, drug overdose, etc.). Can be confused with *dementia,* but its very rapid onset is in itself a sufficiently distinguishing feature. Usually encountered in children and older people.

acute crisis phase First psychological stage through which a dying person passes (as identified by Pattison) characterized by a great anxiety upon realising that death is imminent. This is followed by the ***chronic living-dying phase*** – a period of mourning for what is being lost – and the ***terminal phase*** – an inward withdrawal and resignation/acceptance.

AD *Alzheimer's Disease.*

AD-MID A *dementia* in which the patient displays symptoms of *dementia of the Alzheimer type* and *multi-infarct dementia* simultaneously.

adaptation In *Piagetian* theory, the integration of *assimilation* and *accommodation*. Or, 'the accord of thought with things' – the understanding of a situation and its integration into a person's mental *schema* (see *accommodation*). Is linked with *organization*.

adaptive behaviour (1) The degree to which an individual copes with his/her society. Important in judging degree of *mental retardation* when conventional *IQ* tests might be inappropriate (e.g. in ethnic minorities with poor command of the majority language). (2) Can also refer to the degree to which a minority group has adapted its behaviour in order to survive in a society (this in turn may be used as an explanation for poor intellectual performance).

Adaptive Behaviour Scale (ABS) Rating scale, devised by the *AAMD*, for assessing the degree to which a *mentally retarded* person can adapt into the community. Can be divided into three subscales – measuring how far the subject is self-sufficient in looking after him/herself, how well s/he fits into the community, and how firmly s/he understands the concept of social norms and responsibility.

Adaptive Behaviour Scale – School Edition (ABS-SE) Version of the *Adaptive Behaviour Scale* specifically designed for *mentally retarded* subjects of school age.

adaptive reflex *survival reflex.*

ADD *attentional deficit disorder.*

ADD/+H *attentional deficit disorder* present with *hyperactivity*.

ADD/-H *attentional deficit disorder* present without *hyperactivity*.

ADD-H *attentional deficit disorder with hyperactivity*.

adjunctive behaviour Inappropriate behaviour reinforced by events resulting from the behaviour.

ADL *assessment of daily living.*

adolescence The period of transition between childhood and early adulthood. Commentators differ in setting the parameters of this period, but the period between 12 and 18 years of age is not uncommonly cited.

adolescent egocentricity (1) Term devised by *Piaget* to describe the stereotypical adolescent's belief that the world should conform to ideals, rather than a more pragmatic code. (2) More generally, the preoccupation which stereotypical adolescents are supposed to have with their own thoughts and their self-image.

adolescent spurt Pronounced increase in the rate of growth in early *adolescence*.

adoption study (1) Any study of adopted children. (2) One of the methods used in the *hereditarian versus environmentalist theories of individual differences* debate. Adopted children's scores on a test are correlated with (a) those of adoptive family members and (b) those of their natural mother (and, where possible, other genetic relatives). A high correlation with the former favours the environmentalist viewpoint, and a high correlation with the latter supports the hereditarian argument. The method can be used to assess a wide variety of psychological phenomena (e.g. *IQ* schizophrenia, depression, etc.).

adrenogenital syndrome Premature sexual development caused by an overactive adrenal gland.

adualistical thought Lack of differentiation between objective and subjective perceptions of the environment.

adult children Adults who experience problems as a result of events which occurred during their childhood (e.g. 'adult children of abusing parents').

adult development Change occurring between the end of (school) education and the onset of old age or retirement.

adult executive Family in which both parents share the decision-making processes. Compare with *family executive* and *single adult executive.*

adult offspring *adult children.*

adult survivors Adults who suffered a traumatic event (e.g. sexual abuse) when children.

Advanced Progressive Matrices (APM) See *Raven's Progressive Matrices.*

adventitious Caused by accident. Hence, adventitious blindness, etc.

aerial perspective (1) In conventional art, the technique of conveying depth by imitating the haziness of the atmosphere (first discovered by Ancient Roman painters, and rediscovered by Leonardo da Vinci). (2) In some studies of children's drawing, the portrayal of an object as if seen from overhead, with hidden parts of the object made visible (e.g. an overhead view of a cow with the left and right legs 'splayed' on either side of her body).

affect attunement State in which two people are sensitive and responsive to each other's affect (emotional state). Term used in studies of parent–child interaction.

affectional bond *Bond* of considerable (or permanent) length with a specific person.

affiliation motivation A drive to belong to a group, form friendships, etc.

affiliative need (nAff) The need to belong to a group, family, etc.

affordances In *direct perception theory,* a piece of visual information signifying the object's use. This can work at several levels – some visual information indicates that what can be seen can be moved through, or alternatively, that it will block movement; that it can be eaten; that it can be picked up; that it will cause pain if touched, etc.

AFP screening *alphafetoprotein (AFP) screening.*

age-appropriate behaviour *social age.*

age-as-leveller The argument that old age diminishes the perceived differences between socioeconomic/ethnic groups.

age bias *age discrimination.*

age cohort A group of people born and raised in the same period of time/history. Generally, the age range of such a group increases the older its average age. E.g. an acceptable grouping of newborn babies would not include a three-month old; a group of year-old babies would not include a 5-year-old, but a group of 'old' subjects could have a 20-year age range of 60–80-year-olds.

age discrimination Unfair bias against a person because of his/her age.

age-equivalent scale Test scores expressed in terms of the proportions of an age group who typically possess them. Thus, whether a person is advanced or retarded for their age can be assessed.

age grade placement American term for *age grading.*

age grading (1) In education, the principle that there are set *chronological ages* at which pupils should be learning particular items of knowledge. While this benefits the majority, there are obvious problems for pupils whose *mental ages* are appreciably greater or smaller than their chronological age. See *streaming*. (2) The societal pressures which determine what is considered appropriate for different *social ages*.

age norm The mean score on a test for a given age group, and hence the score one would expect an average child of that age group to achieve.

age normative effect A factor which influences the majority of people at the same point in their lives.

age of acquisition (AOA) The age at which a particular skill or piece of knowledge was first acquired.

age scale *age-equivalent scale*.

age score *mental age*.

age set *age cohort*.

age-specific mortality rate Proportion of people in an age group likely to die before they get too old to be in the said age group.

age stratification Dividing the lifespan into a series of *social ages* or other age groups.

age thirty transition (ATT) See *early adult transition*.

age x complexity effect The phenomenon whereby the difference between the abilities of older and younger adults gets disproportionately larger the more complex the task set. See *age x treatment interaction*.

age x process interaction *age x treatment interaction*.

age x treatment interaction The phenomenon whereby some psychological skills decline more than others in old age (see *differential preservation* and *preserved differentiation*). For example, it has been argued that if skill 1 requires mental process X and skill 2 process Y, but skill 1 declines disproportionately more than skill 2 in old age, then process X must be more affected by ageing than is process Y. This is not the same as the *age x complexity effect*, which argues that changing the complexity of items which the same skill has to process has a disproportionate effect on older subjects.

AGECAT A computerized package for assessing the mental state of older patients.

ageing Process of change occurring with the passage of time. Usually restricted to changes (often perceived as negative) which occur after adolescence. See *biological age, chronological age, distal ageing effects, primary ageing, probabilistic ageing, proximal ageing effects, secondary ageing, social age,* and *universal ageing*.

ageing/aging Either spelling is acceptable. American English favours 'aging', and British English, 'ageing'.

ageism *age discrimination* (usually refers to discrimination against older people).

agenesis (1) Reproductive sterility. (2) *congenital* absence of an organ.

agerasia Having a *biological age* considerably younger than would be predicted from one's *chronological age* (loosely, looking 'well preserved').

aging See *ageing/aging*.

AIDS dementia *Dementing* symptoms found in some patients in the terminal stages of acquired immune deficiency syndrome (AIDS).

alcoholic dementia Old (and misleading) synonym for *Korsakoff's syndrome*.

alexia A complete failure to read or to recognize words or letters (in *dyslexia* there is a partial ability). Only usually seen in brain-damaged individuals.

alleles See *genetic dominance*.

alliteration sensitivity The degree to which a subject can detect that words begin with the same sound – is a good indicator of ability to process *phonemes*, and thus of *phonic mediation* ability. See *rhyme sensitivity*.

allocentric Outside the body. Sometimes used to describe the senses of sight and hearing. Compare with *autocentric*.

allophone An alternative pronunciation of a phoneme, which is noticeable but which does not alter the word's meaning (e.g. the 'l' and 'r' sounds in Japanese).

Allport's theory of personality development A principal component of the theory by Gordon Allport (first advanced in the 1960s) argued that children do not possess personalities as much as a collection of behaviours, which vary according to the needs of the moment (e.g. children behave radically differently with their friends and their parents). The behaviours eventually coalesce into *selves*, which are sets of behaviours consistently used in different settings (e.g. the child has a 'home self', a 'school self', etc.). An individual reaches maturity when the selves in turn coalesce into a 'personality', which is relatively stable across situations.

alphafetoprotein (AFP) screening Assessing a 16–18-weeks-pregnant mother's blood for unusually high levels of alphafetoprotein – this can be indicative of abnormal brain development in the *foetus*.

alphabetic literacy The ability to read a language which uses a limited set of *graphemes* to represent *phonemes* (e.g. English, French, Italian, etc.). This is contrasted with **non-alphabetic literacy**, which is the ability to read a language in which each printed character represents a different word (e.g. Chinese).

alphabetic method Method of teaching reading in which the child is taught the names of the letters of the alphabet, and is then left pretty much on his/her own to work the rest out for him/herself. The method was widely used until the last century, when it fell out of favour.

aluminium theory of dementia of the Alzheimer type Brain cells of Alzheimer patients show unusually large concentrations of aluminium, and the incidence of the disease appears to be higher in areas where there is a greater concentration of aluminium in the water. This has led to the theory that the principal cause of *dementia of the Alzheimer type* is the 'poisoning' of the brain with aluminium contamination. However, recent work suggests that this may be an artifact of the manner in which the cells are analysed.

alumni education American term for education schemes for former students (alumni) of an institute of higher education. The courses are intended for intellectual enrichment, rather than for specific postgraduate qualifications, such as a Masters or PhD degree.

Alzheimer-type dementia *dementia of the Alzheimer type (DAT)*.

Alzheimer's Disease (AD) *dementia of the Alzheimer type (DAT)*.

Amala and Kamala Two *feral children* found in India, apparently reared by wolves.

ambiguous loss Phenomenon usually encountered in severely *demented* patients, whereby the afflicted individual exists only physically – there is no sign of a sentient being occupying the body.

ambivalent and insecurely attached *resistant and insecurely attached.*

amenity migration Moving from one country or area of the country to another because of better amenities/lifestyle, etc. The term is often used to describe retired people moving to a 'nice place in the country'.

American Association for Mental Deficiency (AAMD) American group promoting the rights and needs of *mentally retarded* people.

American school system Some children begin school at 5 with kindergarten. The 'official' entry age is 6 years, with each year in school called a *grade: elementary school* (grades 1–3), *grammar school* (4–8), and *high school* (9–12). Sometimes grades 7–8 are spent in *junior high school.*

amnesia A failure of memory, usually abnormally severe, arising from e.g. *stroke,* head injury, illness (e.g. *dementia*), or poisoning. The term is occasionally used for memory loss which is normal or not unduly serious in its effects (e.g. *childhood amnesia*).

amniocentesis A sampling of *amniotic fluid* during early pregnancy which can reveal chromosomal defects (particularly *trisomy-21*) in the *foetus.*

amnion Sac containing *amniotic fluid.*

amniotic fluid The fluid by which the *foetus* is surrounded in the womb. When the baby is born, some amniotic fluid is trapped in the middle ear, which dampens hearing in new born babies until it drains away after a few days.

anal stage See *Freud's theory of development.*

analogical reasoning Reasoning/problem solving in which an answer is sought by considering another problem with a similar structure whose solution is already known.

analysis See *Bloom's taxonomy of educational objectives.*

Analysis of Coping Style (ACS) Measure of social skills in subjects aged 5–18 years.

anaphoric reference Referring to an item mentioned earlier, usually by its pronoun. E.g. 'The man sat down. It was a hot day, and he was tired after the long walk.'

anatomical age *Biological age,* measured through the relatively gross state of the body (e.g. bone structure, body build, etc.) rather than through *physiological age.* See *carpal age.*

anatomically detailed dolls Dolls possessing genitalia, used by therapists in e.g. cases of *child abuse,* to enable children to describe the nature of the abuse.

androgynous personality A personality combining the 'better' attributes of stereotypical 'masculine' and 'feminine' behaviours (e.g. being gentle but independent, tough-minded but succouring, etc.). Compare with *undifferentiated sex role identity.*

Angelmann syndrome Genetic disorder whose symptoms include *hyperactivity.*

anger at prospect of dying stage See *denial of dying stage.*

animate environment The living components of an environment.

animism *Piaget's* theory that in the *preoperational subperiod,* children believe that many non-living objects are alive. Towards the end of the subperiod, the belief is restricted to objects which can move. It is argued that animism is an expression of *egocentrism* (i.e. the child attributes his/her state to others).

animistic thinking *animism.*

aniseidominance Eyesight defect in which the image in one eye is brighter than that in the other. Compare with *aniseikonia.*

aniseikonia Eyesight defect in which objects create retinal images of unequal size in either eye. Has been linked with reading problems. Compare with *aniseidominance.*

anniversary reaction Usually, negative feelings engendered by the anniversary (or general time of year) of an event distressing to a subject (e.g. death of a close friend or relative). The term can also refer to positive feelings associated with the anniversary of a more cheerful event.

Anomalous Sentences Repetition Test (ASRT) Measure designed to distinguish between patients in early stages of *dementia* and those with *pseudodementia*. Subjects are required to repeat 'nonsense' sentences spoken by the tester.

anomy Absence of morality.

anorexia Undereating, although an ample food supply is readily available, for reasons other than a conventional reduction diet. The disorder can have many causes: the most common are some forms of cancer and *anorexia nervosa.*

anorexia nervosa A mental disorder in which the patient wilfully starves/seriously undereats, in the erroneous belief that s/he is overweight and has an unattractive body shape. The illness is largely (but not solely) confined to females, usually in adolescence. Compare with *bulimia* and *bulimia nervosa*. See *anorexia.*

anoxia A lack of oxygen – if this occurs at birth, then *mental retardation* can result. Brain damage tends to be in the brain stem and 'lower' areas of the brain, rather than in the cortex. Thus, newborn babies suffering severe anoxia most commonly have impaired motor skills. The symptoms of mild anoxia usually disappear by circa seven years.

answer until correct (AUC) score Marking system for a multiple choice test, in which a subject makes as many attempts as necessary until s/he obtains the right answer; the more attempts made, the fewer points scored. See *inferred number right (INR) score.*

antediluvian ageing myth Myth that at some distant time (antediluvian meaning 'before the flood'), a (usually virtuous and pious) race of people existed, who had incredibly long lifespans. See *hyperborean ageing myth.*

anticholinergic Anything which blocks the action of the cholinergic system. This can lead to severe memory loss, and this information is one of the cornerstones of the *cholinergic hypothesis.*

anticipatory grief Preparing for the death of a loved one. The term has been used for the state of a mother with a very premature and/or sickly infant.

anxious-avoidant attachment *avoidant and insecurely attached.*

anxious-resistant attachment *resistant and insecurely attached.*

AOA *age of acquisition.*

apathetic (personality) See *passive-dependent personality.*

Apgar score Named after its inventor, Dr Apgar. A scaled measure of a newborn baby's physical condition. Takes five criteria – heart rate; respiratory effort (i.e. how well s/he is breathing); muscle tone; reflex irritability (i.e. how well baby responds to an irritating stimulus); and colour (for caucasians, the pinker the better). Each measure is scored on a three point scale, and provides a quick indicator of the baby's health.

aphasia Failure of language. The term usually refers to *acquired aphasia* – i.e. the patient has acquired it through accident or illness resulting in brain damage, and prior to this s/he had normal linguistic abilities (e.g. aphasia is common in many of the *dementias*). *Developmental aphasia* is a *congenital* condition.

APM *Advanced Progressive Matrices.*

apnoea Temporary suspension of breathing, usually in sleep. Most common in the very young and the very old. There are several possible causes.

application See *Bloom's taxonomy of educational objectives.*

apportioned grandmother Category of grandmother identified in a taxonomy by Robinson as having both a social and a personal set of expectations for her grandchildren. Other types include: *symbolic grandmother* – has a social set of expectations; *individualized grandmother* – has a set of personal expectations; and *remote grandmother* – relatively detached from the whole idea of being a grandmother.

appraisal-focused coping Dealing with a life crisis by trying to understand why and how it happened. See *emotion-focused coping* and *problem-focused coping.*

approach-avoidance conflict (1) The conflict a subject feels when s/he desires to perform an act which s/he knows has previously been punished. (2) In young children, the simultaneous desire to approach and to avoid a stranger. (3) The behaviour shown by some *abused children* to their abusing parent(s).

Approaches to Study Inventory (ASI) Questionnaire of study habits, divided into 16 subscales, assessing a range of study skills (e.g. over-reliance on details, ability to comprehend broad issues, etc.).

approaching objects paradigm Any paradigm in which infants are shown a visual display of an object coming towards them, and their reaction to this is measured. If the infant shows alarm at an object apparently about to hit him/her, or alternatively shows a lack of response if the object is apparently going to miss, then it is argued that the infant shows a sophisticated movement judgement. However, the method has been criticized, not least because the reactions of the infants may be to other, subtler, aspects of the display, unrelated to movement perception per se.

aptitude test A measure of what the subject is potentially capable of, even though s/he may not currently attain such heights (e.g. an *IQ* test might show that a child's teaching is not stretching him/her sufficiently). Compare with *achievement test.*

aptitude-treatment interaction The interaction between a pupil's or a subject's aptitude (including intellectual skills, personality, and level of motivation) and the task itself (including method of instruction) and the effect this has on the subject's performance.

armoured approach personality *defensiveness personality.*

armoured-defensive personality Personality type found in some older people – possessors are either *holding on* (maintaining a high level of activity to 'defeat' ageing); or *constricted* (dwelling on what they have lost through ageing).

arteriosclerotic dementia *Dementia* resulting from cardiovascular causes (e.g. *stroke* and *multi-infarct dementia*).

articulation (1) Clarity of speech. (2) In education, the degree of continuity between the teaching programmes of institutions at different levels in the education system.

articulatory loop See *working memory*.

artificialism Term by *Piaget* for children's belief that everything (including objects and thoughts) were directly made by people or God.

ASI *Approaches to Study Inventory*.

ASI-S Shortened version of *Approaches to Study Inventory*.

ASL American Sign Language.

Asperger's syndrome Named after its discoverer, Asperger. A condition quite similar to, and currently generally classified as, a form of *autism* (sometimes the two illnesses are found in the same family, indicating a possible genetic component). The principal differences between the conditions are that the Asperger patient possesses near-normal language, and usually has a higher degree of social skills. Sufferers are often perceived as normal, if eccentric.

ASRT *Anomalous Sentences Repetition Test*.

Assessing Reading Difficulties Reading skills test for subjects aged 5–8 years. Subjects are given an *odd man out test*, in which all but one of a list of words have the same sound in common – the subjects have to name the 'odd one out' (e.g. 'cat, hat, rat, man'). The test claims to assess *phonemic awareness*, and thus, the subject's ability to use *phonic mediation*.

assessment of daily living (ADL) A n y method of measuring daily activities, usually with the purpose of identifying memory slips, ability to cope independently, etc.

assimilation See *accommodation*. Also, see *assimilation of schemes, recognition assimilation*, and *reproductive assimilation*.

assimilation of schemes In *Piagetian* theory, building larger *schemes* by integrating smaller ones.

associativity When used in connection with *Piagetian* theory – see *group*.

Aston Index Reading skills test battery for subjects aged 5–14 years. Includes picture recognition, a vocabulary test, the *Goodenough Draw-a-Man Test*, the *Schonell Graded Word Reading Test*, various tests of *phonological* skills, and memory. It is primarily designed to assess poor readers with suspected *dyslexia*.

at risk children/infants Children/infants with a heightened risk of suffering a deleterious change. Although a popular media shorthand for 'at risk from parental abuse', the term also refers to threats from disease, environmental factors, etc.

ateleiosis Failure of sexual development due to hormonal deficiency.

atomism In *Piagetian* theory, the concept that any element is composed of minute particles ('atoms'). In a *conservation of quantity* task, for example, a child possessing atomism might realize that although the clay has changed shape, it still contains the same number of atoms as before, and thus correctly answer the question set.

ATT *age thirty transition*.

attachment *Affectional bond*; used especially of parent–child bond.

'Attachment and Loss' Important and influential trilogy of books by John Bowlby, dealing with children's attachment to parents and the effects of temporary and permanent separations. Argues for the importance of *monotropy*. Volume 1 – 'Attachment' (1969); Volume 2 – 'Separation: Anxiety and Anger' (1973); and Volume 3 – 'Loss: Sadness and Depression' (1980). See *Bowlby's theory of attachment*.

attachment behaviours Behaviours involved in the formation and maintenance of *bonds*.

attainment test *achievement test*.

attention seeking behaviour Behaviour, often unpleasant (e.g. very late night or otherwise inconvenient telephone calls), used to attract the attention of others. Usually an expression of the need for help.

attentional deficit disorder (ADD) Severe failure to concentrate on the task at hand, with obvious deleterious effects on the ability to learn. ***Attentional deficit disorder with hyperactivity (ADD-H)*** has the added symptom of *hyperactivity*.

attentional deficit disorder with hyperactivity (ADD-H) See *attentional deficit disorder*.

attentional inertia The phenomenon whereby the longer one attends to a stimulus, the higher the probability that one will continue to attend to it. Hence the scientific explanation for the 'couch potato'.

attic child Generic term for a child reared in virtual or total isolation from normal fellow humans. Inevitably such children are seriously emotionally and intellectually retarded. Some (although not all) recover when given appropriate care. See *feral child*.

attribution of beliefs task *Sally–Anne task*.

attunement See *facilitation*.

AUC score *answer until correct (AUC) score*.

auditory evoked potential See *evoked potential*.

augmentative communication *facilitated communication*.

authoritarian parents Parents who expect their children blindly to obey their set of rules. Compare with *authoritative parents* and *permissive parents*.

authoritarian teacher Teacher who governs by rigid discipline and motivates by rewards and punishments. Compare with *democratic teacher* and *laissez-faire teacher*.

authoritative parents Parents who raise their children with a firm (but not dictatorial) set of rules. The child is made aware of the reasoning behind the rules. Compare with *authoritarian parents* and *permissive parents*.

autism (1) An obsessional interest in the self to the exclusion of others. (2) Rare (approx. 4 per 10,000 live births) but serious disturbance of thought processes arising in infancy. First identified in the 1940s by Kanner, although an independent and contemporaneous paper by Asperger also identifies the condition. The *autistic* child usually avoids social contact, and may have lacked *cuddliness* as a baby. S/he often seeks a monotony of environment and action (resulting in repetitive stereotyped movements) which appear to provide some comfort. There is usually a strong linguistic handicap, and social skills are poor. Media coverage of autistic children with remarkably good (by any standards) artistic or arithmetical talents can create the impression that the disease always has compensations. However, most autistic children appear to have poor abilities, and are often diagnosed as suffering from *mental retardation*. Autism is usually inherited, but cases resulting from brain damage have been reported. A case has been made for it being the product of faulty parenting methods (see *fragile X syndrome* and *refrigerator parent*), but this has been largely discounted. The disease is four times more common in males. In earlier terminology, 'autism' referred to schizophrenia, and later the term was used synonymously with *childhood schizophrenia* (the degree of division between autism and schizophrenia is still debated). The immediate explanation of what is wrong with autistic patients is still not fully resolved, but an ingenious recent theory is that they cannot create representations of how other people think (see *mind, theory of (autism)*). This was neatly demonstrated in the **Sally–Anne task**. The subject is told a tale of how, when Sally went out of the room, Anne took Sally's toy from where Sally had left it, and hid it in a new place. Sally returns to the room – where will she look for her toy? Non-autistic subjects correctly reason that Sally will look for the toy where she left it. Autistic patients argue that Sally will look for the toy where Anne hid it – they seem incapable of putting themselves in the mind of another person. This failure to understand the needs and views of others may explain the autistic patient's profound linguistic and social problems (also see *Smarties task*). See *Asperger's syndrome* and *mind, theory of (autism)*.

autistic Adjective derived from *autism*.

autobiographical memory Memory for events peculiar to one's own life, as opposed to past events which everyone has experienced (i.e. events which have been 'in the news', such as general elections, train crashes, etc.). See *flash-bulb memory, observer memory*, and *Piaget's 'kidnapping'*.

autocentric Within the body – sometimes used to describe the senses of taste, smell, etc. Compare with *allocentric*.

autoimmune theory of ageing Theory that the ageing body's autoimmune system falters, and begins to attack the body's own cells as if they were infections. See *disposable soma theory of ageing, free radical theory of ageing, Hayflick phenomenon*, and *somatic mutation theory of ageing*.

autonomous level *post-conventional level*.

autonomous parenting Parenting style in which the children are perceived as independent individuals.

autonomous standard Judging one's achievement by comparing one's current performance against past performance. Compare with *social comparison standard*.

autonomy See *Piaget's theory of moral development*.

autonomy-control Scale for judging the degree of freedom and self-expression permitted to children by their parents.

autonomy versus shame and doubt See *Erikson's theory of development*.

autosomes All *chromosomes* other than the *sex chromosomes*.

avoidant and insecurely attached See *strange situation*.

awareness of dying The degree to which a person is aware s/he has a fatal illness.

B

babbling The initial production of *phonemes*, syllables and word-like sounds by a baby (typically 4–9 months, although other commentators specify other periods – e.g. 5–12 months) as s/he begins to produce controlled *vocalizations*. Babbling contains not just some of the syllabic sounds of the baby's parents' language, but also other 'foreign' vocal sounds which are lost when the baby begins to speak. Some commentators restrict the term to a more specific set of criteria. See *reduplicated babbling, variegated babbling* and *speech development stages*.

Babinski reflex A type of *primitive reflex*. If a baby's foot is tickled, the toes fan out and then curl. Possibly reflects humanity's ape ancestors – in tree-dwelling primate species with longer toes, such a reflex would cause the foot to grip whatever it touched (e.g. a branch), thereby avoiding a fall. However, note that this explanation has been disputed. The reflex usually disappears at 8–12 months of age. Its retention after this time probably indicates neurological damage.

Babkin reflex A type of *primitive reflex*. Pressure applied to a baby's palms causes him/her to open his/her mouth.

baby biography *Diary study* of a baby's development kept by a *caregiver*.

'baby blues' *post-natal depression*.

Baby Talk Register (BTR) Non-sexist (but less memorable) synonym for *motherese*.

back-channel feedback Non-verbal simple verbal signals such as 'uh-huh', when listening to a speaker. Tends only to be used in the conversations of relatively mature speakers.

back to basics Educational movement stressing the virtues of educating pupils in the traditional 'basic skills' (primarily the *three Rs*).

backward child Largely outdated term for a child whose abilities fall appreciably below his/her *age norm*.

backward reader Individual whose reading abilities fall appreciably below his/her *age norm*. No cause for this state of affairs is inferred (i.e. the term is not synonymous with *developmental dyslexia*).

backward speller Individual whose spelling abilities fall appreciably below his/her *age norm*. No cause for this state of affairs is inferred (i.e. the term is not synonymous with *developmental dysgraphia*).

balance problem Experiment by *Piaget* to demonstrate the differences between *formal operational thought* and *concrete operational thought*. Subjects were asked to balance a beam balance (a rod on a pivot, from which weights of varying mass can be hung at different distances from the pivot). Although a concrete operational child might achieve a balance by trial and error, Piaget argued that only a child in the formal operational stage could learn and appreciate that the force pulling down on a side is calculated as mass x distance from the pivot. Hence, if a weight of 300 grams is hanging 20 cm from one side of the pivot, a weight of 150 grammes will have to be placed 40 cm from the pivot on the opposite side if the beam is to balance. Since such a calculation involves abstraction of the problem into a symbolic form, Piaget argued that this is only accessible to the formal operational mind.

Baldwin's theory of developmental psychology James Mark Baldwin (1861–1934), psychologist. Influential work was performed in his early professional life before a scandal led to his resignation from his chair at Johns Hopkins University in 1909. The theories were neglected in the period immediately after his professional decline, but later proved highly influential. Baldwin argued that development occurs through *circular reaction*. Children learn by responding to feedback from the results of their actions. This allows the development of more refined and more elaborate skills. Mental representations of items and events were described as *schemes*. Another general theme (particularly in his theory of social development) was the growth from an *egocentric* state to one of wider, more abstract awareness. The work thus has clear links with *Piaget's* work. However, Baldwin's work was often purely theoretical, with no empirical support. Accordingly, he is often best regarded as a generator of ideas rather than proofs.

Bandura's theory of social learning Albert Bandura (1925–), psychologist. Bandura observes that in many situations, people (especially children) learn skills simply by observing others performing them, and then copying. Often the very first attempt at imitation is very accomplished – an example of *no-trial*

learning. Bandura identifies various factors which influence the success of *social learning*. Obviously, the person must attend to the to-be-copied activity, and be physically capable of replicating it (e.g. it is no use an infant watching someone toss the caber in the hope of being able to imitate the action). The person must also be able to retain a memory of the task. Bandura argues that this is often done with a verbal code (e.g. 'right hand hold sprocket, then left hand turn screw') which is more flexible than a visual image. Children under five years lack this code, and so are more restricted in what they can learn. The motivation for learning and, more importantly, performing the task, largely depends upon whether it is perceived as rewarding. This can be learnt by *vicarious reinforcement* (observing if others are rewarded or punished for performing the same actions). In one study, children were shown a film in which aggression was either rewarded, punished, or ignored. Left to play afterwards, children who had seen aggression rewarded were significantly more likely to behave violently to toys than were children in the other two conditions. There is a considerable debate over the range of learning situations for which Bandura's methods are applicable. See *Bobo doll studies*, and *reciprocal determinism*.

Bangor Dyslexia Test (BDT) Test battery of dyslexic symptoms, for subjects aged 7 years and above. Little direct emphasis on reading. Subjects are tested for e.g. knowledge of which is the left or right side of their bodies; they have to repeat polysyllabic words, perform various arithmetical tasks, recite the list of months forwards and backwards, etc.

Bannatyne-WISC categories
Regrouping of *WISC* sub-test scores into three categories – Spatial, Conceptual and Sequential (these are essentially maths skills).

bargaining at prospect of dying stage
See *denial of dying stage.*

barking at print Reading without understanding – used to describe most beginning readers, and a smaller number of older and less gifted ones.

Barking Reading Project (BRP)
Reading research project centring on schools in Barking, U.K.

BAS *British Ability Scales.*

basal reading (1) Reading teaching scheme in which the books and other materials are graded in a hierarchy of difficulty through which the child progresses in a (relatively) fixed pattern. (2) A minimum acceptable standard of reading.

Basic Achievement Skills Individual Screener (BASIS) Measure of scholastic attainment for subjects aged 5–13 years.

Basic Number Diagnostic Test (BNDT)
See *Basic Number Screening Test.*

Basic Number Screening Test (BNST)
Standardized group test of numerical skills for children aged 7–12 years. A related test – the *Basic Number Diagnostic Test (BNDT)* is for individual testing to identify older children with problems with numeracy (or to identify normal numeracy skills in children aged 5–7 years).

basic skills Education's equivalent of *primary mental abilities* – the educational skills which must be present if the education process is to succeed (i.e. basic literacy, numeracy, etc.).

basic trust versus mistrust See *Erikson's theory of development.*

BASIS *Basic Achievement Skills Individual Screener.*

Battelle Developmental Inventory (BDI) A test battery assessing development from 0–8 years in five principal areas: adaptation to the environment, cognitive skills, communication skills, motor skills and social skills.

Batten's disease Rare genetic disorder in infants and young children, causing a variety of physical ailments and *dementia*. Patients rarely live beyond circa 5 years of age.

battered child syndrome Pattern of behaviour which may result from being a victim of physical *child abuse*; includes inability to form adequate relationships and poor self-image.

Bayley Scales of Infant Development (BSID) *Test battery* of mental, motor and behavioural skills/attributes of infants and young children (up to 36 months) used particularly to identify abnormal development. A revised version (Bayley Scales II) was published in 1993.

BBCS *Bracken Basic Concept Scale.*

BCDP *Bracken Concept Development Programme.*

BDI *Battelle Developmental Inventory* .

BDS *Blessed Dementia Scale.*

BDT *Bangor Dyslexia Test.*

beanpole family Family in which there are relatively few members of each generation.

becoming one's own man (BOOM)
See *early adult transition.*

bedwetting *nocturnal enuresis.*

Behaviour Rating Scale (BRS) See *Clifton Assessment Procedure for the Elderly.*

behavioural checklist A measure of assessment which grades a subject's behaviour as to whether it matches up to a set of criteria.

Behavioral Summarized Evaluation (BSE) A measure of behaviour and behavioural problems in *autistic* children.

behavioural genetics Study of how genetic factors influence behaviour (and more generally, differences between individuals).

behaviourism In its rigid form, the belief that psychologists should only study what can be objectively measured. All voluntary acts can be seen as a response to some form of stimulation. Of the various stages in this process, the stimulus can be measured, as can the strength and/or correctness of the response, but the thought processes used to do this cannot. Hence, behaviourism concentrated on the stimulus and response, and rigorously excluded discussion of mental processes. The theory had a very strong hold on psychology from the 1920s to the late 1950s, but was eventually recognized as being too limited in its scope, and researchers began to create models of mental processing. With its emphasis on stimulus and response and *operant conditioning*, behaviourism gave rise to a number of theories of educational practice, which essentially worked by more or less explicitly *conditioning* the child (see *learning theory* and *stimulus-response learning*). Critics have argued that the methods were too harsh and mechanistic – in part, objections may stem from the fact that symbolically identical conditioning techniques can be used to train laboratory animals. See *Skinner's theory of child rearing, token economy, Watson's theory of child rearing.*

Bender-Gestalt Test A test of visuo-spatial skills. The subject is required to copy geometric shapes of increasing complexity. Test is suitable for subjects aged 8 years and over. Part of the *Bender Visual Motor Gestalt Test* battery.

Bender Visual Motor Gestalt Test (BVMGT) Battery of visual and motor skills, including the *Bender-Gestalt Test.*

bending rods problem Measure of *formal operations* by *Piaget*. Subjects were shown rods (posed like fishing rods angled out over water) varying in length, thickness, cross-sectional shape and materials. By adding different weights to one end, each rod would bend. The subjects' task was to see what made the rod bend far enough to touch the surface of the water beneath the rod. Subjects in the *concrete operational sub-period* could not systematically examine the problem, while subjects exhibiting formal operational thought could.

Benton Revised Visual Retention Test Measure of visual skills. For subjects aged 8 years and over.

Bereiter and Engelmann nursery education Nursery school programme for children from disadvantaged homes. The scheme assumes that such children are retarded in most intellectual skills, particularly language and concept formation. Accordingly, emphasis is very much on remedial training. Play periods are included, but very much with 'educational' toys and games. The *Engelmann–Becker programme* is a revised form of this model.

Berkley Growth Study American *longitudinal study* begun in the 1930s, of psychological and physical development from birth to adulthood.

BHP behaviour problem.

bi-univocal See *grouping III.*

bidirectional/bidirectionality Going in both directions – sometimes used as shorthand for the development of skills resulting from the interactions between the child and those around him/her.

Bigg's Study Process Questionnaire *Study Process Questionnaire.*

billiard balls problem Study by *Piaget,* demonstrating the properties of *formal operations.* Subjects were given the task of hitting one billiard ball with another, using a pin-ball type plunger. The ball had to be rebounded off a surface before hitting the target, thereby testing the subjects' knowledge of angles, and the ability to formulate a simple 'law of rebounds'.

Binet/Binet–Simon Scale O r i g i n a l (French) version of the *Stanford–Binet Scale/Test.* Alfred Binet (1857–1911), psychologist and playwright. Early work on cognitive development, particularly mnemonic skills, emphasizing the importance of realistic rather than laboratory-bound studies. He viewed development as a complex sequence of interactions, in which the mind, and intelligence in particular, are flexible to new ideas, and accordingly can be shaped and improved by appropriate training. Binet is best remembered for his work on intelligence. He devised the first standardized intelligence test (1905) – the Binet Scale – which remains a standard test in the psychologist's repertoire.

Binswanger's disease *Dementia* w h o s e origins are disputed, but whose symptoms are akin to those of *lacunar dementia* (some commentators have argued that they are the same condition).

biogenetic theories of development Theories which emphasize *inherited* and physiological influences on development.

biographical approach (creativity) T h e analysis of the lives of pre-eminent members of professions, etc., to see if there are any common factors to explain their greatness. Has been widely used in *creativity* research.

biological age The body's state of physical development/degeneration. This is gauged against the state of an average person of the same *chronological age.* See *anatomical age, physiological age.*

biological parents Parents who physically sired the child in question (as opposed to e.g. adopting or fostering him/her).

biological theories of development Theories which stress the role of genetic inheritance, hormonal changes, or other biological factors in development.

birth cohort A group of people born in the same period of time. See *cohort.*

birth cry (1) The noise most babies make when born (it helps clear the lungs of *amniotic fluid*). (2) Term used by some commentators (e.g. Lenneberg) to denote the vocalization of babies typically aged 0–3 months, which begins as an undifferentiated yell, and refines into a range of cries expressing different needs.

birth injury Injury occurring during birth (e.g. *anoxia,* damage from delivery forceps, etc.).

birth order Siblings arranged in order of age. Was held to be an important predictor of intelligence and other personality factors (the older children were supposedly brighter, more likely to be leaders, etc.). However, the evidence is now disputed.

birth rate Ratio of births to total size of population.

BLAT *Blind Learning Aptitude Test.*

Blessed Dementia Scale (BDS) A simple test of intellectual impairment and functioning, usually employed in the assessment of *demented* patients. The test requires the patient to answer some simple memory questions (e.g. 'what is your name?', 'who is the current Prime Minister?') and to perform some simple intellectual tasks (e.g. 'count backwards from twenty'). Details of how capable the patient is of looking after him- or herself are collected from a *caregiver*. The test provides a useful 'ready reckoner' of how intellectually impaired a patient is, and how much professional nursing care and assistance is required. The Blessed Dementia Scale (named after its author, Dr Blessed) is a British test. The American equivalent is the *Mental Status Questionnaire*, which has nearly the same format.

Blind Learning Aptitude Test (BLAT) Non-verbal intelligence test for visually handicapped children, using only tactile skills. Subjects must distinguish between shapes by touch, and identify the 'odd one out'. The shapes increase in complexity as the test progresses.

blood bond (False) belief that there is an *innate* attachment between a child and his/her *biological parents* (particularly the mother).

'blooming, buzzing confusion' Phrase by William James, describing the young infant's perceptual world.

Bloom's taxonomy of educational objectives First described by Bloom and colleagues in the 1950s. (1) *knowledge* – basic recall of facts. (2) *comprehension*

– retention of an interpretation of a piece of knowledge. (3) *application* – the ability to relate comprehension of a piece of knowledge to other situations. (4) *analysis* – the ability to identify and describe relationships. (5) *synthesis* – the ability to discover relationships, given basic information. (6) *evaluation* – the ability to judge the worth of a piece of information or argument.

BNDT *Basic Number Diagnostic Test.*

BNST *Basic Number Screening Test.*

Bobo doll studies Series of experiments by Bandura et al. in the 1960s, demonstrating *Bandura's theory of social learning*. Children were shown an adult behaving aggressively or not towards a large inflatable doll of 'Bobo the Clown' (a well-known American children's character). When left alone to play with Bobo, the children imitated the aggressive actions towards Bobo which the adult had shown. Children who had not seen the adult being aggressive were not aggressive towards the doll.

Boder Test of Reading-Spelling Patterns Measure of types of reading handicap, including a separation of *developmental dyslexia* from motivational or perceptual problems.

body transcendence versus body preoccupation The (beneficial) realization that in old age, bodily fitness and health can no longer be a prime cause of self-esteem.

Boehm-PV *Boehm Test of Basic Concepts – Preschool Version.*

Boehm-R *Boehm Test of Basic Concepts – Revised.*

Boehm Resource Guide for Basic Concept Teaching Essentially a collection of teaching aids for developing certain concepts in young (3 years and over) and retarded children.

Boehm Test of Basic Concepts – Preschool Version (Boehm-PV) Test of 3–5-year-old children's comprehension of 26 basic concepts. See *Boehm Test of Basic Concepts – Revised.*

Boehm Test of Basic Concepts – Revised (Boehm-R) Test of 4–7-year-old children's grasp of basic concepts. See *Boehm Test of Basic Concepts – Preschool Version.*

bond (1) Emotional attachment – in lay terms, a 'relationship', with a set of societal expectations on how it should be conducted (e.g. mother–child bond). (2) The verb for the same process.

bonding The formation of a *bond.*

BOOM *becoming one's own man* .

'booming, buzzing confusion' Frequent misquotation of *'blooming, buzzing confusion'.*

Borke Interpersonal Awareness Test Two part measure of children's awareness of others' emotions. Part I: emotion-inducing situations are described to the subject, who must decide which emotion would be elicited. Part II: the subject hears stories in which s/he is described as behaving in various ways towards another child. The subject must judge how that child would feel.

Botel formula *Readability* formula. Readability is defined as the median level of difficulty of the words in the text sample (calculated from a graded word list). The grading is claimed to be effective up to *grade* 12.

bovine spongiform encephalopathy (BSE) Degenerative disease of the nervous system in cattle, colloquially known as *mad cow disease.* Probably contracted from animal feed containing *scrapie.* At the time of writing, there is strong circumstantial evidence (but no firmly-proven link) that the disease may be transferrable to humans through infected beef/beef products, producing an illness whose symptoms are most akin to *Creutzfeldt-Jakob Disease (CJD).* There are differences, however –victims of the 'new' disease are on average younger than 'traditional' CJD patients, typically first exhibit anxiety and depression before intellectual and movement impairment, the disease takes a longer course, and brain cell death has a different appearance. At the time of writing, laboratory evidence suggests that it is difficult to infect human nervous tissue with BSE, so a future epidemic of *dementia* is perhaps less likely than the Jeremiah-like prophecies of the popular media suggest. A similar disease to BSE has been found in other species – e.g. *feline spongiform encephalopathy (FSE)* affects cats.

Bowlby's theory of attachment J o h n Bowlby (1907–1988). Central tenet of his theory was *monotropy* (belief that a child has a drive to maximally *bond* to only one person – usually the mother). Attachment develops in four phases (the following are Bowlby's own terms – less unwieldy terminology is used by some commentators). Phase 1: *orientation and signals without discrimination of figure* (circa 0–3 months). The baby will respond to any adult or stimulus. Phase 2: *orientation and signals directed towards one (or more) discriminated figure(s)* (circa 3–6 months). The baby begins to focus his/her attentions on familiar people. Phase 3: *maintenance of proximity to a discriminated figure by means of locomotion as well as signals* (circa 6 months–3 years). The baby/child actively seeks to maintain contact with his/her mother/principal *caregiver*. Phase 4: *formation of a goal-corrected partnership* (3 years and over). The formation of other bonds, and the toleration of separation from the mother/primary caregiver. Bowlby also studied children's responses to being separated from their mothers (e.g. on entering hospital), and identified phases of response by the child, collectively called *protest, despair and detachment.* The *protest* phase consisted of crying, and generally protesting at the separation, to be succeeded by *despair* (the child was generally miserable), and finally came *detachment* (the child was disinterested in his/her parents, and appeared content, although could be inwardly insecure). Bowlby's views are most famously expressed in 'Child Care and the Growth of Love' (the book publication of a 1951 report for the World Health Organisation) and 'Attach ment and Loss'.

Bowman Test of Reading Competence Reading test for 7–10-year-olds. Uses *cloze procedure.*

BPVS *British Picture Vocabulary Scale.*

Bracken Basic Concept Scale (BBCS) Measure of concept acquisition in children aged 2 years 6 months–8 years. Consists of a group screening test and a more searching diagnostic test done on a one-to-one basis.

Bracken Concept Development Programme (BCDP) Teaching aid consisting of instructional materials to aid concept development in young children (2 years 6 months and over).

bradykinesia Very slow movement. A common feature of *Parkinsonism.*

bradylexia Very slow (but not necessarily inaccurate) reading.

Braille Named after its inventor, a writing system for the blind, in which embossed dots, detectable by touch, represent letters or letter combinations. See *Braille Grade One* and *Braille Grade Two.*

Braille Grade One *Braille* system in which all words are fully spelt out. See *Braille Grade Two.*

Braille Grade Two *Braille* system in which common letter sequences, syllables, and words are represented by special symbols. More advanced, and once mastered, faster to read than *Braille Grade One.*

Brazelton Scale Measure of newborn infant's mental state, by measuring reactions to a variety of stimuli (light, rattle, etc.), reflexes, etc. Used to identify possible brain damage, mental retardation, etc. An amended version – the **Neonatal Behavioural Assessment Scale with Kansas Supplements (NBAS-K)** is also in wide use.

brick test Semi-serious term for a *creativity test* in which the subject must think of novel uses for an everyday object (often a house brick, hence the name).

bridging See *instrumental enrichment (IE).*

Bristol Social Adjustment Guides (BSAG) Measure of the degree to which school age children are able to adjust to social situations.

British Ability Scales (BAS) Test battery to assess 2–17-year-old children's intellectual abilities. The test can be used as a straightforward measure of overall intelligence, and can also provide a profile of abilities.

British Picture Vocabulary Scale (BPVS) Updated version of the **English Picture Vocabulary Test (EPVT)**. Test of vocabulary in young children. Subjects are shown four pictures and are asked which best represents a word provided by the experimenter. The words increase in difficulty as the test progresses. The original (American) version of the test is known as the *Peabody Picture Vocabulary Scale*.

British school system Children typically begin school at 4–5 years. The ordering of state schools is *infant school* (years 1–3), *junior school* (4–7/8), *secondary school* (7/8–14). Infant and junior schools are sometimes amalgamated into a *primary school* (although confusingly, this term applies in some regions only to a junior or to an infant school). The types of secondary school are detailed under the entry for *grammar school*. Private schools (which educate about 10% of British children) are generally termed *public schools*. The private junior school is often called a *preparatory school* or *prep school*, because its principal purpose is to prepare pupils for entry into private secondary education (see *Common Entrance Exam*). Children may begin school before the age of 5 years at kindergarten (nursery school), often attached to the infant school. The minimum school leaving age is 16 years. Remaining at school after this age is usually dependent on scholastic attainment. See *sixth form*.

broken glass experiment *chipped beaker experiment.*

Brooklands experiment Study of a training and caring scheme for *mentally retarded* children.

BRP *Barking Reading Project.*

BRS *Behaviour Rating Scale.*

Bruininks-Oseretsky Test Test of children's (4–14 years) motor skills.

Brunet-Lézine Test Test battery of infant's motor, adaptive, linguistic and social skills.

BSAG *Bristol Social Adjustment Guides.*

BSE (1) *bovine spongiform encephalopathy.* (2) *Behavioral Summarized Evaluation.*

BSID *Bayley Scales of Infant Development.*

BTR *Baby Talk Register.*

BUGGY *Computer aided instruction* programme for correcting errors in subtraction problems.

bulimia Gross over-eating. The cause may be due to organic changes in the brain (e.g. a tumour or *Pick's disease*) but the most common reason is *bulimia nervosa*, where the over-eating may take the form of episodes of binge eating, rather than constant over-eating.

bulimia nervosa The urge to eat unnaturally large quantities of food (usually binge eating, followed by self-induced vomiting). Patients are usually teenage and young adult women. An appreciable proportion (some studies record circa 50%) of patients have previously suffered from *anorexia nervosa*. See *bulimia*.

burst-pause Term sometimes used to describe an infant's feeding pattern when sucking a nipple/teat. Some commentators argue that the pauses between bursts of sucking are the first occasion when interaction occurs between the mother and child, helping strengthen the mother–child *bond*.

Burt Word Reading Test Reading test for 6–12-year-olds. Requires subjects to read out loud single words, which increase in difficulty as the test progresses.

BVMGT *Bender Visual Motor Gestalt Test.*

C

CA *chronological age.*

CAB *Comprehensive Ability Battery* .

cafeteria study Any study which gives subjects a range of foodstuffs to choose from. The aim is usually to see if subjects select a balanced diet. Some studies (not without criticism) report that young children are capable of doing this.

CAH *congenital adrenal hyperplasia.*

CAI *computer aided instruction.*

California Infant Scales Forerunner of the *Bayley Scales of Infant Development.*

callosal agenesis *Congenital* defect in which the patient is born without a corpus callosum (the principal pathway connecting the left and right cerebral hemispheres).

Camphill Movement Worldwide therapeutic movement for training and treating *mentally retarded* people (children and adults). A particular feature are 'Camphill Villages' – therapeutic working communities for adults.

canalization Development shaped by *inherited* as opposed to environmental factors.

canonical bias *intellectual realism.*

canonical orientation *intellectual realism.*

CAP *Colorado Adoption Project.*

capacity, mental *mental capacity.*

capacity stage (of career choice) See *fantasy stage (career choice).*

CAPE *Clifton Assessment Procedure for the Elderly.*

cardinal number The concept that different sets of objects can contain the same number of items, regardless of other properties of the set (e.g. 'three mice' has the same cardinal number as 'three elephants'). See *ordinal number.*

cardination test Measure of ability to judge if two or more rows of items have equal numbers of elements. Subjects are instructed to do this by visual comparisons, without explicitly counting. Often used as a measure of *conservation of number.*

career awareness Knowledge of what a particular career or type of career entails.

caregiver A person who looks after a patient or child.

caregiver burden The psychological and material demands and stress placed on a *caregiver.*

caregiver speech *motherese.*

Caregiver Strain Index (CSI) Measure of stress and strain in *caregivers* (usually caregivers of older patients).

caretaker (1) *caregiver.* (2) For the benefit of American readers – 'caretaker' is commonly used in British English to denote a janitor, particularly of a school.

carpal age *Chronological age* calculated through state of wrist (carpal) bones.

Carver Word Recognition Test Reading test for subjects aged 4–8 years. Subjects must choose the printed representation of a word spoken by the experimenter, from a list of alternatives.

CAS *Cognitive Assessment Scale.*

Casati-Lezine Scale French version . of *Uzgiris-Hunt Scale.*

cascade model of ageing Model of ageing which argues that changes begin in a relatively slight fashion, and then gather momentum and accelerate in severity.

CAT (1) *Children's Apperception Test.* (2) *Cognitive Abilities Test.*

cataracts A progressive opaqueness of the lens, ultimately causing blindness. Has several causes, including diabetes and kidney failure. Cataracts are found most frequently (although not exclusively) in older people.

catastrophe theory Theory that ageing is attributable to a faulty genetic code causing faulty cell replacement.

catchment area Area whose inhabitants are treated, educated etc. at a particular hospital, school, etc.

categorical self *objective self.*

cathartic play Play as a relief from stress or other negative emotions.

Cattell Culture-Fair Test (CCFT) Intelligence test, which by avoiding measures of linguistic skills and general knowledge, supposedly measures intellectual skills equally accessible to people of all cultural/linguistic backgrounds.

Cattell Infant Intelligence Scale Companion to the *Stanford–Binet Scale*, for infants aged 3–30 months.

CBRSC *Comprehensive Behaviour Rating Scale For Children.*

CBS *chronic brain syndrome.*

CCFT *Cattell Culture-Fair Test.*

CD (1) congenitally deaf. (2) *conduct disorder.*

CDR *Clinical Dementia Rating.*

CE *Common Entrance Exam.*

CEC Council for Exceptional Children (American).

cellular garbage model Model of ageing which argues that ageing occurs because of the accumulation of metabolic waste products.

central executive See *working memory.*

centration Opposite of *decentration* – i.e. in *Piagetian* terms, the illogical emphasis on subjective impressions of a situation, without regard to other viewpoints, leading to a biased and hence erroneous appraisal. See *egocentrism.* Similarly, overly concentrating on one aspect of a stimulus to the exclusion of others.

cephalocaudal development Development from the head downwards. This contrasts with **proximodistal development**, which is from the centre of the body outwards. The terms are used to describe the general pattern of development of control over the body in developing infants.

cerebral cortex Usually known by its abbreviated name of *cortex.* The cerebral cortex is the characteristic wrinkled surface of the brain. It is divided into two linked *hemispheres* and can be divided into four regions or lobes which have different functions. The cerebral cortex is responsible for most higher intellectual functioning.

cerebral haemorrhage Bleeding in the brain. See *subdural haematoma.*

cerebral palsy General term for any defect in control of movement resulting from brain damage.

CF *current family.*

CFF *critical flicker fusion.*

CFQ *Cognitive Failures Questionnaire.*

chaining See *signal learning.*

changing environment effect *cohort effect.*

Charteris Reading Test Reading test for 10–13 year olds.

CHE community home with education on the premises.

chemistry problem See *formal operations*.

child abuse Deliberate psychological or physical mistreatment of a child, sometimes by his/her parents and/or other caregivers. Compare with *child neglect*.

child as scientist Phrase sometimes applied to the mental frame of mind a child must adopt to solve *Piagetian* tasks.

'Child Care and the Growth of Love' Book by John Bowlby (1951), dealing with child rearing and problems of delinquency. Controversial because it was (mis)interpreted as arguing that all mothers should stay at home, rearing their children. See *Bowlby's theory of attachment*.

child caregiver *Caregiver* who looks after a child or children. Not a child who is a caregiver, as might be reasonably interpreted.

child-centred relationship Any familial relationship from the child's viewpoint (e.g. mother, father, grandfather, etc.). See other-centred relationship.

child-contingent Aimed advantageously at the child.

Child Language Data Exchange System (CHILDES) Depository of recordings of child language for use in research.

child minder See *family day care*.

child neglect Psychological or physical damage befalling a child, resulting from lack of care, usually by his/her parents and/or caregivers. Compare with *child abuse*.

CHILDES *Child Language Data Exchange System*.

childhood amnesia The loss of memories about early childhood which is disproportionately greater than would be predicted from simple forgetfulness.

Originally thought (e.g. by Freud) to be due to suppression of emotionally fraught memories, more recent explanations have taken a cognitive approach (e.g. young children are intellectually incapable of storing memories efficiently, so they are forgotten).

childhood disintegrative disorder A decline in psychological, motor and/or social skills after conventional development for at least 2 years.

childhood neurosis Rather nebulous term denoting a neurosis-like illness occurring in childhood.

childhood onset pervasive developmental disorder Disorder which begins in childhood, and whose symptoms appear to be a mixture of *autism* and *childhood schizophrenia*. Among the symptoms are: an abnormally low desire for normal social contacts, distress at changes in surroundings, sudden temper tantrums, and a lack of emotion.

childhood psychosis Psychosis whose onset is in childhood. The term includes *autism* and *childhood onset pervasive developmental disorder*.

childhood schizophrenia Schizophrenia whose onset is in childhood. The term is now largely outmoded (the nearest *DSM* – perhaps the most widely accepted taxonomy system – classification is *childhood onset pervasive developmental disorder*). In some older texts, the term is used fairly interchangeably with *autism*.

Children's Apperception Test (CAT) Test of children's beliefs and motivations. The subject is shown a series of pictures and is asked to make up a story about each one. These are supposed to reveal the child's attitudes.

Children's Television Workshop (CTW)
American television production company of children's programmes with a high educational content. Most famous creation is 'Sesame Street'.

Chinese readers and spellers P e o p l e who tend to read and spell by the visual shape of the word, without paying much attention to what it sounds like. Refers to average individuals, but symptoms in extremis are akin to *phonological dyslexia.* Compare with *Phoenecian readers and spellers.*

chipped beaker experiment
Experimental method devised by Light and colleagues, criticizing the experimental methodology used to support *Piaget's* original *conservation of quantity* experiments. Children were shown two identical beakers containing identical quantities of pasta shells. The experimenter then observed that one of the beakers had a chipped rim, so the contents of the chipped beaker were transferred to another, differently shaped, beaker. More children accept that the quantities have been conserved in this experimental design than in the traditional *Piagetian* paradigm. It has been argued that this is because the child can more readily understand the logic of transferring the contents in this experiment, and so is less likely to be confused into changing his/her answer.

cholinergic hypothesis T h e o r y that much of the memory loss in *dementia of the Alzheimer type* can be attributed to depletion of the cholinergic system (neurons in the brain which transmit signals using the chemical acetyl choline). See *ganglioside, ondansetron,* and *tacrine.*

chorionic villus sampling (CVS)
Taking a sample of tissue from the chorion (the tissue surrounding the *foetus* and placenta), in women 8–10 weeks pregnant, where there is a high risk of abnormal foetal development. Used to test for a variety of abnormalities.

Chowchilla kidnapping A mass kidnapping of 26 children, aged 5–14 years, who were in a bus on their way to a summer school in Chowchilla, U.S.A. The children were entombed in a buried bus, until they dug their way out and escaped. The incident has been the subject of several studies of trauma in children.

chromosomes Found in every cell nucleus is a set of chromosomes which are composed of sets of *genes* which provide the complete 'genetic blueprint' for 'making' the living being in question. The size of a complete set of chromosomes varies between species – humans normally have 46, arranged in 23 pairs. In sexual reproduction, the pairs split, and one half of each pair of the father fuses with a complimentary set from the mother (see *genetic dominance*). A person's sex is determined by the **sex chromosomes**, labelled X and Y. Normally, females possess two X chromosomes and males one X and one Y chromosome (however, see *XYY syndrome*). The functions of the genes on each chromosome are not fully known, although abnormalities in some chromosomes are known to cause disability (e.g. *Down's Syndrome*).

chronic long lasting.

chronic brain disorder Any long-lasting (although not *congenital*) disorder of mental efficiency, usually resulting from a long-standing cause (e.g. malnutrition/vitamin deficiency from a poor diet). Can produce *dementia*-like symptoms, or can 'flare up' relatively suddenly into *acute confusional state*.

chronic brain syndrome (CBS)
Long-term degeneration of brain tissue, resulting in severe impairment of personality and/or intellectual functioning. Largely synonymous with *dementia*.

chronic living-dying phase (of dying)
See *acute crisis phase*.

chronological age (CA) The length of time a person has been alive.

chronological age matching
Comparing groups with the same *chronological ages*. Any differences between the groups thus cannot be attributed to age per se. See *mental age matching*.

circular action *circular reaction*.

circular reaction Term originally describing behaviour which created similar behaviour (see *Baldwin's theory of developmental psychology*). However, adapted by *Piaget*. See *sensori-motor stage 2 et seq.*

CJD *Creutzfeldt-Jakob Disease*.

class inclusion The logical rule that the number of members of a sub-group cannot exceed the total size of the set, where the sub-group is totally enclosed in the set (e.g. there cannot be more poodles than there are dogs). *Piaget* devised a series of experiments to demonstrate the failure of class inclusion in children in the *preoperational subperiod* (and in particular, the failure of *grouping*). In perhaps the best known study, children were shown a set of flowers, of which the majority were tulips. The children were asked if there were more flowers or more tulips. The preoperational children tended to answer 'more tulips', thereby indicating, Piaget argued, that they thought that the subset

was bigger than the total group. However, as with most of Piaget's experimental work, the study has been criticized for being over-complicated, and confusing the child into giving the wrong answer.

classical conditioning A method of training subjects to make a response to a stimulus which in itself would not elicit the response, because the stimulus is associated with another stimulus which normally elicits the response. The technique was first objectively studied by the Russian physiologist Ivan Pavlov in the early years of the twentieth century. Dogs salivate when presented with food – Pavlov discovered that if a bell was rung (or in other experiments, a light was flashed) just before the presentation of the food, then after several days, the dogs began to salivate simply on hearing the bell (presumably because they expected food to follow). The technique is used in certain forms of training. See *operant conditioning*.

classification In *Piagetian* theory, grouping items on the basis of shared feature(s).

classroom dynamics General term for the interactions and patterns of behaviour exhibited in teaching situations.

Clifton Assessment Procedure for the Elderly (CAPE) Test battery consisting of two 'sub-batteries' – the ***Cognitive Assessment Scale (CAS)*** and the ***Behaviour Rating Scale (BRS)***, measuring intellectual skills and personality respectively, in older subjects (particularly hospital patients and the institutionalized older people).

climacteric menopause.

Clinical Dementia Rating (CDR) A 'checklist' for assessing the level of functioning a patient suspected of *dementia* is capable of on various tasks. From this, his/her level of impairment, and hence the severity of the dementia can be calculated.

clinical method Term used by *Piaget* to denote observing children in naturalistic (as opposed to more artificial laboratory-based) settings.

clinical retardation Very severe *mental retardation* which is apparent at birth or soon after. Contrast with *sociocultural retardation*.

cloaca concept The erroneous belief of some children that they were born through the anus.

closed family Family whose members 'keep themselves to themselves', and who tend to seek help within the family. Opposite of *open family*.

cloze procedure Reading test method – subjects have to insert appropriate words into blanks in a passage of text (e.g. fill in the blank in 'the cat sat on … mat'). The term (devised by Wilson Taylor in the 1950s) is meant to indicate a link with the Gestalt concept of closure (the hypothesized drive to mentally fill in missing gaps in an image). Scores on cloze tests correlate well with more conventional reading measures, but the procedure can be criticized as artificial and ambiguous (e.g. what counts as an acceptable answer – only the word originally intended by the author? is the passage written in a style which will unfairly favour some readers over others?).

Cloze Reading Tests Reading tests for 8–12 year olds, which use the *cloze procedure*.

cluttering Developmental speech disorder characterized by missing/distorted consonants. In severe cases, speech may be incomprehensible. Other linguistic skills may be relatively normal. Symptoms often improve (sometimes spontaneously), although some difficulties may remain, even after treatment.

CMMS *Columbia Mental Maturity Scale.*

CMV *cytomegalovirus.*

co-dominant gene See *genetic dominance.*

co-twin control Method (now rarely used) in which the effects of training are assessed by administering training to one twin only. The subsequent difference in the performances of the trained and untrained twins on a particular task are then (debatably) attributed to the effect of the training.

co-twin study Experimental design in which one twin receives a different treatment from the other.

co-univocal See *grouping IV.*

code switching Shifting from one language or dialect to another.

codification rules See *Piaget's theory of moral development.*

Cognitive Abilities Test (CAT) Intelligence test battery, with a chief subdivision into non-verbal and verbal measures.

Cognitive Assessment Scale (CAS) See *Clifton Assessment Procedure for the Elderly.*

cognitive clarity (reading) *reading awareness.*

cognitive differentiation The ability to create and identify sub-categories from a larger category.

cognitive equilibration *equilibration.*

Cognitive Failures Questionnaire (CFQ) Test, devised by the psychologist Donald Broadbent, which asks subjects to report instances of memory failure in recent everyday life (e.g. forgetting to buy items when shopping, etc.). Used to assess how forgetful people (particularly older people) are in 'real life' (compared with more artificial laboratory tasks).

cognitive slowing *slowing.*

cohort A group of people raised in the same environment and/or period of time, or otherwise sharing a feature. Often used synonymously with *age cohort.*

cohort analysis The process of comparing *cohorts.*

cohort effect A difference between age groups which is better attributed to differences in the ways they were raised and educated than to their ages per se. See *overlapping longitudinal study.*

cohort sequential design *overlapping longitudinal study.*

cohort study Study of a *cohort* (typically, an *age cohort*). If this is of one cohort over time, then it is also a *longitudinal study.*

collateral learning The incidental learning which occurs in the classroom beyond what is being explicitly taught (e.g. social skills, planning skills, etc.).

collective décalage *Décalage* in which the direction of the disparity is the same for all individuals (e.g. for everyone, skill X arises before skill Y). In *homogeneous collective décalage*, the magnitude of the disparity is the same for everyone, whilst in *heterogeneous collective décalage*, the magnitude varies between individuals. See *individual décalage.*

Colorado Adoption Project (CAP) *Longitudinal study* of the development of adopted infants, and infants with their *biological parents.* Among other aims, the study investigates the *hereditarian versus environmentalist theories of individual differences.*

Colorado Childhood Temperament Inventory Battery of scales of aspects of temperament/behaviour (e.g. 'emotionality', 'reaction to foods', etc.).

Coloured Progressive Matrices (CPM) See *Raven's Progressive Matrices.*

Columbia Mental Maturity Scale (CMMS) Intelligence test battery for children aged 3 years 6 months–10 years. Requires no spoken answers and little movement, and is particularly intended for children with restricted movement and/or speech impairment.

combinatorial analysis See *formal operations.*

combinatorial rules Linguistic rules governing the correct order of word sequences.

combinatorial task The *chemistry problem* in *Piaget's* theory of *formal operations.*

Common Entrance (CE) Exam Examination for entrance into a British *public school*, good performance in which can be a basis for scholarships or other remuneration.

communicative intent Term used by some commentators (e.g. Lenneberg) to denote a stage in speech acquisition (typically, 2 years 6 months–3 years) characterized by an 'explosion' in vocabulary and use of more complex utterances).

commutativity Property of a process which is the same whatever order it is expressed in (e.g. $5+2 = 2+5$).

compensation General and often ill-defined theory that older people can compensate for failings in one (usually *fluid intelligence*-based) skill by increasing their reliance on another (usually *crystallized intelligence*-based). See *molar equivalence (ME).*

competence (1) The hypothesized level of ability which would be displayed under perfect conditions. (2) The term is also used in its everyday sense.

complex learning Theory by Norman that learning a topic requires three processes: *accretion* (basic learning of new information), *restructuring* (making sense of the new information and creating/adapting *schemas*) and *tuning* (automatizing the knowledge so that it becomes 'second nature'; although note some related theories use this to describe relatively minor changes in knowledge).

complexes stage See *vague syncretic stage*.

complexity effect *age x complexity effect*.

complexity preference The phenomenon whereby (at least in babies) a complex stimulus is preferred over a simple one, and that the level of preferred complexity increases with age.

complimentary substitutions Also known as *vicariances.* See *grouping II.*

component efficiency hypothesis Hypothesis that the decline in a skill is due to a decline in one or more of the 'basic' sub-skills governing it.

componential intelligence See *triarchic theory of intelligence*.

composition When used in connection with *Piagetian* theory – see *group*.

compositional word acquisition Theory that the meanings of words are learnt bit by bit. See *holistic word acquisition*.

comprehension See *Bloom's taxonomy of educational objectives*.

comprehension learning See *operation learning*.

Comprehensive Ability Battery (CAB) Intelligence test battery for children.

Comprehensive Behaviour Rating Scale For Children (CBRSC) Measure of behaviour of schoolchildren aged 6–14 years.

comprehensive school Most common form of British state school, which accepts pupils of all abilities (hence its name) from circa 11 years up to leaving age. The school may be linked to a *sixth form college*, or may undertake post-16 years teaching itself. See *grammar school*.

Comprehensive Test of Adaptive Behaviour (CTAB) Measure primarily of coping and housekeeping skills in subjects (5–60 years) with potential problems.

computer aided instruction (CAI) Any educational method involving the use of a computer. Typically refers to software packages where the computer presents the pupil with a series of problems to solve. See *response-sensitive instruction*.

computer literacy Ability competently to use a computer.

concealment of effort Phenomenon whereby some pupils/students work hard, but cover up their efforts in order not to appear over-keen.

concept learning See *signal learning*.

concrete operational period The *Piagetian* theory of intellectual development of children aged between approximately 18 months and 11 years. Divided into two stages – *preoperational subperiod* (circa 18 months–7 years) and the *concrete operations subperiod* (circa 7–11 years). 'Concrete operations' loosely correspond to the ability to (a) mentally represent physical items and (b) to imagine actions which would transform them. Piaget argued that a series of rules of logical and relational groupings are learnt during this period (see *grouping* et seq). A key feature of these is *reversibility* – unlike some of their physical counterparts, mental transformations can be 'run backwards' (e.g. a firework can be imagined exploding and recombining – only the former is physically possible). Thoughts are still tied to real physical items, however (hence the term 'concrete'); truly abstract conceptualization does not arise until the next stage of development – the *formal operations period*.

concrete operations subperiod In *Piagetian* theory, the second and final stage of the *concrete operational period*, occurring between the ages of circa 7–11 years. The problems of the *preoperational subperiod* have been overcome (principally *egocentrism* and the failure of *conservation*). The child is now capable of creating *groups*, *groupings*, and *lattices* of related mental *operations*. These are essentially packages of mental procedures for processing problems. Note that children in this subperiod are restricted to mental representations of physically real items and events – truly abstract thought does not arise until the *formal operations period* which follows.

conditioning Process whereby a subject is trained to respond to a stimulus which previously did not elicit a reaction. See *behaviourism*.

conduct disorder (CD) Nebulous term for serious misbehaviour by children. Can be divided into two sub-categories. *Socialized conduct disorder* describes breaches of social or moral codes (e.g. truancy), whilst *undersocialized conduct disorder* describes offences against other people or objects (e.g. arson). The two sub-categories can be further divided according to whether the acts performed are violent or non-violent.

confabulation Condition in which the patient makes up stories or other implausible explanations to cover up gaps in his/her memory or other skills. Generally, the term is reserved for situations where there is no conscious attempt to deceive.

configurational organization Concept (created by the Gestalt psychologist Heinz Werner in the 1940s) that as the child matures, so s/he comes to recognize complex shapes as formations of simpler shapes and not simply as homogeneous complex shapes or as sets of isolated simpler shapes. E.g., one sees a chess board as a pattern in its own right, but one can also perceive the black and white squares from which it is formed – one does not see only the chess board or only black and white squares. It was felt that many *mentally retarded* individuals were 'stuck' with one of the less satisfactory perceptions.

conflict theory of mental development Theory that a person develops a new (and more sophisticated) mental process because his/her existing theory does not adequately explain the evidence.

confluence model Model of how *birth order* may affect intelligence. Argues that a child's *IQ* is correlated with the average *mental age* of the household. Hence, the household of the first-born child will have the average mental age of the child's parents. However, the second-born child will enter a household with an average mental age of the parents and the first born child. Hence, the average mental age will be lower, and will be lower still for subsequent births.

congenital Born with – includes characteristics which are inherited, but also features acquired during pregnancy and birth (e.g. *Down's Syndrome, foetal alcohol syndrome*).

congenital adrenal hyperplasia (CAH) Inherited (treatable) malfunction – female sufferers are born with male-looking genitals. In rare cases this is undetected at birth, and the patient is raised as a boy, the error not being discovered until puberty. Such cases are obviously of interest to sex difference researchers.

congenital hypothyroidism *cretinism.*

congenital inarticulation *cluttering.*

congenital word blindness Old term for *developmental dyslexia.*

Conners Parent Rating Scale A measure of parental assessment of the emotional and social developent of children aged 3–17 years.

Conners Teacher Rating Scale A 40-item measure of a teacher's assessment of a pupil's behaviour and abilities.

cononical stage Loosely, *reduplicated babbling.*

conservation The knowledge that an item can retain a particular property even though other properties of the item have changed (e.g. a modelling clay ball retains the same volume when it is rolled into a sausage shape). Acquisition of conservation is a key feature of *Piaget's* theory of the *concrete operational period.* Children can be categorized according to their responses to a conservation task. The stages are held to occur in the following developmental order. *Stage Ia children* fail the tasks because they only attend to changes in the height of the transformed item. *Stage Ib children* fail because they only attend to the breadth. *Stage IIa children* attend to either height or breadth, but not both simultaneously. *Stage IIb children* attend to both height and breadth, but cannot adequately calculate how the change in one is offset by a compensatory change in the other. *Stage III children* have attained conservation. Conservation is often considered in terms of the property under discussion – see *conservation of inequality, conservation of length, conservation of number, conservation of quantity, perceptual seduction,* and *pseudo-conservation.*

conservation focusing See *selection strategies.*

conservation of inequality *Conservation*-type task in which the items to be compared are unequal before the transformation is made. The aim is to see if the child recognizes that the inequality remains after the transformation.

conservation of length In *Piagetian* theory, the knowledge that items remain the same length even if they are moved. In the most famous experiment, the child is shown two rods of equal length, and the child agrees that they are so. One rod is moved, and the child is again asked if they are the same length. Children under 7 years often fail at this task. However, the experimental design may be (unintentionally) confusing the children – Piaget's critics observe that if the child is asked if the rods are the same length only once, after one of them has been moved, then the child is far more likely to give the correct answer. This implies that the child can conserve length, but changes his/her answer because s/he thinks the (adult) experimenter wants him/her to. See *conservation.*

conservation of matter See *conservation of quantity.*

conservation of number In *Piagetian* theory, the knowledge that items retain their numerical value even if the pattern of their grouping changes. E.g. a child in the *pre-operational subperiod* is shown an equal number of red and blue counters, set in two same-colour rows next to each other. The child agrees that there are as many red counters as blue counters. However, if the experimenter now spreads out one of the rows, then the child, when asked, argues that there are more of one colour counters than there are of the other. This theory has been criticized (as per the *conservation of length* experiment) for confusing the child, and making him/her suppose that the (adult) experimenter wants a change of answer. For example, in the *naughty teddy experiment*, the child is shown the two lines of counters, and then the experiment is disrupted by a 'naughty teddy bear', who (controlled by the experimenter) spreads out one of the lines of counters. The child, if now asked if the two sets of counters have the same number, is far more likely to answer correctly. This implies that whether conservation of number is found or not is very much an experimental artifact. However, more recent evidence suggests that experiments such as the naughty teddy are themselves biasing the child's response, by e.g. distracting him/her. See *conservation* and *provoked correspondence (number conservation)*.

conservation of quantity In *Piagetian* theory, the knowledge that an item contains the same quantity of matter, even though its physical shape has changed. This can take three forms – conservation of matter, weight, and volume. *Piaget* argued that most children are at least 7 years old before they begin to acquire this knowledge. In the archetypal demonstration of this, he asked a child to make a ball of clay 'just as big as and just as heavy' as one provided by the experimenter. Several variants follow from this. To demonstrate *conservation of matter*, one of the balls is rolled into a sausage shape, and the child is asked if the two balls still contain the same amount of clay (typically, children are 7–8 years old before they correctly answer 'yes'). This task is also known as the *solid continuous quantity task*. The experiment can also be performed using liquid. In the *liquid continuous quantity task*, the child is shown two beakers containing the same quantities of liquid. The contents of one of the beakers are poured into a differently shaped glass, and the child is asked if the contents are still equal. In a variation on this – the *discontinuous quantity task* – beads, rather than liquid, are used. To test *conservation of weight*, the child weighs the two balls (as in the conservation of matter experiment) in a balance to ensure they are the same weight. One of the balls is rolled out, and then the child is asked if the two pieces of clay still weigh the same. Children are typically 10 years old before they correctly answer 'yes'. To test *conservation of volume*, the children put the two balls separately into a water filled glass container, and observe that the water level rises by the same amount in both cases (i.e. an equal amount of water is displaced). One ball is rolled out, and then the child is asked if the two pieces of clay will still cause the same rise in water level (i.e. displace the same volume of water). A correct 'yes' answer is not usually given until the child is about 12 years old. Conservation of matter, weight and volume are three facets of the same basic knowledge, and the age difference in their acquisition is an example of *horizontal décalage*. One of the methods by which a child might gain insight into conservation is through *atomism*. Another is to perceive that although the clay changes shape, any decrease in its height is compensated for by an increase in its width (this is akin to the concept of multiplying relative features of a set cited in *grouping VII*). The experiments are the most cited of all Piaget's work. Another very elegant (although less well known) experiment assessing the same issues is the *dissolving sugar experiment*.

conservation of volume See *conservation of quantity*.

conservation of weight See *conservation of quantity*.

consolidation stage Term used in some descriptions of the lifespan, denoting the period when career advancement reaches a peak (typically in the thirties and forties).

constricted personality See *armoured-defensive personality*.

constructionist theory Also called *constructivism*. Term sometimes applied to (e.g. *Piaget's*) theories which argue that knowledge and thought processes are constructed through the interaction of the child's mental mechanisms and the environment. See *neoconstructivism*.

constructive play See *functional play*.

constructivism See *constructionist theory*.

contact comfort Receiving comfort from the texture of an object being touched.

content criterion The minimum mark a subject must attain on a test to be deemed to know the topic being tested in sufficient depth. See *criterion-referenced tests*.

content specific teaching skills Skills which are only appropriate to a particular lesson or section of the curriculum (e.g. ability to explain the periodic table, the Treaty of Westphalia, etc.). See *general teaching skills*.

context-bound word Characteristic of some of an infant's early words whereby they are only used in a particular and inappropriately narrow context (e.g. 'dog' may only refer to the family pet feeding, and not e.g. when it is running, going walkies, etc.). See *decontextualization*.

contextual cues In reading, semantic and other cues other than those from the to-be-read word itself which help identify a word.

contextual intelligence See *triarchic theory of intelligence*.

contingency awareness The realization that a particular action has a particular effect.

continuation education Education of people who have 'dropped out' from the conventional education system.

continuous development Development in which the skill, once acquired, remains qualitatively the same, and improves at a reasonably steady rate until a terminal plateau is reached (i.e. the subject has reached a peak of performance which s/he cannot improve on). Compare with *discontinuous development*.

continuous quantity task See *liquid continuous quantity task* and *solid continuous quantity task*.

contraction stage See *expansion stage*.

conventional level Middle level of moral reasoning in *Kohlberg's theory of moral development*.

convergence analysis Complex statistical technique combining findings from a variety of different methods of study (e.g. of *longitudinal studies* and *cross-sectional studies*) to determine a general rule.

convergent strabismus See *strabismus*.

convergent thinking See *divergent thinking*.

cooing Term given by some commentators to the repeated sounds made by infants of up to circa 4 months of age.

cooperation board Measure of cooperation in children. Subjects sit at fixed positions around a table, each holding a piece of string attached to an object. The object (usually a pen) has to be moved around a sequence of targets (e.g. a track) drawn on the table. This can only be done if the children cooperate, and pull in pre-agreed sequences – if they all pull at once, the object does not move.

cooperation rules See *Piaget's theory of moral development*.

cooperative play *Play* in which the child interacts with other children. Develops after earlier stages of *solitary play* and *parallel play*.

Copernican revolution Copernicus was the astronomer who provided the first coherent argument that the Earth revolves around the sun, rather than vice versa. *Piaget* used this as an analogy for the process of *decentration* in *sensori-motor development*.

coping skill The ability to handle a severe disruption to one's life (e.g. accident, death of friend or relative, etc.). See *appraisal-focused coping*, *emotion-focused coping*, and *problem-focused coping*.

cops and robbers task *policeman experiment*.

corneal reflection technique Method of measuring eye movements by shining an (invisible) infra-red beam onto the subject's eyeball, and by measuring the angle at which the beam is reflected back, calculating where the subject's eye is directed.

cortex *cerebral cortex*.

cortical dementias *Dementias* in which the principal damage occurs in the *cortex* of the brain (e.g. *dementia of the Alzheimer type*, *multi-infarct dementia*). Compare with *sub-cortical dementias*.

cortical thickening The phenomenon whereby animals raised in stimulating environments have thicker brain *cortices* than those raised in unstimulating environments. See *plasticity*.

covert curriculum That which is learnt at school, although it is not explicitly taught (e.g. many study skills). Also called *collateral learning*. See *hidden curriculum*, and *overt curriculum*.

CPM *Coloured Progressive Matrices*.

creative play *Play* in which symbolic or 'pretend' attributes are given to objects or situations.

creativity Largely synonymous with *divergent thinking*. The term generally refers to any ability to produce novel ideas. Note that the term has a less 'dramatic' meaning than the layperson's use – i.e. it is usually not confined to great artists, writers, etc.

creativity test Any measure of ability to produce original ideas. Usually there are caveats that the ideas should be plentiful and feasible. Frequently used measures include the *brick test*, a *verbal fluency measure*, ability to create narratives on a given theme, etc.

cretinism A *congenital* form of *mental retardation* caused by an underactive thyroid gland. If identified early (before 3 months of age), the illness can be largely successfully treated.

Creutzfeldt-Jakob Disease (CJD) A very rare *dementia* (affecting circa 1 person per million per year), possibly contracted through contact with infected nervous tissue. In addition to archetypal *demented* symptoms of intellectual and mnemonic impairment, there are severe disturbances of gait and movement. CJD can strike at any age in adulthood, but is typically found in middle aged and older people, probably because in most cases there is a long incubation period (e.g. decades). In recent times, CJD has been associated with ***bovine spongiform encephalopathy (BSE)***.

cri du chat *Inherited* condition with physical and psychological handicaps, and characterized by the strange cat-like sounds made by patients as babies.

crisis nursery A nursery where parents may leave their children for a short period when they feel they are in danger of abusing their child.

crisis theory Any theory which seeks to explain how people cope with severe (and usually negative) disruptions to their lives (e.g., accident, death of friend or relative, etc.).

criterion-referenced tests *Achievement tests* in which subjects' scores can be compared to a particular standard or criterion. The nature of this criterion is an absolute value, independent of considerations of e.g. age group norms.

critical flicker fusion (CFF) The slowest rate at which a flickering light is perceived as a 'continuous' light. The rate decreases in old age (i.e. an old person cannot perceive as fast a rate of flicker).

critical loss Pertaining to the *terminal drop model*, the theory that in old age, declines in some intellectual abilities can be endured, but falls in others constitute a 'critical loss' which heralds death.

critical period (1) The time during which *imprinting* to a stimulus must take place, or the animal will thereafter fail to respond to the stimulus as intended. E.g. if a newborn (non-human) animal is only given contact with humans rather than its own species, it tends to *bond* itself to the humans it encountered even if subsequently returned to its own species. (2) More generally, the period of development during which the subject must be exposed to a particular skill if it is to be learnt. See *sensitive period*. (3) See *plasticity*.

cross-linking theory of ageing Theory that the physical decline of the older person's body can be attributed to a loss of elasticity of tissues (skin, muscles, etc.).

cross-modal matching Recognizing an object previously only experienced in one sensory modality in another modality (e.g. feeling an object and then recognizing it by sight alone).

cross-modal transfer *cross-modal matching.*

cross-sectional mesosystem See *microsystem.*

cross-sectional research/samples/study The experimental method of testing different groups (usually different age groups) in the same test period and comparing their performances. Contrast with *longitudinal research/samples/study*. See *overlapping longitudinal study*.

crying cat syndrome *cri du chat.*

crystallization Term used in several models to denote the period in which a skill or an interest is formed into its final or near-final state.

crystallised intelligence The amount of factual (as opposed to autobiographical) knowledge a person has acquired during a lifetime – roughly corresponds to the lay term 'general knowledge'.

CSI *Caregiver Strain Index.*

CTAB *Comprehensive Test of Adaptive Behaviour.*

CTW *Children's Television Workshop.*

cuddliness The degree to which a baby positively responds to being cuddled by its mother/ *caregiver* – some babies repel cuddles, which may indicate mental illness (e.g. *autism*).

Cuisenaire rods Educational toy/instructional materials for promoting mathematical skills. Consists of a set of wooden sticks of differing colours and lengths, representing different numbers. The rods are proportional to the numerical values they represent – thus the '4' rod is twice the length of the '2' rod, and half the length of the '8' rod, etc. By playing with the rods, the children come to appreciate the relationships between numbers.

cultural amplifier *Cultural tool* which serves to improve intellectual performance.

cultural deprivation Lack of an intellectually stimulating environment. Can result in a lowering of intellectual abilities. Compare with *maternal deprivation.*

cultural determinism The belief that a person's cultural environment is a principal determinant of his/her development.

cultural development, general law of *general law of cultural development.*

cultural puberty Time period during which a child/adolescent acquires an understanding of, and begins to practise, the cultural norms of the adult world.

cultural tool Tool/intellectual skill peculiar to or originating in a particular culture (e.g. slide rule, writing system, etc.). See *cultural amplifier.*

culture-fair test Test which is equally fair to all subjects, no matter what their cultural background (e.g. *Cattell Culture-Fair Test*). See *culture-specific test.*

culture-specific test Test which is specifically targeted at individuals from one (usually minority) culture. See *culture-fair test.*

cumulative difference Difference whose size increases over time.

current family (CF) Family in which a child is currently being reared. Contrast with *family of origin.*

CVS *chorionic villus sampling.*

cytologic theory Theory of ageing that the bodily decline can be attributed to 'poisoning' by toxins (including the waste products of metabolic processes). Compare with *wear and tear theory.*

cytomegalovirus (CMV) Viral infection which in a pregnant mother may lead to physical damage and *mental retardation* in her baby.

cytoplasmic inheritance The cytoplasm is the cell material surrounding the nucleus, including that of sperm and egg cells. It contains DNA, and contributes to the genetic inheritance of the *foetus*. Since the egg is larger than the sperm, the majority of cytoplasmic inheritance is from the mother.

D

DA *desired act.*

DAF *Draw a Family Test.*

Dale-Chall formula *Readability* measure. Calculated by the formula: readability = (0.1579 x percentage of unfamiliar words) + (0.0496 x mean no. of words per sentence) + 3.6365. The result is expressed as the earliest *grade* in which an average child could read the text (to express the result as *reading age*, add five to the result). The calculation of 'unfamiliar words' is too lengthy to describe here – consult an appropriate textbook. Considered most reliable for texts aimed at 11–16 year olds.

DAM test *draw-a-man test.*

Daniels and Diack reading tests *Standard Reading Tests.*

DARD *Durrell Analysis of Reading Difficulty.*

DAS *Differential Ability Scales.*

DAT (1) *dementia of the Alzheimer type.* (2) *Differential Aptitude Tests.*

DDST *Denver Developmental Screening Test.*

death preparation Preparing for the psychological and practical impact of the death of oneself or of a loved one. Usually helps to lessen the negative effects of the event. To some extent, 'passive' death preparation increases with age, as the probability of dying increases.

DEBQ *Dutch Eating Behaviour Questionnaire.*

DEBUGGY *Computer aided instruction* programme for correcting errors in subtraction problems.

décalage *Piagetian* term for the development of skills relative to each other, and the fact that the same skill can become more refined and/or be more widely used as the child develops. Has several manifestations – *collective décalage, horizontal décalage, individual décalage, oblique décalage,* and *vertical décalage.*

deceleration stage Stage in the lifespan when career and some other interests begin to wane (typically, circa 60 years).

decentration In *Piagetian* theory, the broadening of thought from a too limited perspective. In infancy, the baby must learn that s/he is a part and not the cause of the environment (see *sensori-motor development*). In early childhood, s/he must learn that many situations must be perceived from several viewpoints and not just one (see *concrete operational period*). Also broadly describes the growth of thought by which the child can think beyond the narrow confines of here and now to more abstract representations of other places and times, through conjectural thoughts on everyday life (e.g. 'what if...' type problems) to pure abstract thought.

decentre To perform *decentration.*

decision-making pattern How decisions are made within a group (e.g. a family). For examples, see *adult executive, family executive* and *single-adult executive.*

decontextualization Ceasing to use a word as a *context-bound word,* and correctly using it across a variety of appropriate situations.

deductive reasoning See *inductive reasoning*.

deep approach (learning) L e a r n i n g which seeks to discover the underlying structure of a problem. This contrasts with the *surface approach*, in which the treatment is relatively superficial and/or consists of memorizing the surface appearance of the situation.

deep play Term devised by Jeremy Bentham to denote play in which the risks are too great for a sensible person to consider (e.g. car 'joyriding').

deep structure Term devised by Noam Chomsky to denote his argument that although languages obviously differ in surface detail, they all can be transformed (hence the term *transformational grammar*) to the same essential relationship of noun phrases and verb phrases, and from these, meaning can be extracted. Chomsky argued that knowledge of the deeper structures was *innate*, and without such a *language acquisition device (LAD)*, a child could not learn a language. This was in opposition to the *behaviourist* model of language acquisition, which argued that learning took place by simple association. Chomsky's work is widely quoted, although his views have been criticized.

deep study reading An attempt to understand the author's aims and intentions, and the overall structure of the passage, as well as the basic facts. See *surface study reading*.

defectology Outmoded term for the study of children with physical/mental handicap.

defence mechanisms See *Freud's theory of development*.

defensiveness personality Personality type found in some older people – those possessing it have a strong urge to carry on working to 'prove' they are still young.

deferred circular reaction Arises in *sensori-motor stage 3* – the baby plays with an object, does something else, and then returns to the object again, finding it with no apparent difficulty. *Piaget* argues that the child remembers the object through remembering the actions needed to encounter it, rather than remembering the location of the object itself (i.e. the phenomenon is not taken as evidence of *object concept*).

deferred imitation See *sensori-motor stage 6*.

Defining Issues Test Measure of moral reasoning, based on *Kohlberg's theory of moral development*.

deictic gesture Pointing at, showing, or otherwise indicating, a particular object.

deictic words Words denoting where an object is relative to another one (e.g. 'here', 'yours', 'that', etc.).

deixis Use of *deictic words*.

delayed speech The very late arrival or complete non-arrival of a particular *speech development stage*.

delinquent (Usually) under-age breaker of the law.

delirium *acute confusional state.*

Delirium Rating Scale (DRS) A test assessing the likelihood that a patient's symptoms indicate *delirium* (*acute confusional state*) rather than an illness with which it can be easily confused (e.g. *dementia*).

demented Describing the state associated with *dementia.*

demented dyslexia A condition found in some *demented* patients, who can read aloud perfectly normally, and yet have no understanding of what they are reading.

dementia A global deterioration of intellectual function, resulting from atrophy of the central nervous system. In some (older) textbooks, 'dementia' applies purely to *pre-senile dementia* and *senile dementia* to the over-60s. This distinction is now largely disregarded. The illness takes many forms (the most common are *dementia of the Alzheimer type (DAT)* and *multi-infarct dementia*), but in all cases it characteristically kills the person before the body (*ambiguous loss*). Patients in the later stages of the disease lack any sign of memory (and hence recognition of friends and relatives), intellect, personality, and often language. Diagnosis of the types of dementia is difficult, and post-mortem studies of patients have found that up to 70% of them have been misdiagnosed during life (this is currently only of academic interest, because there are no cures for dementia). See *acute confusional state, Blessed Dementia Scale, bovine spongiform encephalopathy (BSE), chronic brain disorder, chronic brain syndrome (CBS), cortical dementias, Creutzfeldt-Jakob Disease (CJD), Pick's Disease, pseudodementia, pre-senile dementia, pugilistic dementia, senile dementia, sub-cortical dementias*, and *Wernicke's dementia*.

dementia of the Alzheimer type (DAT) The commonest form of *dementia*, first described by Alois Alzheimer in the early twentieth century. Typically, the first symptom is *amnesia*, followed by *aphasia*, and a general loss of intellectual functioning. Disturbance of language and visuo-spatial skills also typically occur early in the course of the disease. *Senile dementia of the Alzheimer type* (held only to afflict patients aged over 60 years) was at one time felt to be qualitatively different from the disease contracted by younger patients, but this distinction is now largely ignored. See *aluminium theory of dementia of the Alzheimer type*, and *cholinergic hypothesis*.

dementia praecox Now outmoded term for the illness now known as schizophrenia. The term means 'pre-senile dementia', but should not be confused with the condition now graced with that name.

dementia pugilistica *pugilistic dementia.*

democratic family Family group high in emotional warmth, allowing children freedom of expression, although not without controls, as with *permissive parents*. Very much the opposite of *authoritarian parents*.

democratic teacher Teacher who allows pupils to share in some of the decision making, and is generally 'open'. See *authoritarian teacher* and *laissez-faire teacher*.

denial of dying stage First of the psychological stages exhibited by dying people, as identified by E. Kubler-Ross. consisting of denying the possibility of death. These are followed by *anger*, *bargaining* (pleas to the deity, fate, etc.), *depression*, and finally, *acceptance*.

dental age Calculation of *chronological age* from the state of the subject's teeth. Useful for dead humans and live horses.

Denver Developmental Screening Test (DDST) Test battery for detecting delayed development in infants. Based on the *Gessell Developmental Schedules*.

dependency ratio The ratio of working to non-working members of the population.

dependent personality Personality type found in some older people – possessors have some life satisfaction, but rely on others to help them.

depression at prospect of dying stage See *denial of dying stage*.

deprivation Strictly speaking, 'deprivation' is the removal of something once owned or experienced, and *privation* the complete lack of something (i.e. it has never been owned or experienced). However, the two terms tend to be used interchangeably, especially in studies of *maternal deprivation*.

deprivation amblyopia Poor vision in children resulting from an uncorrected obstruction to vision (e.g. cataract). If the obstruction is not removed very early in life, then amblyopia (poor vision) is inevitable and irrevocable.

deprivation dwarfism Small stature and retarded physical development, sometimes found in children deprived of adequate psychological interaction (even though nutrition may be adequate).

deprivation of maternal care See *maternal deprivation*.

deprivation study Any study in which a young/infant subject is deprived of something which would normally occur in his/her environment. The aim is usually to see if development is normal if the stimulus is absent, and thus whether the development is *innate* or reliant on environmental input (see *hereditarian versus environmentalist theories of individual differences*). Because such studies are of necessity depriving a sentient being of a normal development, and can often cause stress, a large question of ethics hangs over this work.

derivational reading error Misreading a word for one with the same root (e.g. 'run' for 'runs').

derived score See *raw score*.

describer thinking See *explainer thinking*.

desired act (DA) The act someone wants in a *request for action*.

despair In discussion of *maternal deprivation*: see *Bowlby's theory of attachment*.

detachment In discussion of *maternal deprivation*: see *Bowlby's theory of attachment*.

deterioration quotient (DQ) Measure of rate of intellectual decline associated with ageing, first devised by Wechsler. Sections of the *WAIS* (and many other intelligence test batteries) can be divided into those measuring *crystallized intelligence* (held to be unaffected by ageing), and those measuring *fluid intelligence* (held to decline with ageing). These can also be referred to as **hold tests** and **don't hold tests** respectively. The DQ is calculated as {[(score on hold tests) - (score on don't hold tests)]/(score on hold tests)} x 100. A phenomenon of the WAIS is that hold and don't hold scores are equal in early adulthood. Hence, the bigger the gap in an old person's hold and don't hold test scores, the greater the deterioration. The DQ expresses this change as a percentage. See *efficiency quotient*.

developmental age Age at which a particular set of characteristics normally first appears. Strictly speaking, *mental age* is a facet of this, but usually developmental age refers to changes other than purely those of the intellect. More generally, the stage of development, as opposed to *chronological age*.

developmental aphasia A *congenital* failure of language. In its 'pure' form, it refers to a condition in which the child suffers *delayed speech* and linguistic skills in general, which cannot be attributed to hearing impairment, damaged vocal cords, *mental retardation, autism,* or environmental factors (e.g. being an *attic child*). However, the term is often used to denote congenital language failure, regardless of whether other symptoms are present or not.

developmental disability *Developmental disorder,* usually refers particularly to a *learning disability.*

developmental disorder Any disorder present at birth or which first appears in infancy, childhood or adolescence.

developmental dysgraphia A profound difficulty in spelling, or more generally, writing, and in learning to spell, or more generally, write, which the person appears to have been born with.

developmental dyslexia A profound difficulty in reading and in learning to read, which the afflicted person appears to have been born with. *Developmental dysgraphia* almost always appears in conjunction with it. See *developmental phonological dyslexia, dyseidetic dyslexia,* and *dysphonetic dyslexia.* Contrast with *acquired dyslexia.*

developmental dysphasia A profound language difficulty, which the afflicted person appears to have been born with.

developmental phonological dyslexia *Developmental dyslexia* in which the subject is unusually bad at *phonological* skills.

developmental psychology The study of psychological processes across the lifespan. Traditionally, developmental psychology has been concerned with development from birth to adulthood. and studies of life-long patterns of change are often grouped under the term *lifespan development.*

developmental psychopathology T h e study of the development of abnormal behaviour.

developmental quotient (DQ) Calculated as for *intelligence quotient,* except that general physical and mental development, rather than purely intellectual development, is calculated.

developmental range The range of ability which a child can display at the same task under different conditions. *Functional performance level* refers to the best a child can do on his/her own; *optimal performance level* to how well s/he can do when following instructions; and *scaffolded performance* level refers to how well s/he can do it when an adult (or other more gifted person) is directly helping with the task. See *zone of proximal development.*

developmental scaling (1) Measuring developmental changes. (2) Generally, the problem with placing a detailed measure of developmental change when the rate of change is slow and/or occurs across a large time period (e.g. over 5 years for the *pre-operational sub-period*).

developmental tasks (1) Tasks which show a change in performance with the age of the subject. (2) The term is used by some commentators (e.g. R. Havinghurst) to denote goals to be attained at particular stages in the lifespan.

Developmental Test of Visual-Motor Integration Measure of visual perceptual abilities in 3–13-year-olds.

developmental validity The property of a process which, having been developed in one time and place, can be appropriately used in future times and in different situations.

developmental view of mental retardation See *mental retardation – the developmental versus the difference debate.*

Devereaux Elementary School Behaviour Rating Scale Measure of social and emotional development in 5–12-year-olds.

Devereaux formula *Readability* formula. Readability = (1.56 x word length in character spaces) + (0.19 x no. words per sentence) – 6.49. This gives the earliest *grade* at which an average child could read the text in question. To find the result expressed as reading age rather than grade level, add five to the result.

deviation IQ The degree to which a person's intelligence test score deviates from the norm. See *intelligence quotient*.

Dewey's paradox of ageing J o h n Dewey, philosopher, argued that 'we are...in the unpleasant and illogical condition of extolling maturity and depreciating age' (Dewey 1939, in the Introduction to E.V. Cowdry's 'Problems of Aging', first edition).

diacritical marking system (DMS) Reading teaching system – symbols printed alongside letters in *irregular words* indicate how they should be pronounced.

Diagnostic and Statistical Manual (DSM) A system of classification of mental illness, devised by the American Psychiatric Association. The first DSM *(DSM-I)* appeared in 1952, followed by *DSM-II* in 1968, and *DSM-III* in 1980, later revised *(DSM-III-R* 1987). The current version, *DSM-IV,* appeared in 1994. The classification system is not the only one in use (see e.g. *WHO classification of diseases*) but it is the most widely accepted, particularly in the USA, and other classificatory systems are usually very similar in structure (indeed, the DSM-IV has sought to increase its compatibility with the WHO system). The current version is divided into five axes. Axes I and II describe the disease the patient is suffering from. Axis II consists of two types of mental disorder: problems in development (other than learning and and motor skills development disorders, which are on Axis I) and all *personality disorders*. Axis I consists of all other mental disorders. Axes III and IV provide information on factors which may exacerbate or ameliorate the condition. Axis III describes all other physical conditions the patient may suffer from, and Axis IV rates the severity of recent events in the life of the patient on a scale of one (none) to six ('catastrophic'). Axis V describes the highest level at which the patient coped in the past year, on a scale of one (serious danger of death/hurting self or others) to 90 (practically normal coping).

Diagnostic Interview for Children and Adolescents (DICA) *Structured interview* format, assessing the mental status of child and adolescent psychiatric patients.

Diagnostic Interview Schedule (DIS) *Structured interview* format, assessing the current status and mental health of subjects. There is also a ***Diagnostic Interview Schedule for Children (DISC)***, which divides into ***DISC-C***, which is administered to the child, and ***DISC-P***, which is administered to the child's parents.

Diagnostic Interview Schedule for Children (DISC) See *Diagnostic Interview Schedule (DIS)*.

Diagnostic Language Tests (DLT) Test battery of six language skills (including punctuation and written expression). Part of *Metropolitan Diagnostic Tests* series.

Diagnostic Mathematics Test battery of six mathematical skills (including computation, graph skills, and statistics). Part of *Metropolitan Diagnostic Tests* series.

Diagnostic Reading Tests (DRT) Reading test battery assessing 11 aspects of formally taught reading skills (letter recognition, comprehension, grapheme-phoneme conversion, etc.). Part of *Metropolitan Diagnostic Tests series*.

Diagnostic Spelling Test Spelling test battery for subjects aged 7–11 years. Tests a variety of spelling skills – producing spellings, 'proof reading', dictionary use, etc.

Diagnostic Spelling Tests Spelling test battery for subjects aged 9 years and over. Consists of several 'Levels', which assess increasingly complex spelling rules.

diary study (1) Study of contents of a person's diaries, for changes in writing style, topics of interest, etc., as the person ages. (2) Method of assessing *autobiographical memory*. Subjects complete a diary, and they are subsequently asked what they can recall of particular events, days, etc. The diary is used as an accuracy check. (3) Method used to assess a particular aspect of a person's activity for the purposes of research and/or therapy (e.g. recording how much and what type of food is eaten, etc.).

DICA *Diagnostic Interview for Children and Adolescents.*

dichromacy Colour blindness resulting from the absence of one of the three types of colour receptor in the eye. The most common form results in a failure to distinguish between greens and reds. There is some evidence that young infants are virtually dichromatic until about 3 months old (they have considerable difficulty with blues). See *trichromacy*.

didactic Pertaining to teaching and education.

difference view of mental retardation See *mental retardation – the developmental versus difference debate.*

Differential Ability Scales (DAS) Test battery of intelligence and (in appropriately aged subjects) educational achievement. For children aged 2 years 6 months–18 years.

Differential Aptitude Tests (DAT) Test battery of a variety of intellectual skills, including verbal and numerical abilities, mechanical reasoning, and 'clerical perception'. The battery is primarily intended to identify the careers a pupil is best suited for.

differential preservation The theory that some intellectual skills may be preserved better than others in ageing. However, see *preserved differentiation*. See *age x treatment interaction*.

difficult child See *New York longitudinal study*.

dimensional control structures See *sensorimotor control structures*.

direct dyslexia *demented dyslexia*.

direct perception theory Theory proposed by James Gibson (1904–1980) and subsequently developed by his wife Eleanor. Gibson argued that we perceive the world directly, without cognitive processing or the need for interpretation. See *invariants, distinctive features* and *affordances*.

direct route reading *visual reading*.

directed reading Any form of reading (but almost always the term refers to the early stages) where the pupil is reading texts set or recommended by the teacher.

DIS *Diagnostic Interview Schedule.*

DISC *Diagnostic Interview Schedule for Children.*

DISC-C See *Diagnostic Interview Schedule.*

DISC-P See *Diagnostic Interview Schedule.*

discontinuous development (1) Development in which a skill is acquired at one level of competence, continues to be practised at roughly the same level, until there is a sudden 'jump' to performing the skill at a higher level. In other words, growth by fits and starts. Compare with *continuous development.* (2) The term is often used significantly differently to denote developmental changes in which one method of functioning is replaced by another, qualitatively different one. An example of this is *Piaget's* theory of stages of development. Indeed, the phrase is often a synonym for *stage theory.*

discontinuous quantity task See *conservation of quantity.*

discovery learning Teaching system in which the pupils are encouraged to discover information for themselves, rather than having it dictated to them by the teacher.

discrete emotions theory Belief that all basic emotional responses are present at or soon after birth.

discrimination learning See *signal learning.*

disease cohort A group of people suffering from the same disease. See *cohort* and *patient cohort.*

disembedding Extracting an abstract concept or principle from an item or items.

disengaged (personality) See *integrated personality.*

disengagement theory The theory that older people seek to lose much of their contact with the outside world, in preparation for death. Contrast with *activity theory.*

dishabituation The state exhibited when a subject recognizes a new stimulus after exposure to a stimulus s/he has become used to (habituated to). See *habituation technique.*

disorganized personalities Personality type found in some older people — possessors are not capable of normal functional behaviour.

display rotation task Measure of *position constancy* in infants/young children. Typically, the subject is seated in a room, is shown how to find a target item, and the display is then rotated (usually by 180°). The correct solution is to search in the opposite location from the previous trials (e.g. if the subject was shown an array of containers, one of which contains a toy, and the toy had previously been in the furthest container from the subject, the correct solution would now be to search in the nearest container). See *observer rotation task.*

disposable soma theory of ageing The theory that the body 'sacrifices' replacing all somatic (non-reproduction) cells lost through natural 'wear and tear' to concentrate on reproductive fitness. This, it is argued, is the evolutionary force which 'causes' ageing. See *autoimmune theory of ageing, free radical theory of ageing, Hayflick phenomenon,* and *somatic mutation theory of ageing.*

dissolving sugar experiment Devised by *Piaget* to assess *conservation of quantity.* The child is shown some sugar lumps which are added to a glass of water, and dissolve. The child is asked if the addition of the sugar will make the weight change and whether the volume will change. Children in the *concrete operations subperiod* show three responses —

the youngest think that the sugar will not affect these quantities, the slightly older argue that the weight (but not the volume) will alter, whilst only the oldest children can correctly judge that the volume will alter. The results are thus reminiscent of the more famous clay ball experiments (see *conservation of quantity*).

distal ageing effects Ageing changes attributable to relatively distant events (e.g. poor self-image in old age because of childhood bullying) or events which are only felt through several intermediaries. See *proximal ageing effects*.

distinctive features (1) In *direct perception theory*, the knowledge that certain objects possess characteristic features (such as eyes and teeth signifying a face, etc.). (2) A feature of an object which can be distinguished from other parts of the object.

disuse theories of ageing Theories which argue that intellectual skills worsen in old age because they are not used frequently enough.

divergent strabismus See *strabismus*.

divergent thinking Ability to create new ideas based upon a given topic. The term is largely interchangeable with *creativity*, and is assessed with the *creativity test*. Divergent thinking is contrasted with *convergent thinking*, which is the ability to find a single principle behind a collection of information (i.e. the former takes a single point of reference and diverges from it, whilst the latter converges several strands of thought into a single premise).

diversive play *Play* as a relief from boredom or other unappealing situations.

dizygotic (DZ) From two eggs – see *dizygotic twins*.

dizygotic (DZ) twins Twins formed from two separately fertilized eggs (i.e. non-identical twins). Compare with *monozygotic twins*.

DLT *Diagnostic Language Tests*.

DMS *diacritical marking system*.

Doctor Fox effect The phenomenon whereby in most circumstances, students' ratings of a course are most heavily influenced by the lecturer's level of expressiveness.

dolls test Test of children's racial attitudes. Children are given a choice of coloured and caucasian dolls and asked which are the nicest to play with.

domain referenced test Test in which performance is gauged against a criterion of maximum performance on the skill being assessed. See *norm referenced test*.

domain specificity The degree to which something only applies to one situation or domain.

dominance hierarchy The hierarchical order determining which members of a group exert power over others (i.e. the 'pecking order').

dominant gene See *genetic dominance*.

don't hold tests See *deterioration quotient (DQ)*.

Doren Diagnostic Reading Test of Word Recognition Skills Test battery of various reading-related skills, for subjects aged 6–9 years. Concentrates particularly on phonological skills and word recognition.

double ABCX model An attempt to account for the stress induced in a family by a major crisis befalling one of its older members. The letters refer to variables expressing the seriousness of the crisis, the amount of available help, etc.

double jeopardy Term sometimes used to describe the state of subjects belonging to two minority groups (e.g. older coloured people).

Down's Syndrome (DS) A *congenital* condition, named after its nineteenth century discoverer, John Down. Symptoms include a characteristic flattened face, extra folds of skin on the eyelids, stubby fingers, unusual folds of skin on the soles and palms, and an overlarge tongue. Severe *mental retardation* is a frequent but not inevitable symptom. Life expectancy is poor (a maximum of 40–50 years) – in the terminal stages, the Down's Syndrome patient's intellectual state may resemble that of a *dementia of the Alzheimer type* patient (there are tentative suggestions that the two illnesses may be genetically linked). Down's Syndrome is caused by faulty cell division soon after fertilization – about 90% of patients have an extra chromosome 21 (*trisomy 21*). The incidence of the disease rises with the age of the mother – there is a fairly high (but by no means overwhelming) risk in mothers over 40.

DQ (1) *developmental quotient.* (2) *deterioration quotient.*

Dr Fox effect *Doctor Fox effect.*

dramatists Children who, when playing, use toys to act out stories. Compare with *patterners.*

Draw a Family Test (DAF) *Projective* test in which the subject draws a picture of his/her family. See *Kinetic Family Drawing.*

draw-a-man (DAM) test *Goodenough Draw-a-Man Test.* Not to be confused with the *draw-a-person test.*

draw-a-person test Test requiring a subject to draw a person and make up a story about their creation. The test can be used to assess if unusual emphasis/lack of emphasis is placed on certain features, and may be of use in assessing some mentally ill patients. Not to be confused with the *draw-a-man test,* or the *Goodenough draw-a-person test.*

drawbridge experiments Series of ingenious studies by Baillargeon, assessing *object concept.* The apparatus consists of a hinged flap which at the start of the experiment lies flat on the table at which the infant is seated, with the hinge parallel to the edge of the table. When raised, the flap moves upwards and away from the infant (akin to a drawbridge being raised), so that the infant's view of anything on the table becomes *occluded.* In some conditions, the infant has seen that there is a block or other object in the flap's path. As the flap is raised, it blocks the infant's view of the object. If *Piaget's* view of object concept is valid, then the infant should suppose that the object has ceased to exist. If the flap stops at the point where the object would be expected to block the movement of the flap, then the infant expresses no surprise. However, if the flap moves through 180 degrees (i.e. appears to move through the hidden object – which in reality the experimenter has removed whilst it was hidden from view) then the infant does express surprise, indicating that s/he expected the object to be there, and to block the flap's movement.

DRS *Delirium Rating Scale.*

DRT *Diagnostic Reading Tests.*

DS *Down's Syndrome.*

DSM *Diagnostic and Statistical Manual.*

DSM-I See *Diagnostic and Statistical Manual.*

DSM-II See *Diagnostic and Statistical Manual.*

DSM-III/DSM-III-R See *Diagnostic and Statistical Manual.*

DSM-III-R On-Call Computerized version of the *DSM-III-R.*

DSM-IV See *Diagnostic and Statistical Manual.*

DTVP *Marianne Frostig Developmental Test of Visual Perception.*

dual career family Family in which both parents have jobs. See *role cycling.*

dual monologue 'Conversation' where the two speakers are talking about different topics.

dual route reading The concept that reading can use both *visual reading* and *phonic mediation* skills.

dualistic personality *androgynous personality.*

Duke Longitudinal Study 20-year *longitudinal study* of community residents aged 50 years and over in Raleigh-Durnham, North Carolina, U.S.A.

duplicated syllable babbling Infants' repetition of the same syllable (e.g. the familiar 'dada' or 'mama').

Durrell Analysis of Reading Difficulty (DARD) Reading test battery, designed to identify early and pre-readers' areas of difficulty/strength.

Dutch Eating Behaviour Questionnaire (DEBQ) Measure of eating habits, with three scales assessing restrained eating, eating in response to emotion, and eating in response to external cues.

dyad Pair (usually refers to mother and child).

dyadic Between two subjects. See *polyadic.*

dyadic unit *dyad.*

dying trajectory (1) The speed with which a person is likely to die. (2) The emotional and intellectual states associated with dying.

dysarthria Disorder of muscular control of speech (and often of skills associated with the same muscles, such as eating and drinking).

dyscalculia A profound problem with arithmetical skills. Can be developmental or acquired as the result of brain damage in adulthood.

dyseidetic dyslexia *Developmental dyslexia* in which there is a profound failure in *visual reading* – every word has to be (laboriously) read by *phonic mediation* and *irregular words* are consistently mispronounced. Compare with *dysphonetic dyslexia.*

dysfunctional Not working optimally. The term is particularly used of poor or maladaptive psychological performance, either by an individual or by a group.

dysgraphia A profound spelling (or more generally, writing) problem (although note there is evidence of some spelling ability). The syndrome can be inherited *(developmental dysgraphia)* or can be acquired through brain damage *(acquired dysgraphia).*

dyslexia A profound reading problem (although note there is evidence of some reading ability). The syndrome can be inherited *(developmental dyslexia)* or can be acquired through brain damage *(acquired dyslexia).* A child is typically diagnosed as dyslexic if his/her *reading age* is appreciably (usually this means at least two years) below his/her *mental age* and *chronological age.* See *dyslexia – qualitative versus quantitative debate.*

dyslexia – qualitative versus quantitative debate The qualitative theory argues that *developmental dyslexic* children possess a set of skills which are radically different from (and significantly less efficient than) those of non-dyslexic readers. The quantitative theory argues that *dyslexic* readers possess the same set of skills as normal readers, but that they are significantly less competent at using these same skills.

dyslogia (1) Poor spoken articulation. (2) Used (inaccurately) by some developmental psychologists as a synonym for *developmental aphasia* in general.

dysphasia A profound spelling problem (although note there is evidence of some spelling ability). A child is typically diagnosed as dysphasic if his/her *spelling age* is appreciably (usually this means by at least two years) below his/her *mental age* and *chronological age*. Dysphasia is usually seen in conjunction with *dyslexia.*

dysphonetic dyslexia *Developmental dyslexia* in which there is an almost total failure of *phonic mediation – visual reading* is the only feasible strategy. Compare with *dyseidetic dyslexics.*

dysphonia Disorder of voice production.

dyssynchronous child Child with *learning disabilities.*

DZ *dizygotic.*

DZ twins *dizygotic twins.*

E

EARLI European Association for Research on Learning and Instruction.

early adult transition (EAT) The transition from adolescence into adulthood, during which careers and lifestyle plans are established. This is followed by the *entering the adult world (EAW)* stage, in which the patterns laid down in EAT are consolidated. The plans are then 'tuned' during the *age thirty transition (ATT)*, leading into a phase known as *becoming one's own man (BOOM)*. Following on from this are the *mid-life transition* and *late adult transition*.

early childhood The period between 18 months and 6 years of age (note that commentators differ about the precise boundary ages).

Early School Inventory – Developmental (ESI-D) Test assessing general physical and psychological development in 4–6-year-old children.

Early School Inventory – Preliteracy (ESI-P) Test assessing 4–6-year-old children's *reading readiness*.

EASI Temperament Survey Test battery of aspects of temperament/behaviour. 'EASI' stands for emotionality (fear and anger), activity, sociability, and impulsiveness.

easy child See *New York longitudinal study*.

EAT (1) *early adult transition*. (2) *Eating Attitudes Test*.

Eating Attitudes Test (EAT) A *self-report questionnaire* assessing the eating habits of patients, particularly those suffering from *anorexia nervosa* and *bulimia*.

EAW *entering the adult world*.

echelon structure A 'power structure' of a partnership ruling any on lower power levels. Thus, another way of describing a two parent family.

echolalia (1) Abnormal repetition of what has just been said by a person with mature speech patterns. (2) Term used by some commentators (e.g. Lenneberg) to denote a baby's vocalizations at the stage (usually reached at 9–12 months) where there is an obvious 'playing with sounds' and an indication of comprehension of some simple words.

eclectic reading teaching Using a mixture of teaching strategies – typically, combining aspects of *phonics (reading teaching)* and *whole word (reading teaching)*.

ecogenic An event not tied to a particular historical epoch. See *epogenic*.

ecological theory Term sometimes applied to theories which argue that knowledge and thought processes are primarily constructed through the environment.

ecological validity How 'realistic' and relevant to 'real life' an experiment or study is.

economy (in drawing) Using the same symbol/shape for more than one item (e.g. in children's drawing, the same shape is often repeated for arms and legs).

Edinburgh Picture Test (EPT) Test of reasoning skills using pictorial material, for children aged 6–8 years.

Edinburgh Reading Test Reading test. Has four 'Stages' commensurate with the age group under consideration. Stage 1: 7–9 years; Stage 2: 8.5–10.5 years; Stage 3: 10–12.5 years; Stage 4: 12–16 years. Each stage is a battery of tests of different skills. Obviously, these increase in difficulty across the Stages, but they also assess increasingly complex and 'mature' reading skills (e.g. there is a greater emphasis on story comprehension and interpretation, rather than simple word recognition).

educable mentally retarded (EMR) American term for persons of low *IQ* (50s–60s) who can benefit from some form of very simple academic education. Compare with *trainable mentally retarded (TMR)*.

education(al) age The average age at which the skills a child possesses are usually learnt (i.e measures how much more or less a child knows than his/her peers).

Education Priority Area (EPA) Area of social deprivation in which schools are given extra teaching staff, equipment provision, etc.

education(al) quotient Akin to *intelligence quotient*, save that *education age*, rather than intelligence test score is entered into the equation. In effect, it measures how much a child has learnt in comparison with his/her peers.

Educational Resources Clearing Centre (E.R.I.C.) An American institution which catalogues virtually all contemporary research on education (and to lesser extent, developmental and educational psychology). Operates a computerized journal search system.

educationally subnormal (ESN) British term for persons of low *IQ* who require a simpler than normal education if they are to benefit at all from schooling.

Edwards' Reading Test Reading test for subjects aged 6–13 years. Consists of measures of pronunciation of words, reading speed, and comprehension.

effectance motivation The motivation to do something because it is known that there are results from this effort. Has been used of infants learning that their actions bring results. Related to *contingency awareness*.

efficiency quotient (EQ) Measure of an older person's intellectual abilities relative to the performance of young adults, who are assumed to be at the peak of their abilities. Basically, it is the *IQ* which the young adult would be recorded as possessing, if s/he had the same *raw score* as an older subject. E.g. an older man has a raw test score of 95, which is good for his age group, and gives him an IQ of 130. However, a score of 95 would be a poor score for a young adult, and would give him/her an IQ of 70. The older person's EQ is therefore classed as 70. By comparing EQ with IQ, a measure of the extent of a person's age-related decline in intelligence can be calculated. However, a more useful single measure is probably the *deterioration quotient*.

ego See *Freud's theory of development*.

ego differentiation versus work-role preoccupation In some theories of ageing, coming to terms with retirement, and realizing that status is no longer conferred by one's employment.

ego integrity versus despair See *Erikson's theory of development*.

ego transcendence versus ego preoccupation In some theories of ageing, (beneficially) coming to terms with the fact that one is inevitably going to die.

egocentric rules See *Piaget's theory of moral development*.

egocentrism The error of assuming that one's subjective impression of a situation equates to its objective reality, or (erroneously) believing that other people's perceptions and knowledge bases are the same as one's own. The term is used particularly in *Piagetian* theory. E.g. children in the *preoperational subperiod* use linguistic expressions which make little or no concession to listeners unacquainted with the subject matter. Again, children are poor at (literally) seeing other's points of view, as demonstrated by the *three mountains experiment*. In *Piaget's* theory, much of the *concrete operational period* is spent reducing egocentrism and hence increasing *decentration*. See *animism* and *realism*. See *adolescent egocentricity*.

einstellung See definition (3) of *learning set*.

ELA *expressive language age.*

elaborated code See *restricted code*.

ELBW infant *extremely low birth weight (ELBW) infant.*

elder abuse Abuse of older people, particularly those who are mentally enfeebled. The abuse can be physical, but also psychological or financial (e.g. extorting money). See *granny bashing*.

eldering Ageing in terms of *social age*.

elderspeak The use of patronizing 'baby talk' by younger people talking to older people.

elective mutism Deliberately choosing not to speak, without any clear physiological cause (e.g. sore throat). Most often found in children, usually with another, underlying psychological problem. Can be a symptom of *autism*.

electroretinograph (ERG) Measure of eye movements from electrical activity around the eyes. Has been superseded in many instances by the *corneal reflection technique*.

element When used in *Piagetian* theory – see *grouping I*.

elementary school See *American school system*.

eleven plus See *grammar school*.

elicited imitation Asking a subject to repeat an experimenter's utterance.

embryo In human *prenatal development*, the organism 2–12 weeks after conception.

'Emile' See *Rousseau's theory of human development*.

emotion-focused coping Dealing with a life crisis by trying to control the emotions created by it. See *appraisal-focused coping* and *problem-focused coping*.

emotional maturity The degree to which emotional expression is appropriate for the subject's age.

empathic arousal The arousal of *empathy* – used to describe how one infant or young child crying can set off others within hearing distance.

empathic distress Feeling distressed because someone else is. Particular form of *empathic arousal*.

empathy Experiencing the emotions of another person in response to their emotional state.

empirical bias Allowing experience of how the real world appears to cloud judgement of hypothetical and 'unrealistic' problems. Sometimes used as an explanation of children's failing in intellectual tasks.

empiricism Belief that psychological abilities are acquired primarily through experience. Opposite of *nativism*. See *hereditarian versus environmentalist theories of individual differences.*

empty nest syndrome Set of negative feelings created in parents (usually the mother in particular) when their children have grown up and moved out of the family home.

EMR *educable mentally retarded.*

enactive gesture Imitating or symbolically expressing an action or sequence of actions.

enactive thought Term devised by Bruner for thought which uses neither language nor imagery, but works through actions (e.g. learning motor skills). *Iconic thought* uses mental imagery (but not language), whilst *symbolic thought* uses both mental imagery and language, and is capable of abstract representation. Bruner argues that the thought processes develop in the order described; the early processes are not rejected (as in *Piaget's* theory) and individuals continue to use all three types as and when appropriate throughout life.

encopresis faecal incontinence. See *enuresis.*

endogenous Within the person. Sometimes used as a synonym for *inherited.* See *exogenous.*

Engelmann–Becker programme See *Bereiter and Engelmann nursery education.*

English Picture Vocabulary Test (EPVT) See *British Picture Vocabulary Scale (BPVS).*

enmeshed family Family whose individual members are heavily reliant on each other.

enrichment Any process providing a subject with better education/richer opportunities, etc.

enrichment programme The method by which *enrichment* takes place (e.g. *headstart programme*).

entering behaviour *readiness.*

entering the adult world (EAW) See *early adult transition.*

entrainment (1) The process of adapting an internal drive to limitations imposed by the environment. (2) The complementary synchronization of two people's movements (usually refers to mother–baby/child interaction). (3) The combined effect of several strands of influence over time.

enuresis urinary incontinence See *nocturnal enuresis* and *encopresis.*

environment of adaptedness The environment in which the subject was brought up. See *environment of evolutionary adaptedness.*

environment of evolutionary adaptedness The environment for which evolutionary pressure has shaped a set of behaviours. Since the last thousand or so years have witnessed enormous changes in living patterns in humans, and such a time span is far too short for evolution to have adapted to these changes, it may be argued that many human behaviours are not optimally designed for the current world. The theory has been used by several researchers in various guises (e.g. *Bowlby's theory of attachment*).

environmental determinism *environmentalist theory of individual differences.*

environmentalist theory of individual differences The belief that people's psychological skills are primarily determined by their upbringing, rather than any genetic factors.

EPA *Education Priority Area.*

epigenesis The belief that an organism develops from a few basic 'building blocks', which develop into more complex structures by interactions between themselves and the environment. Accordingly, *Piaget's* term for the development of new methods of thinking.

epigenetic theory *epigenesis*.

epogenic An event unique to a particular historical epoch. See *ecogenic*.

EPT *Edinburgh Picture Test.*

EPVT *English Picture Vocabulary Test.*

EQ *efficiency quotient.*

equilibriation Process of attaining *equilibrium*.

equilibrium In *Piagetian* theory, the balancing of conflicting forces resulting in a mental *schema* (e.g. see *accommodation*). Equilibria are held to be fairly unstable in early childhood, but to become progressively more immovable as the person gets older.

equivalence principle In *Piaget's* theory of cognitive development, the understanding that if A=B and B=C, then A=C.

ERG *electroretinograph.*

E.R.I.C. *Educational Resources Clearing Centre.*

E.R.I.C. Clearing House *Educational Resources Clearing Centre.*

Erikson's theory of development Erik Erikson (1902–1994), psychoanalyst/*humanistic psychologist*. A psychoanalytical theory of development, based upon Freudian theory. Central to the model is Erikson's concept of eight 'general stages', which are conflicts between two opposing beliefs (one positive, one negative) which have to be resolved at different stages of development. These are also known as *nuclear conflicts*. The resolution is not simply a matter of the positive and beneficial belief overcoming the other, but rather, of the individual coming to appreciate the uses of both, although ultimately the more positive belief must be dominant, giving the individual the drive to advance, with the darker, more negative value adding a degree of necessary cynicism and caution. The eight stages are: (i) *basic trust versus mistrust* (0–1 year 6 months). A baby learns that parents/*caregivers* will reliably feed, comfort, change nappies, etc., and hence can be trusted. However, the baby also learns that sometimes his/her needs are not met, leading to mistrust. Accordingly, the baby learns trust and also recognizes that all needs are not automatically met. (ii) *Autonomy versus shame and doubt* (1 year 6 months–3 years). The child wishes to acquire independence, and to do things for him/herself. This is set against the realization that these actions may look ridiculous to others, and that they might perform the same acts better. (iii) *Initiative versus guilt* (3 years–6 years). The child begins to make plans and generally takes initiatives. However, this is offset against the awareness that some plans are doomed to failure (e.g. in boys, the famous *Oedipus complex*). Thus, the child must learn to curb his/her ambitions to take account of reality. (iv) *Industry versus inferiority* (6–11 years). The child must acquire skills by dint of working hard, although this can be marred if s/he is made to feel inferior to other, brighter, children or adults. (v) *Identity versus role confusion* (adolescence). The attempt to create one's own personality and behavioural standards, and to identify one's aspirations are set against the knowledge that one is rejecting some of the values of one's upbringing (and hence of family/caregivers). This general process can lead some adolescents (such as Erikson himself) to take a *psychological moratorium*. This is a process of temporarily 'dropping out' from society in order to 'find oneself'. A connected issue is the fear of *identity foreclosure*, or accepting/creating an identity too soon. (vi) *Intimacy versus isolation* (early adulthood). Assuming that marriage is the prime desirable state, intimacy is obviously a prime consideration. However, this cannot be developed until the partners 'know themselves' – marrying before this state is achieved means that they will be absorbed in discovering themselves rather than their partners, and this, according to Erikson, is a recipe for disaster. (vii) *Generativity versus stagnation* (adulthood). There is a need for individuals to be productive – producing and successfully raising children and/or creating a better world for the next generation to live in. A failure to do this results in a feeling of stagnation. (viii) *Ego integrity versus despair* (old age). The conflict between whether to come to terms with one's past, or to feel that past events cannot be amended. Erikson's theory has fallen foul of the usual criticisms of psychoanalysis, and also of the at times vague arguments used.

erogenous zone See *Freud's theory of development*.

error analysis (reading) *miscue analysis*.

error catastrophe theory Model of ageing which attributes bodily decline in old age to faulty replication of proteins.

ESI-D *Early School Inventory – Developmental*.

ESI-P *Early School Inventory – Preliteracy*.

ESN *educationally subnormal*.

establishment stage Stage of career development in which the subject is beginning his/her choice of career.

ethnogerontology The study of ageing in different ethnic/cultural groups.

ethological-adaptational developmental theories Any theories which view development primarily from the viewpoint of how they are shaped by *inherited* factors, and in turn how these are shaped by evolutionary pressures (e.g. *Bowlby's theory of attachment*).

evaluation See *Bloom's taxonomy of educational objectives*.

evoked potential Brain or nervous activity resulting from exposure to a stimulus. A common measure in neurophysiological and related studies, and sometimes used to gauge mental processes where the subjects cannot give a coherent response/account of their thoughts (e.g. babies and *demented* patients). The term is usually prefixed according to the sensory modality the stimulus is presented in – e.g. *auditory evoked potential, visual evoked potential*, etc.

EVS *eye-voice span*.

exceptional children Collective term for any children who are out-of-the-ordinary (principally *gifted children* and children with *mental retardation*). As there is little in common between many of the sub-groups, the term has only a specious unity.

executive process In many models of mental functioning, that part of the model controlling the workings of other parts.

exercise In *Piagetian* theory, using items without abstracting information about them. See *logicomathematical experience* and *physical experience*.

existential self *subjective self*.

exogenous From outside the person. Sometimes used to describe any factors in the environment causing changes. Compare with *endogenous*.

exosystem See *microsystem*.

expansion-restriction model Model of lifespan development which depicts a person as at first expanding his/her horizons and interests, and then contracting them again when middle age is reached.

expansion stage In some models of speech development, the phase between circa 4 and 7 months when there is an explosion in the range of *vocalizations*. This is later met by a contraction stage (10–14 months) when the infant begins to concentrate upon those sounds specifically needed in his/her language.

experience-dependent system See *experience-expectant system*.

experience-expectant system Section of the brain/nervous system hypothesized to be relatively *hard wired*, and pre-prepared to process information. This contrasts with the *experience-dependent system*, which is hypothesized to require input from the environment, and which is *soft wired*.

experiential intelligence See *triarchic theory of intelligence*.

explainer thinking The ability to explain causality. This contrasts with *describer thinking*, which is the ability to describe a situation, without being able to explain causality.

exploratory play *Play* in which the characteristics of an object are identified.

expository teaching Teaching method in which the desired principle is explicitly taught to the pupil. Compare with *inductive teaching*.

expressive language (1) Language which can be produced. (2) *expressive vocabulary*.

expressive language age (ELA) *Age norm* for which the level of *expressive language* would be appropriate.

expressive language style A tendency to use people's names, words for actions, and strings of words. See *referential language style*.

expressive vocabulary The total range of language which can be produced.

extended family Family unit of parents, children, and other relatives. See *joint family* and *nuclear family*.

external contour The 'outline' of a pattern.

extinction (1) Forgetting (2) More precisely, a lowered probability of making a previously learnt response to a stimulus.

extrafamilially adopted child See *intrafamilially adopted child*.

extremely low birth weight (ELBW) infant Baby weighing under 1000 grams. Such a low weight carries an appreciably heightened mortality risk.

extrinsic reinforcement See *intrinsic reinforcement*.

eye–voice span (EVS) In reading aloud, the amount of text which the eye has seen but the mouth has not yet spoken. Measured by getting subjects to read aloud, and then (without warning) taking the text away from them. To the subjects' surprise, they can usually remember the next one or two phrases beyond the phrase being read when the text was removed. The measure provides a relatively crude method of assessing how much information is being processed at one time. The EVS increases the more proficient and intelligent the reader, and accordingly, in children, rises with age. However, in old age, there is some evidence that it declines. EVS length is also determined by the type of text. Phrases with a lot of redundant 'filler' words, such as 'and', 'the', etc., tend to be processed in larger chunks (probably because the reader doesn't bother to process the filler words to any great depth).

F

facilitated communication (FC) A n y form of communication in which a conventional method of communication is aided by other means (e.g. use of gestures, or of keyboard operated computers). The term is principally applied to the augmentation of communication in children with physical and/or mental disadvantages whose communicative abilities might otherwise make them unintelligable.

facilitation Development of a skill accelerated by environmental factors (though the ultimate level of development is the same as would be gained without this input). This contrasts with *attunement,* in which the environment boosts development above its 'natural level', and *maintenance*, in which environmental input prevents the loss of an already-established skill.

facilitator A teacher or fellow pupil acting as a catalyst for a pupil's developing ideas/learning.

failure to thrive A failure to develop as expected, often with the added implication that no physical cause can be discerned.

family-centred therapy *family therapy.*

family day care U.S. term for day care of a group of children in a family home by an adult (usually paid and often with children of his/her own). The U.K. equivalent term is a *child minder.*

family executive Family in which all members take part in the decision process. Compare with *adult executive* and *single adult executive.*

family of origin (FO) Family in which a child (e.g. an adopted child) was originally reared. Contrast with *current family.*

family method Method used in origins of illnesses or other phenomena – members of the patient's family are examined to see how many of the symptoms they share in common with him/her, and the extent to which the illness can be attributed to genetic factors.

Family Relations Test (FRT) *Projective test* using a set of model figures of members of a family. The test is available in different formats for younger children (3–7 years), older children (7–15 years) and adults.

family therapy Any therapy in which all of the family is treated, rather than just the most obviously afflicted member. Follows the rationale that a person's psychological problems are not purely self-made, but are formed through interactions with those close to him/her.

Famous Names Test (FNT) A measure of *remote memory*. Subjects are presented with a list of names of people famous for brief periods of time since the 1920s, and are asked to identify those names which they can remember being 'in the news' at some point in the past. Included in the list are some fictitious names, to prevent subjects confabulating and saying 'yes' to every name on the list. The test also includes a set of very famous names (Margaret Thatcher, Winston Churchill, etc.) who have been famous for appreciable periods of time. One would normally expect these names to be recognized, but they may cause problems for some patients suffering from certain types of *amnesia* or *dementia*.

fantasy stage (career choice) S t a g e identified by Super as being typical of early childhood – simply wanting to be something glamorous (e.g. astronaut, lion tamer, psychologist) without regard to practicalities. This is followed by: *interest stage* of late childhood – wanting a career which fits in with interests; *capacity stage* of adolescence – wanting a career which fits in with abilities; and *tentative choice stage*, where the subject adjusts aims according to the job market, availability of places, etc.

Fantz's face recognition experiment Form of *preference study* in which the infant subjects preference for faces or face-like patterns over non-face-like patterns is studied. Named after the experimenter who first devised the experimental procedure (often it is the original study which is being referred to).

Farr–Jenkins–Paterson formula *Readability* measure. Simplified version of the *Flesch* reading ease (RE) formula. RE = 8.4335 + (0.0923 x mean no. words per sentence) + (0.0648 x no. one syllable words per 100 words). The score indicates the *grade* where an average child would correctly answer 50% of comprehension questions on such a passage.

FAS *foetal alcohol syndrome.*

FAST model Model describing seven stages of progressively worsening intellectual deterioration found in patients suffering from *dementia of the Alzheimer type*.

father involvement (1) Used in many situations simply to denote the level of father's involvement in the running of the family. (2) In a slightly more specialized manner, refers to the father's level of emotional and practical commitment to his partner's pregnancy and giving birth.

FC facilitated communication

feeble minded See *mental retardation*.

feeling of knowing (FOK) *metaknowledge.*

fencing posture See *tonic neck reflex*.

feral child A child reared by wild animals or generally 'in the wild'. A few (sometimes dubious) cases have been reported, the best known being the *Wild Boy of Aveyron*.

fetal American spelling of *foetal*.

fetus American spelling of *foetus*.

FEU further education unit.

Feuerstein Instrumental Enrichment *instrumental enrichment (IE).*

fictional play See *functional play*.

figurative thought In *Piagetian theory*, collections of facts. Groups of facts are termed *schemas*. See *operative thought*.

fine motor skills See *motor skills*.

first age childhood. *Second age* refers to young adulthood; *third age* to active old age; and *fourth age* to (usually later) old age with dependency on others.

first pretend play *pretend play*, definition (2).

fis phenomenon Phenomenon whereby children learning to speak do not recognize their (incorrect) pronunciations of words when they are spoken by others. The term derives from an anecdote that a young boy called a toy fish a 'fis'. When an adult asked 'is this your fis?', the child would reply 'no, it's my fis', but if asked 'is this your fish?', he would reply 'yes, it's my fis'.

Fisher's model of development Fisher, in the 1980s, proposed a *stage model of development*, which regards development as progressing through levels of skill, which increase in complexity. Skills may be learnt faster in some fields than in others.

flashbulb memory An *autobiographical memory* of a key event in one's life, which is perceived as being unusually vivid, like a photo taken with a flashbulb. There is considerable debate over whether such memories are qualitatively different from others, or whether they have simply been recalled many more times, therefore making them appear unusually vivid.

Flesch formula *Readability* measure. Calculated by the formula: readability = 206.835 − (0.846 x mean no. of syllables per 100 words) − (1.015 x mean no. of words per sentence). The result is expressed as a 'reading ease score' (RE): 90+ is 'very easy'; 80–90 'easy'; 70–80 'fairly easy'; 60–70 'standard'; 50–60 'fairly difficult'; 30–50 'difficult'; and 0–30 'very difficult'. Considered most reliable for texts aimed at 11–18 year olds. There is a related measure of *human interest (HI)*, which = (3.635 x mean no. personal words per 100) + (0.314 x no. personal sentences per 100 sentences). The *Farr–Jenkins–Paterson formula* and the *Powers–Sumner–Kearl formula* are revised and simplified versions of the RE measure.

fluid intelligence The ability to solve problems for which there are no solutions derivable from formal training or cultural practices. There is usually an added assumption that to have a high level of fluid intelligence, a person must solve the said problems quickly. Fluid intelligence roughly corresponds to layperson's concepts of 'wit' (as in 'quick witted', rather than humour).

FNT *Famous Names Test.*

FO *family of origin*

focus gambling See *selection strategies.*

focused (personality) See *integrated personality.*

focusers See *selection strategies.*

foetal Pertaining to the *foetus.*

foetal alcohol syndrome (FAS) *Mental retardation* (and often slight physical deformity, particularly of the face) resulting from the mother's alcohol abuse during her pregnancy.

foetal position 'Curled up' position adopted by newborn babies. See *posture and locomotion development of infant.*

foetus Unborn infant. Usually refers to infant 12 weeks after conception up to birth.

FOG formula *Readability* measure. Calculated by the formula: readability = 0.4 x (mean no. of words per sentence + percentage of polysyllabic words). This provides the earliest *grade* in which the average child could read the text. To express the result as *reading age*, add five to the result.

FOK *feeling of knowing.*

FOME *Fuld Object Memory Evaluation.*

fontanelles Gaps between the bones of the skull in new-born babies, protected by a tough membrane. Principally, they allow the brain to grow and the head to be squashed during birth. The fontanelles disappear by circa 18 months as the bones grow and knit together.

FORCAST formula *Readability* formula, primarily designed for assessing readability of texts directed at adults. Formula is simple: readability = 20 − (no.

of single syllable words per 150 words, divided by 10). This provides the earliest *grade* in which the average person could read the text. To express the result as *reading age*, add five to the result.

force du leurre Literally, 'strength of the lure'; *perceptual pregnance.*

forced choice preferential looking (FPL) technique Experimental method for assessing infant perception, which is very similar to the *preference study*. The infant is shown two or more displays, and if s/he looks more at one display than the others, then it is assumed that s/he prefers this one, and hence can tell it apart from the others.

forced responsiveness to stimuli Part of the *Strauss Syndrome*, the phenomenon whereby some (particularly brain-damaged) children will be distracted by any new stimulus.

foreclosure Deciding upon something before weighing up all the evidence. Is used particularly of selecting a belief system. See *identity foreclosure.*

formal game Game fitting the following criteria: (a) voluntary; (b) a contest between powers; (c) confined by rules; (d) has a disequilibrial outcome (i.e. some win, some lose); and (e) players seek to attain such an outcome.

formal operational schemata Problem-solving methods identified by *Piaget* as being possessed by subjects in the *formal operations* period. The schemata can be described symbolically as deriving from combinations of the *INRC group* and *lattice structures.*

formal operations In *Piaget's* theory of cognitive development, the period from approximately 11 years onwards when the child begins to think in genuinely abstract terms. In the *concrete operations period* which preceded it, s/he can imagine sequences of actions, but they have to be feasible and concrete. Now thoughts can be of literally 'impossible' events and items as well. Furthermore, the child can theorize, identifying the underlying logic of events and projecting hypothetical situations. In short, s/he becomes capable of what is generally considered to be mature thought. Several new thought processes can be identified. *Hypothetico-deductive thought* is the ability to identify the best hypothesis from a set of alternatives. *Propositional thought* is the ability to express relationships in terms of symbolic (and hence abstract and more manipulable) propositions. *Combinatorial analysis* is essentially the ability to break down a problem into its constituent (and more manageable) parts, and to recombine them. There are several demonstrations of formal operational thought. One of the best known is the *chemistry problem*. The subject is shown how adding a colourless liquid x to another colourless liquid creates a yellow liquid. The subject is then given four liquids A,B,C, and D, plus liquid x, and is told to replicate the demonstration. The correct solution is to add x to a mixture of A and C. A subject in the concrete operational period will typically add x to A,B,C, and D in turn, and failing to find a result, will give up. The formal operational child will try each liquid in turn, before trying various combinations of the four. According to Piaget, having found the correct solution, s/he will often carry on, and try other combinations, to see if s/he has found the only possible answer to the problem. Other experiments of Piaget's demonstrated formal operational subjects' superiority at solving *syllogisms* and geometric problems. Replications of

Piaget's work have often found relatively small proportions (as low as 15–30%) of teenagers (even as old as 18) in possession of formal operational thought. See *balance problem, bending rods problem, billiard balls problemn, and pendulum problem*. For representation of formal operational thought in logico-mathematical terms, see *group, lattice, 16 binary operations* and *INRC group*.

formation of a goal-corrected partnership Phase 4 of *Bowlby's theory of attachment*.

formula blindness An inability to extract meaning from mathematical formulae.

foster-child/fostering fantasy The common childhood (mis)belief that one is adopted.

Foundation Skills Assessment (FSA) Test battery for subjects aged 16 years and over. Assesses basic literacy, numeracy and problem-solving skills.

four-group *INRC group*.

fourth age See *first age*.

FPL *forced choice preferential looking technique*.

fragile X syndrome Genetic disorder in which the *X chromosome* is damaged. This results in moderate to severe *mental retardation* and often *autistic* symptoms in the majority of cases. Particularly affects boys.

fra(X) *fragile X syndrome*.

free drawing Drawing which is not to a theme set by a teacher or other adult.

free radical theory of ageing Free radicals are ions (charged atomic particles) which are produced in chemical reactions in the body. The theory argues that the free radicals damage the cells and their *chromosomes*, thereby causing physical degeneration. Some theorists argue that consuming extra daily quantities of vitamin C will offset these effects. See *autoimmune theory of ageing, disposable soma theory of ageing, Hayflick phenomenon*, and *somatic mutation theory of ageing*.

Freud's theory of development Sigmund Freud (1856–1939), founder of psychoanalysis. Created a very rich theory of human psychological behaviour. Not interested in development for its own sake, but principally for its effect on future adult behaviour. At the heart of the theory is the belief that the human personality is empowered with *psychic energy*, which when it builds up, has to be released in the form of an appropriate action (e.g. if the drive is to eat, then eating is an appropriate release). The *pleasure principle* states that there will be an attempt to do this as soon as possible, but the *reality principle* attempts to ensure that the release only occurs in a socially appropriate form (e.g., a frustrated employee may have an urge to hit his/her boss, but the drive may be channelled into being nasty to an office junior – not commendable, but preferable in terms of social survival). The psychic energy drives three forces. The *id* is a primitive collection of urges with which a baby begins life. It is capable of projecting some basic thoughts of desirable goals *(primary process thought)*. In order to cope more efficiently, the ego develops. This loosely corresponds to rational thought *(secondary process thought)*, decides on appropriate goals, and attempts to keep a check on the id and the *superego*. The latter arises in later childhood, and is a collection of (often over-harsh) ideals. It acts like an internalized set of moralistic parents. If the ego feels threatened by the id and the superego, then various *defence mechanisms* are available. E.g. the famous *repression*, where an unpleasant thought is blocked (in extreme cases by e.g. hysterical deafness). Freud argued that the id, ego, and superego develop as a consequence of several psychosexual stages of development. Each is centred on an *erogenous zone* – an area of the body providing sensual (and not necessarily exclusively sexual) satisfaction. *Oral stage* (0–1 year) – sensual satisfaction primarily through the mouth. *Anal stage* (1–3 years) – sensual satisfaction primarily through the retention and expulsion of faeces. *Phallic stage* (3–5 years) – according to Freud, a boy in this stage realizes that he has a penis, and desires his mother (the *Oedipus complex*). However, he fears that this desire will cause his father to punish him by castration. This leads him to cease desiring his mother, and to identifying more with his father. A girl at this stage discovers that she lacks a penis, but desires one *(penis envy)*. She feels that she once had one, but that it has been cut off as a punishment. She blames her mother for this loss, weakening her identification with her, and increasing her liking for her father. *Latency period* (5 years–adolescence) – energy is channelled into non-sexual development of intellectual and social skills. *Genital stage* (adolescence onwards) – the individual now aims for 'mature' sexual satisfaction with a permanent partner of the opposite sex. However, 'faulty' development prior to this stage will lead an individual to choose a particular type of partner (e.g. the archetypal case of the man with the unresolved Oedipus complex who chooses a partner just like his mother). 'Faulty' development affects more than choice of partner, however. For example,

a baby in the oral stage who bites at the nipple will develop a 'biting' and sarcastic sense of humour in later life. The above is a very simplistic gloss of a very rich theory, which has influenced a large number of researchers (e.g. *Erikson's theory of development*) as well as other fields (notably surrealist artists and the stream-of-consciousness novelists). Freud's theories have been very heavily criticized for, amongst other things, being post-hoc and untestable explanations, as well as being sexist (e.g. women are portrayed as having 'naturally' weaker personalities). Freud himself developed no explicit theories of ageing, and rarely examined psychological problems in children (although see *Little Hans*). Freud's place in the history of psychology is assured, but whether he will be ultimately remembered as more than a founding father (in the same manner as alchemists are honoured in chemistry) is open to doubt.

Frostig Developmental Test of Visual Perception *Marianne Frostig Developmental Test of Visual Perception.*

FRT *Family Relations Test.*

frustration reading level See *functional reading level.*

Fry graph Method of assessing *readability*. The average number of sentences per 100 words is plotted against the average number of syllables per 100 words on a specially devised graph, from which the readability score (expressed as the lowest *grade* level at which the average child could read the text) is derived (to express it as *reading age*, add five to the result).

FSA *Foundation Skills Assessment.*

Fuld Object Memory Evaluation (FOME) Memory and naming test for older subjects, who are given objects to recognize, first by touch, and then by sight. Subjects must then recall the items several times over, interspersed with a *verbal fluency task*.

full-term infant Infant born after a usual (i.e. full-term) period of pregnancy.

functional age The average age at which a particular set of abilities is found (i.e. it measures how well an individual performs relative to his/her age group).

functional asymmetry See *Gessell's maturational theory*.

functional literacy (1) The basic level of reading skills required for a particular occupation or lifestyle. E.g., for most unskilled jobs, a *reading age* of 11 is the maximum required. See *functional reading*. (2) *functional reading*.

functional parenting See *symbolic parenting*.

functional performance level See *developmental range*.

functional play Term devised by Buhler to denote *play* which involves the practice of a skill. Other types are: *fictional play* (with toys, etc, in which objects are assigned roles in the play's 'story'); *receptive play* (in which the child listens to/watches a story); and *constructive play* (play in which items are made (e.g. play with toy bricks)). The types of play are argued to arise in the order described.

functional reading The ability to read basic instructional materials at the barest level of proficiency expected by the society in which the subject is living. See *functional literacy* and *functional reading level*.

functional reading level The maximum difficulty of text a pupil can competently read. Can be subdivided into *independent reading level* (maximum diffi-

culty coped with alone) and *instructional reading level* (maximum difficulty when teacher's help available). Generally, making fewer than 5% errors/*miscues* and comprehending the majority of the text's meaning is taken as the functional level (although note that some researchers adopt much more lax criteria). Related to this is the *frustration reading level*, which is the level where the text becomes too difficult to read.

functional thought See *Piaget*.

functionalist language theory Theory that emphasizes the social nature of language and its usefulness in establishing greater social contact as a driving force in language acquisition.

G

g General intellectual capacity – a term devised by Charles Spearman (early twentieth century) to describe an ability he felt underpinned all intellectual skills. Today often used more loosely to denote subjects' general level of intelligence.

GAMT *Graded Arithmetic-Mathematics Test.*

Ganda infants study 1960s study of the children of the Ganda tribe of Uganda. The study found that *posture and locomotion development of infants* was several months ahead of Western norms, and that this resulted from cultural practices which encouraged the practice of motor skills, rather than an innate superiority. The *developmental quotient* was found to be on a par (or even behind) Western norms by the time the infants reached 3 years.

ganglioside Drug whose effects include the enhanced release of acetyl choline (a key neurotransmitter in the brain – see *cholinergic hypothesis*). Has been cited as a possible treatment for patients suffering from *dementia*. See *ondansetron* and *tacrine*.

GAP Reading Comprehension Test Reading test for 7–12 year olds. Uses *cloze procedure*.

GAPADOL Reading Comprehension Test Reading test for 7–16 year olds. Uses *cloze procedure*.

garden variety poor readers Individuals with reading problems as part of a general intellectual deficit (by far the most common cause of poor reading – hence the name). Contrast with *developmental dyslexia*.

Gates-Macginitie Reading Test Reading test. Consists of several 'Levels', commensurate with the age of the subjects: R: 5–7 years; A: 5–7; B: 7–8; C: 8–9; D: 9–12; E: 13–16; F:16–18. All measure size of vocabulary and comprehension abilities, (with the exception of 'R', which also measures letter recognition and ability to recognize letter sounds).

gateway drugs 'Soft' illegal drugs (marijuana, etc.) which are often the first illegal substances used by drug users who subsequently 'graduate' to taking 'hard' drugs (e.g. heroin etc.). The general theory of this progression is also known as the *stepping stone theory*. It should be noted that the majority of 'soft' drug users do not follow this path.

Gc/gc Symbol for *crystallized intelligence.*

GDS (1) *Gessell Development Schedules.* (2) *Geriatric Depression Scale.*

gender consistency The awareness that in all situations, one retains one's gender (e.g. a man 'in drag' is still a man).

gender constancy The awareness that a person's gender remains the same throughout life and across all situations.

gender identity The awareness in boys that they are male and in girls that they are female. Compare with *sex role identity*.

gender identity disorder The adoption of stereotypically 'inappropriate' behaviours for one's sex (e.g. a boy playing with dolls). The degree to which this is greeted with concern has diminished with the advent of saner attitudes about what is 'correct' behaviour for males and females.

gender role The expression of one's gender through stereotypical behaviours (e.g. girls playing with dolls, boys playing with toy soldiers).

gender salience The degree to which stereotypically 'correct' gender roles are important to an individual (e.g. how strongly a person (dis)approves of female lorry drivers, male *infant school* teachers, etc).

gender stability *gender constancy.*

gene The basic functional unit out of which *chromosomes* are made. One gene by itself can usually do little – it is the coordinated action of groups of genes which typically determines physical characteristics. However, it is often too convenient to talk of 'the gene' to denote the workings of genetic inheritance.

general identity See *grouping I.*

general law of cultural development See *Vygotsky's theory of development.*

general learning disability See *learning disability.*

general learning skill General ability to learn skills. The concept can be used to compare individuals or species. Compare with *specific learning skill.*

general slowing hypothesis *speed hypothesis.*

general symbolic function The ability to use an object to symbolise another item (e.g. using a doll to represent a real baby).

general teaching skills Skills appropriate to all or most teaching situations (e.g. voice, ability to keep discipline, etc.). See *content specific teaching skills.*

generate and test thought *hypothetico-deductive thought.*

generational effect *cohort effect.*

generationally-biased stimuli Stimuli which will only be recognized by, or be most familiar to, a particular *age cohort.*

generativity versus stagnation See *Erikson's theory of development.*

genetic co-dominance See *genetic dominance.*

genetic counselling The provision of information to potential and expectant parents about genetic complaints they may pass on if they have children.

genetic dominance In sexual reproduction, a complete set of *genes* (grouped in *chromosomes*) controlling the *phenotype* are inherited from both the mother and the father. Some aspects of the phenotype are solely controlled by the genes of either the mother or the father. Where this occurs, the genes responsible are said to be ***dominant***, and the genes which fail to exert an influence are ***recessive***. [Note that when writers discuss a 'dominant gene' or a 'recessive gene', they do not invariably mean that only one gene is controlling the phenotype. The phrase is a convenient figure of speech, and often a group of genes is involved]. Far more common in humans is ***genetic co-dominance***, where genes from both parents control the phenotype (e.g. skin colour – this can be witnessed in children of parents of different races, who almost inevitably have a skin colour somewhere between the colorations of their parents). The mother's and father's genes controlling the same aspect of the phenotype are called ***alleles***.

genetic epistemology The belief that the principal drive to acquire knowledge is the need to explain apparent anomalies in one's understanding of the environment, and accordingly, to become more adapted to the environment. It is felt that these changes require active work by an individual (i.e. the development of knowledge is not purely dictated by one's genes). The term 'genetic' primarily refers to its older meaning of 'growth', rather than the more modern use of the word. The best-known exponent of this theory was *Piaget*.

genetic expression The manner in which the *phenotype* is formed from the *genotype*.

genetic psychology developmental psychology.

Genevan School Loose term given to *Piaget* and (more usually) his followers, particularly those based in his research institute in Geneva, Switzerland. See *Piagetian*.

Genie *Attic child*, rescued in 1970, at the age of 13 years.

genital stage See *Freud's theory of development*.

genogram family history.

genome The total *genes* contained in a full set of *chromosomes*.

genotype The genetic composition of an organism. Compare with *phenotype*.

Geriatric Depression Scale (GDS) A 'yes/no' questionnaire measuring the level of depression in the respondent. The questions are geared to match the symptoms and lifestyles typically found in depressed older people.

Geriatric Mental State (GMS) A standardized interview package for assessing the mental state of older patients.

geriatrics Medical treatment and study of ageing. See *gerontology*.

germ cells Sperm and egg cells.

German measles *rubella*.

geronting Ageing in terms of *psychological ageing*.

gerontologists Practitioners of *gerontology*.

gerontology The study of old age. The term is usually restricted to psychological and sociological aspects of ageing. See *geriatrics*.

Gessell Development Schedules (GDS) Test battery measuring development in infancy and early childhood – largely requires observation of child's behaviour and physical measurement, rather than more conventional psychological tests. Principal author – Arnold Gessell (see *Gessell's maturational theory*).

Gessell Preschool Schedules (GPS) *Gessell Development Schedules*.

Gessell's maturational theory Arnold Gessell (1880–1961), psychologist and medical doctor. Central tenet of his theory is that development is primarily controlled by genetic, rather than environmental factors, a process Gessell termed *maturation*. The implication is that children will progress when they are ready (i.e. when their genes will allow). Gessell concentrated on babies, and argued that their development consists of an increased sophistication in integrating movements ('patterns'). E.g. *reciprocal interweaving* – combining left and right hand sided body movements; and *functional asymmetry* – developing a favoured side (e.g. being left- or right-handed). He also argued that babies display *self-regulation* – e.g., left free to sleep and demand food when they want it, babies will display a logical and sensible pattern of activity. The term also refers to the observation that children develop new concepts and then consolidate their knowledge before progressing (reminiscent of *horizontal décalage*). Gessell's theory eased parental neuroses that the development of baby and child must be constantly monitored and shaped (viz. the rigid feeding and sleeping times prescribed by 'baby experts' of the day). However, much of his theory has been criticized for being too deterministic.

gestational age Length of time since conception.

Gf/gf Symbol for *fluid intelligence.*

gifted children Children with exceptional talents. Often used 'merely' to denote children with high *IQs*, rather than the truly exceptionally gifted.

Gilmore Oral Reading Test Reading test for 6–14 year olds.

GLA *Group Literacy Assessment.*

glaucoma An excess accumulation of fluid in the eyeball, increasing pressure on retinal cells, leading to their (permanent) destruction. Found most commonly in older people.

g.l.b. *greatest lower bound.*

global reading strategy *Visual reading,* with emphasis on recognizing the overall shape of the word.

GM-1 *ganglioside.*

GMS *Geriatric Mental State.*

GMT *Group Mathematics Test.*

goal directed behaviour Activity which is modified because its outcome was not the desired goal. See *goal terminated behaviour.*

goal terminated behaviour Activity which ends when its aim is achieved. See *goal directed behaviour.*

gonadotrophic hormones Hormones involved in the development of sexual organs at puberty.

'good boy-nice girl' orientation See Stage 3 of *Kohlberg's theory of moral development.*

Goodenough Draw-a-Man Test Test for children aged up to 12 years. The subject is required to draw a picture of a man or woman, which is marked for detail, accuracy, etc. The measure gives a rough indication of *IQ.* See *Goodenough Draw-a-Person Test.*

Goodenough Draw-a-Person Test Modified *Goodenough Draw-a-Man Test* with a non-sexist title. However, do not confuse with the *draw-a-person test.*

Goodenough-Harris Drawing Test *Goodenough Draw-a-Man Test.*

goodness of fit The degree to which a subject is successfully incorporated into a particular environment.

gooing stage Term used by some commentators to denote speech development between 2 and 4 months, characterized by early attempts to link vowels and consonant-like sounds. See *speech development stages.*

Gordon Musical Aptitude Profile A measure of basic musical skills (e.g. ability to spot similarities and differences in pieces of music).

Gorham Proverb Interpretation Test Measure of intelligence through ability to interpret proverbs. See *proverb interpretation.*

GORT *Gray Oral Reading Test.*

Gotkin Matrix Game Educational game for young schoolchildren. The pupil is shown an array (matrix) of pictures, and asked to mark the picture showing a particular activity. As the pupil becomes more competent at the task, so the required responses become more complex (e.g. they must mark a series of pictures in a set order, the description of the picture they must find becomes more complex, etc.).

GPC rules *grapheme-to-phoneme correspondence rules.*

GPS *Gessell Preschool Schedules.*

GRA *Group Reading Assessment.*

graceful degradation The phenomenon whereby the cell loss which accompanies ageing is reflected in a gentle loss of memories and level of skill (rather than a wholesale and absolute loss).

grade equivalent score American measure expressing the school *grade* level at which an average pupil can perform the task in question.

Graded Arithmetic-Mathematics Test (GAMT) Standardized test of mathematical and arithmetical skills for subjects aged 6–18 years. Has two forms – Junior (6–12) and Senior (11–18).

graded test Test which consists of several progressively more difficult levels.

Graded Word Spelling Test (GWST) Standardized spelling test for subjects aged 6–16 years.

grades (U.S. school classes) See *American school system*. To convert a grade score to *chronological age* in years, simply add five.

grammar school (1) In some parts of the U.K., a school for the scholastically most gifted pupils aged circa 11 years and over. Assessment is usually based on examination(s), popularly called the *eleven plus* (because of the pupils' age). Slightly less able pupils go to a *technical school* (where education has a strong vocational link towards a skilled manual job), if one is available, or to a *secondary modern school*, which offers a more 'rudimentary' level of education. The system was the norm for the whole of the Britain for much of the twentieth century. However, complaints from many educationalists (although perhaps fewer psychologists) that it was elitist and unfair on low ability pupils to be categorized as 'failures', led to the abandonment of the scheme in much of the country. The system was replaced by the *comprehensive school* system, which judging from media reaction and various official reports, seems to have fared little better. (2) In the U.S.A., a school for 8–12 year olds (see *American school system*).

granny bashing Slang term for physical *elder abuse.*

granny dumping Slang term for the process whereby *caregivers* (usually sons and/or daughters) who cannot cope with looking after an older relative, abandon him/her to the local authorities (sometimes literally leaving him/her on the doorstep of the local hospital/social services office).

grapheme The smallest written symbol whose substitution or removal changes meaning. This means that most graphemes are letters (and many commentators treat 'letter' and 'grapheme' as synonyms), but punctuation marks and commonly-accepted symbols (e.g. '@', '£', etc.) are also included in a rigid definition.

grapheme-phoneme conversion Calculating what letters sound like, and by extrapolation, what the words made from the letters sound like. An essential part of *phonic mediation.*

grapheme-to-phoneme correspondence rules (GPC rules) The rules governing which *phoneme* is represented by which *grapheme* or combination of graphemes (i.e. what letters 'sound like').

graphemic Pertaining to *graphemes.*

graphemic buffer A temporary memory store used in spelling to 'hold' the memory trace of the word to be spelt while it is written. Compare with *phonemic buffer*.

grasping reflex A type of *primitive reflex*. An object placed in the hand of a young baby is automatically grasped. The reflex is replaced at 3–4 months with a voluntary grasp. Like the *Babinski reflex*, it may reflect primate ancestry – automatically grasping at something may prevent a fall (especially useful if the baby is in a tree at the time).

Gray Oral Reading Test (GORT) *Achievement test*, using *oral reading* measures.

greatest lower bound (g.l.b.) See *lattice*.

greying population Term describing the increasing proportion of older people in industrialized nations.

Griffith Scale of Mental Development (GSMD) Test battery, primarily of motor, social, auditory and aural abilities in infants and young children.

ground line In pictures, the orientation (whether made explicit or not) of the ground. In conventional art, the ground line is usually parallel to the base of the picture.

group In *Piagetian* theory, a set of mental operations with four specific properties. *Composition* – the product of two members of the group can only be another member of the same group (e.g. in the group of dogs, breeding two dogs produces dogs, not cats or aardvarks). *Associativity* – three or more elements of the same group can be mixed in any order to produce the same result (e.g. in a group of paint colours, red added to green added to brown will produce the same result as green added to red added to brown). *Identity* – within a group there is an element called the *identity element*, whose addition to another ele-

ment leaves the latter unchanged (e.g. in the group of numbers, 0 is the identity element, since any number added to it remains the same). *Reversibility* – each element in the group has an exact opposite, called the *inverse element*. Adding an element with its inverse creates the identity element (e.g. in the group of numbers, 10 has the inverse element -10. $10 + (-10) = 0$, and 0 is the identity element). The formation of groups is one of the chief activities of the *concrete operational period*, but Piaget also uses the term for sets of actions in stages of *sensori-motor development*. Some actions learnt in *sensori-motor stage 1* and *2* correspond to the *practical group*; stages *3* and *4* to the *subjective group*, and stages *4–6* to the *objective group*. Groups are also formed in the *formal operations period*. Many of these are akin to (and derived from) groups formed in the concrete operational period, but are used for propositions, rather than physically real items. See *grouping*.

Group A/B/C child See *strange situation*.

Group Literacy Assessment (GLA) Reading and spelling test for subjects aged 7–14 years. Requires subject to identify misspellings in a prose passage and to provide the correct spelling. Also contains a *cloze procedure* test, in which the first letter of the to-be-found word is provided).

Group Mathematics Test (GMT) Test of mathematical abilities (divided into orally presented and computational sub-sections) for subjects aged 6–7 years (and also for less able older children).

Group Reading Assessment (GRA) Reading test for subjects aged 7–9 years (specifically, children in their first year at U.K. *junior school*). Requires subject to identify a word spoken by the tester, to find the word best suited to a given sentence, and to find homophones [same sounding but differently spelt words] of a given word.

Group Reading Test (GRT) R e a d i n g test for subjects aged 6–12 years. Requires subjects to choose a word to match a picture, and to complete sentences, given a list of alternatives.

grouping In *Piagetian* theory, a mental construct which is an amalgam of a *group* and a *lattice*. Piaget identified nine types of groupings (eight labelled with roman numerals – see *grouping I* to *grouping VIII*, plus *preliminary grouping of equalities*). *Grouping I* describes the basic structure of all the groupings. In *concrete operational* thought, groupings are of membership of real groups. In *formal operations* thought, the groupings can be of propositions of truth or falsehood, which may or may not be 'realistic'. See *class inclusion*.

grouping I The *grouping* consists of a set of classes, arranged in a hierarchy. Each level of the hierarchy can be divided in two, consisting of a class and a group of all the other classes at that level of hierarchy. These are usually denoted as X (the *primary class*) and X′ (the *secondary class*) respectively. E.g. milk (A) and all other types of soft drink (A′). Each level of the hierarchy is a subset of the one above. E.g. skimmed milk (A) + all other kinds of milk (A′); milk (B) and all other soft drinks (B′); soft drinks (C) and all other kinds of drink (C′), etc. Classes can also be called *elements*, and are labelled so that the smallest element is termed 'A'. The grouping's structure resembles a *lattice*, and also resembles a *group* in that all elements obey the rules of *associativity*, *composition*, and *revers-*

ibility. However, the *identity* rule is modified. The *identity element* is said to determine **general identity**. In addition, the grouping possesses two **special identities**. (i) **Tautology** – each element is its own identity element. E.g., skimmed milk added to skimmed milk gives skimmed milk, or symbolically, A + A = A. (ii) **Resorption** – an element added to a **supraordinate element** (an element of which the first element is a subset) produces the supraordinate element only. E.g. if the element 'gin' is added to its supraordinate set of 'alcoholic drinks', nothing new has been added to the latter element. Put symbolically, A + B = B (thus, the smaller element acts like zero, i.e. it acts like an identity element to the supraordinate class). Grouping I's rules form the basis of the structure of *Groupings II – VIII* although their precise operation may differ.

grouping II Each hierarchical level of a grouping consists of a *primary class* (e.g. skimmed milk, or A) and a *secondary class* (all other kinds of milk or A′), which in turn form a larger class (milk, or B). Symbolically, A + A′ = B. In the example, the type of milk which forms the primary class can be altered, without changing the identity of B. E.g. 'A' could be full cream milk, semi-skimmed milk, etc., and A + A′ would still equal B. *Piaget* terms this phenomenon **complementary substitutions** or **vicariances**. Grouping II refers to the process by which this takes place.

grouping III Within a *grouping*, a class can be divided in more than one way. E.g. animals can be divided into whether they are pets, farmed, or wild and can also be divided into whether they have fur, feathers or scales. These two categorizations can be combined (pets with fur, pets with feathers, pets with scales, farmed animals with fur, etc.). Piaget calls this multiplication of different categorizations of the same set, *bi-univocal*, and grouping III describes this process.

grouping IV A *grouping* in which two classes are joined, as in *grouping III*, with the difference that members of one group can belong to more than one subgroup of the second group. This process is called *co-univocal* multiplication.

grouping V A *grouping* where there is an asymmetrical relationship between its members (i.e. one member has a higher value than another). An important feature is the *transitive* relationship between elements (e.g. if A>B, and B>C, then the relationship between A and C can be calculated without direct comparison being necessary).

grouping VI A *grouping* where there is a symmetrical relationship between its members (i.e. one member has the same value as another, or alternatively, the concept of value is meaningless – e.g. in familial relationships).

grouping VII A very complex *grouping* which describes how asymmetrically related members of two or more sets can be multiplied together using *bi-univocal* multiplication (in essence, this is applying the techniques of *grouping III* to *grouping V*).

grouping VIII A complex *grouping* which describes how asymmetrically related members of two or more sets can be multiplied together using *co-univocal* multiplication (in essence, this is applying the techniques of *grouping IV* to *grouping V*).

GRT *Group Reading Test.*
GSMD *Griffith Scale of Mental Development.*

guck-guck da-da See *peek-a-boo.*
GWST *Graded Word Spelling Test.*

H

habituation-novelty technique See *habituation technique.*

habituation rate The speed with which a subject becomes used to (habituates to – see *habituation technique*) a stimulus. In infants, it is sometimes used as a predictor of future intelligence (i.e. the faster the baby can 'take in' a stimulus and habituate to it, the more intelligent s/he is likely to be).

habituation technique An experimental method in infant perception research. Obviously, babies cannot tell experimenters what they perceive. However, they become quickly bored with items they have encountered before (i.e. which they are habituated to), and this behaviour can be utilized. The experimenter presents a stimulus (e.g. a blue card), and the baby looks at it until s/he has habituated to it, and turns his/her attention elsewhere (i.e. s/he stops gazing at it). The experimenter presents a new stimulus (e.g. card in a slightly different shade of blue). If the baby shows renewed interest, then it is argued that s/he perceives the item as a new object, and hence can tell the difference between the old and the new (in the example, s/he can distinguish between the two shades of blue). However, if the baby does not look at it, then it is argued that s/he does not perceive it as a new object, and hence cannot tell the two stimuli apart. By varying the degree of difference between the stimuli, it is possible to measure how sensitive the baby's perceptions are. A variation on this technique is to present the new stimulus in conjunction with the old, and measure whether the baby spends longer looking at the new stimulus. This is called the *habituation-novelty technique*. Measures of interest include length of time an object is looked at, and heart rate monitoring. The latter (*heart rate habituation technique*) assumes that a faster heart rate on being presented with a new stimulus indicates interest, and hence a perception of change. By the same argument, no change in heart rate is held to indicate no perception of change. However, the latter argument, although the most plausible, is not necessarily logically correct. The baby may perceive the change, but it does not interest him/her, so there is no change in response. See *dishabituation, nonnutritive nipple sucking technique* and *preference study.*

Hachinski Ischaemic Score (IS) A diagnostic technique for distinguishing *dementias* of cardiovascular origin, and specifically, *multi-infarct dementia.* Patients are scored on the number of symptoms they display (some, more indicative symptoms are weighted). A score of seven or more is taken to indicate multi-infarct dementia.

Hachinski scale *Hachinski Ischaemic Score.*

Hall's theory of developmental psychology *Stanley Hall's theory of developmental psychology.*

Haptic Visual Matching Test (HVM Test) Assesses children's ability to match visual and haptic (touch) perceptions, and the degree of impulsiveness with which this is done. The child feels (but cannot see) a shape, and is then asked to pick the target by sight from a range of alternatives. The time taken to make the response, as well as accuracy, is recorded.

hard wired Psychological slang (derived from electronics/computing) for a mental system which is relatively fixed and resistant to change (e.g. which is genetically *inherited* in an unalterable form). See *soft wired*.

Harrison-Stroud Reading Readiness Test Test of *reading readiness* for beginning readers.

HAS technique *high amplitude sucking technique*.

Hawthorne effect Term originally used in occupational psychology, but occasionally used of education methods. The phenomenon whereby a change in working conditions will almost certainly improve productivity, at least in the short term, regardless of the true worth of the new regime.

Hayflick limit See *Hayflick phenomenon*.

Hayflick phenomenon Named after its discoverer, Hayflick. Living cells taken from a body can be reared in a laboratory, and will reduplicate a limited number of times (the *Hayflick limit*). The older the animal from which the cells are taken, the lower this number is. This implies that the upper limit of life expectancy may be due to the simple fact that the body's cells can only reduplicate a limited number of times. See *autoimmune theory of ageing, disposable soma theory of ageing, free radical theory of ageing*, and *somatic mutation theory of ageing*.

Head Start *headstart programme*.

headstart programme Extra/remedial education designed to boost the performance of pupils, usually handicapped children or children from underprivileged backgrounds. The term may specifically refer to Project Head Start, an American Government programme begun in 1965 by President Johnson. Alternatively, it may be used generally of any *enrichment programme*.

Healthy Family Functioning Scale (HFFS) As its name implies, a measure of psychological functioning of a family. Used e.g. in *family therapy*.

hearing impairment (HI) Loss of auditory sensitivity sufficient to cause handicap. Often measured in terms of the minimum volume (measured in decibels, or dB) which can be reliably heard (the higher the figure, the worse the impairment). E.g. a hearing loss of 90dB means that the quietest sound which the person can detect is over 90 decibels (approximately the noise level generated by heavy traffic). See *profound hearing impairment* and *severe hearing impairment*.

heart rate habituation technique See *habituation technique*.

hemispheres (cortex) The *cerebral cortex* is divided into two equally sized halves along a vertical axis running from the front to the back of the head. These two halves are known as the hemispheres, and are called the right hemisphere and the left hemisphere. In most individuals, the left hemisphere is principally responsible for linguistic skills and the right for visuo-spatial (although in some individuals, particularly left-handers, this is reversed and other, rarer, people have no simple left-right distinction).

hereditarian theory of individual differerences The belief that psychological abilities are primarily determined by a person's genetic makeup (i.e. people are born 'predestined' to be the way they are).

hereditarian versus environmentalist theories of individual differences The major theme of individual differences research – are people's psychological abilities primarily determined by their genes or by their method of upbringing? The debate has obvious political overtones (e.g. if intelligence is largely innate, then racial differences in intelligence can be seen as 'proof' that some races are inevitably less clever than others), and has generated more controversy and ill-feeling than any other topic in psychology. Methods of assessing the question include *split twins* and *adoption studies.*

hermaphrodism Possession of male and female sexual characteristics. This contrasts with ***pseudohermaphrodism,*** in which the sexual organs are abnormally shaped and may create the appearance of the opposite sex.

heterogeneous collective décalage See *collective décalage.*

heteronomous morality *heteronomy.*

heteronomy See *Piaget's theory of moral development.*

heterozygotic See *homozygotic.*

heuristic Problem-solving method. Often applied to a method which might not be entirely accurate, but will be 'close enough' and will save mental effort (e.g. treating pi as $22/7$).

heuristics (1) Plural of *heuristic.* (2) Attempting to solve problems by applying a sequence of heuristics to it to see which provides the best solution.

HFFS *Healthy Family Functioning Scale.*

HI (1) *human interest* – see *Flesch formula.* (2) *Hearing impairment.* (3) hearing impaired.

hidden curriculum *Covert curriculum*; often refers specifically to the covert teaching of middle class language, social values, etc.

hierarchy of needs *Maslow's hierarchy of needs.*

high amplitude sucking (HAS) technique *nonnutritive nipple sucking technique.*

high risk students Students whose (mis)perception of previous academic failings may lower their motivation, and increase the probability that they will 'drop out'.

high school See *American school system.*

Hirano body A crystalline structure found in some brain cells in older people. The incidence of these increases greatly in some *demented* patients.

Hiskey-Nebraska Test of Learning Aptitude Non-verbal intelligence test battery designed for deaf or hard-of-hearing children.

HIT *Holtzman Inkblot Technique.*

Holborn Reading Scale Reading test for subjects aged 5–13 years. Consists of sentences which increase in difficulty as the test progresses. The test terminates when the subject has made a set number of errors. The *Salford Sentence Reading Test* has a similar format.

hold tests See *deterioration quotient (DQ).*

holding on personality See *armoured-defensive personality.*

holist student Student who builds understanding of a topic through analogies and examples. See *serialist student.*

holistic word acquisition Theory that meanings of words are usually learnt as 'wholes'. See *compositional word acquisition.*

holophrases In early speech, utterances which consist of only one word, but which represent larger concepts (e.g.

'milk' might represent 'please may I have some milk?').

Holtzman Inkblot Technique (HIT) *Projective test* in which subjects (age 5 years and over) describe impressions formed by a series of inkblots.

HOME *Home Observation for Measurement of the Environment.*

Home Observation for Measurement of the Environment (HOME) Measurement scale of influences likely to influence mental development. Uses a combination of tester observation and interviewing.

homogeneous collective décalage See *collective décalage.*

homograph Word with same spelling but two or more different pronunciations (e.g. 'wind').

homophone Word with the same pronunciation but two or more different spellings (e.g. 'sun' and 'son').

homozygotic Pertaining to *genes* from both parents which have the same effect. By contrast, *heterozygotic* refers to genes which have different effects (e.g. different hair colours).

horizontal décalage In *Piagetian* theory, the developmental lag between exhibiting one manifestation of a skill and another (see *conservation of quantity* for an example). See *vertical décalage* and *oblique décalage.*

horizontal growth The increase in the number of skills of the same level of difficulty which can be successfully performed. Compare with *vertical growth.*

horizontal relationship See *vertical relationship.*

hostility personality Personality type found in some older people – those possessing it (illogically) blame others for their present misfortunes.

HPRT syndrome *Lesch-Nyham syndrome.*

HR heart rate.

human interest (reading) (HI) See *Flesch formula.*

humanistic psychology A rather nebulous term for psychological/psychoanalytical theories which, while acknowledging the importance of objective observations, hold the introspections of individuals to be of the greatest importance in analysis of mental life (accordingly, humanistic psychology is often cited as the antithesis of *behaviourism*). Best known humanist developmental theory is *Erikson's theory of development.*

Hunter-Grundin Literacy Profiles Reading test, which assesses several related reading and linguistic skills, including: *cloze procedure*; spelling; creative writing; ability to verbally describe a pictorial scene; and motivation to read. Consists of four 'Levels', commensurate with the age of the subjects: Level 1: 6–8 years; Level 2: 7–9 years; Level 3: 8–10 years; and Level 4: 10 years and over.

Huntington's Chorea Older term for *Huntington's Disease.*

Huntington's Disease An illness with the principal characteristics of disturbed gait and movements. Some patients develop *demented* symptoms. Ultimately fatal, the illness can strike at any age, from childhood through to old age. Strong genetic component.

Hutchison-Gilford syndrome *progeria.*

HVM Test *Haptic Visual Matching Test.*

hydrocephalus Accumulation of fluid in the skull, causing damaging pressure on the brain, which if not treated, can lead to serious and permanent damage, or even death. Symptoms may include *dementia*-like behaviour.

hyperactivity An inappropriately high level of activity, which cannot be voluntarily controlled. Many adults with the condition are better at covering up their problem than are children, who are the most conspicuous sufferers. The definition of hyperactivity is rather over-inclusive, and covers a variety of conditions from 'spoilt brat' through to individuals with genuinely serious problems. See *attentional deficit disorder*.

hyperborean ageing myth Myth that there is a distant land where people have incredibly long lifespans. See *antediluvian ageing myth*.

hyperlexia (1) Reading accurately but with no evidence of comprehension of what is being read. See *demented dyslexia*. (2) Reading at a precociously early age.

hypothesis theory Theory that initial attempts to solve a problem involve applying already learnt hypotheses to it (see *heuristics*). Only if these do not work does the subject attempt to solve from 'first principles'. Obviously, the older and brighter the subject, the more ready-made hypotheses are available, and the more efficiently they can be used.

hypothetico-deductive thought See *formal operations*.

I

IARS *Intellectual Achievement Responsibility Scale.*

iatrogenic Describes any complaint induced by medical treatment (e.g. side-effects of drugs, etc). Can in certain cases cause *acute confusional state* or *dementia*-like symptoms.

I.B.E. International Bureau of Education.

IBR *Infant Behaviour Record.*

iconic thought See *enactive thought.*

id See *Freud's theory of development.*

identification The acquisition of personality and behavioural characteristics which are seen as 'copying' from other people (e.g. parents, teachers etc.).

identity When used in connection with *Piagetian* theory – see *group.*

identity confusion Confusion about what is one's 'true' personality.

identity element When used in connection with *Piagetian* theory – see *group.*

identity foreclosure See *Erikson's theory of development.*

identity principle In *Piaget's* theory of *conservation*, the understanding that the basic attribution of an object does not change, despite any outward alteration in its appearance.

identity versus role confusion See *Erikson's theory of development.*

idiot See *mental retardation.*

idiots savants (Pronounced the French way.) Individuals with a severe *mental retardation* who are surprisingly adept at an isolated intellectual skill (an *islet of intelligence*). E.g. there are some *autistic* children who are (by any standards) extraordinarily talented at a facet of arithmetic or drawing, yet who otherwise have a very low *IQ.*

IDPS *Irlen Differential Perceptual Scale.*

IE *instrumental enrichment.*

Illinois Test of Psycholinguistic Abilities (ITPA) Test battery of twelve measures of psycholinguistic skills, principally vocabulary.

imbecile See *mental retardation.*

impersonal teacher Teacher who deliberately maintains an emotionally disinterested air towards his/her pupils, on the grounds that anything else interferes with work objectives. Opposite of *warm teacher.*

imprinting (1) A period in an animal's life (usually soon after birth) when it is predisposed to learn a particular type of information (probably genetically controlled). Often used of the first few days of life when the young of many species become attached to whoever is rearing them (thus forming a parent–offspring *bond*). The learning is virtually irrevocable. See *critical period.* (2) The term is used in *Bowlby's theory of attachment* in a modified form to denote the formation (over longer periods of time) of the human mother–child *bond.*

inanimate environment The non-living components of the environment.

inborn error of metabolism *Inherited* metabolic disorder (e.g. *PKU*).

Inchkeith experiment An early (and morally dubious) attempt to resolve the *hereditarian versus environmentalist theories of individual differences* debate, with special reference to linguistics. James IV of Scotland had two babies reared in the isolated community of Inchkeith, with only a deaf-mute woman to look after them. Some reports claim the children spontaneously began to converse in Hebrew. However, in all likelihood, their fate (at least regarding linguistic skills) was that of any *attic child*. A similar tale is told of Akbar the Great, a sixteenth century Mogul emperor.

independent reading level See *functional reading level*.

index (Piagetian theory) An item which is part of a larger item, and indicates the presence of that item (e.g. *Piaget* gave the example of a person's voice signalling the presence of the person). This can be contrasted with *symbols*, which are representations of items and which to some extent physically resemble the items (e.g. Piaget cites children using white stones to represent loaves of white bread); and *signs*, which are purely abstract representations.

indirect route reading *phonic mediation*.

individual décalage *Décalage* in which the direction of the disparity can vary between developing individuals (e.g. in person A, skill X may arise before skill Y, while in person B, the reverse applies). See *collective décalage*.

individualized grandmother See *apportioned grandmother*.

individuolet Term used by some commentators (e.g. Lenneberg) to denote the stage in speech development (usually 4 years and over) by which time mastery of basic linguistic rules is virtually complete and there is the beginning of individual idiosyncrasies of speech.

induction disciplining Parental disciplining of children in which the adverse effects of misbehaviour are explained to them.

inductive reasoning Creating a general principle from specific examples. This contrasts with *deductive reasoning*, in which the outcome of a specific example is calculated from a general principle.

inductive teaching Teaching method where the pupil is encouraged to discover the desired principle by working it out for him/herself by working through problems which are examples of the principle at work. Compare with *expository teaching*.

industry versus inferiority See *Erikson's theory of development*.

infancy (1) Commonly classified as the period between birth and 1 year 6 months. However, other definitions (e.g. first year of life) are employed by some commentators. (2) In pre-twentieth century English, the period of life up to circa 7 years (hence *'infant school'*).

Infant Behaviour Record (IBR) Scale within the *Bayley Scales of Infant Development*, which measures the infant's temperament.

infant intelligence tests Misleading shorthand for tests assessing mental development in babies. Such tests can only detect fairly gross levels of functioning, and beyond very broad generalizations (e.g. there is evidence of *mental retardation* or there is not), it is impossible to give a precise indication of future *IQ*. Indeed, many authors of these measures explicitly reject the idea that they have produced intelligence tests.

infant school See *British school system*.

infantile amaurotic idiocy *Tay-Sachs disease*.

infantile amnesia *childhood amnesia.*

infantile marasmus Complaint resulting from severe malnutrition in very young (less than 2 years) children. Psychological symptoms include apathy and high level of irritability.

infantile speech Speech which is at a significantly earlier stage of development than would be predicted from the afflicted person's *chronological age.* Can be a symptom of *mental retardation*, but can also exist in children with an otherwise normal *IQ*.

infarct A 'miniature *stroke*', causing the death of a tiny proportion of brain tissue. Infarcts occur in most older people's brains, but on too small a scale to cause serious damage. However, in *multi-infarct dementia*, the number of infarcts is considerably greater than normal.

inference Extrapolating from existing knowledge to form new pieces of knowledge.

inferred number right (INR) score Traditional scoring system for a multiple choice test, in which the first answer given is the only one accepted. See *answer until correct (AUC) score.*

inflection A grammatical term for an indicator of the grammatical form of the word (e.g. plural, tense, etc).

informal reading inventory (IRI) Reading measure in which the child reads from a variety of books (rather than taking a more formal reading test), primarily to establish his/her *functional reading level.*

information processing (IP) An explanation of cognitive functioning in terms borrowed from computer programming. There are many variants, but essentially, the processing of a piece of information is seen in terms of a se-

quence of mechanisms, each of which manipulates the information so that it is 'readable' by the next process in the chain (often collectively called processing stages).

infra-red corneal reflection technique *corneal reflection technique.*

infralogical operation In *Piagetian* theory, any mental *operation* dealing with measurement. See *intellectual operation.*

Inglis Paired Associate Learning (IPAL) Test Test assessing *paired associate learning* (and hence mnemonic/cognitive efficiency) in older psychiatric patients.

inherited Characteristics which are the result of genetic transmission. Compare with *congenital.*

inherited sinfulness The belief, derived from one interpretation of the fall of Adam and Eve, that humans are inherently evil. Accordingly, the excuse in previous centuries for repressing any signs of 'evil' rebelliousness, boisterousness or signs of independent thought in children.

inhibition theory A theory of cognitive ageing which argues that older people become less proficient at inhibiting extraneous information and concentrating on the target task.

initial teaching alphabet (i.t.a.) Reading teaching method, devised by Pitman (of shorthand fame). Beginning readers learn to read using the *traditional orthography (t.o.)* of twenty-six letters, plus an additional set of phonetic symbols, creating an alphabet of forty-four characters. Each letter or symbol represents one sound only. Accordingly, English words are all spelt logically – there are no *irregular spellings.* Children learn to read very quickly using the i.t.a. method, but critics have observed that unless carefully taught, whatever advantage they have gained over pupils learning to read by conventional methods is lost when they transfer to reading conventionally printed books.

initiative versus guilt See *Erikson's theory of development.*

innate *inherited.*

innate releasing mechanism (IRM) Term derived from ethology (the study of animal behaviour). The phenomenon whereby certain stimuli provoke an unlearnt response in certain animals. E.g. the herring gull chick will 'automatically' peck at the red dot on its parent's beak to elicit feeding. Sometimes used in human infant research to describe certain responses which are thought to be *innate.*

inner speech (1) The 'voice in the head' one is sometimes aware of in thinking or reading. (2) Language-mediated thought in *Vygotsky's theory of development.*

INR score *inferred number right (INR) score.*

INRC group In *Piaget's* theory, a group of mental operations which can be performed on a statement of the truth or falsehood of one statement given the truth or falsehood of another (e.g. 'if p is true then q is false'). The INRC group arises in the *formal operations period.* The name is an acronym for the four properties of the group (sometimes called the *four-group*). Identity (I) refers to the fact that one type of transformation results in no change to the statement (i.e. it acts like the *identity element* in a *group*). Negation (N) reverses all aspects of the argument, including a switching from a conjunction statement (i.e. 'if p then q') to a disjunction statement (i.e. 'if p, then q', or, 'if not p then not q', or 'if q then not p' and other permutations). Reciprocal (R) reverses a statement from being positive to negative (or vice versa),

but leaves statements as conjunctions or disjunctions. Correlative (C) is the reverse of the Reciprocal operation – conjunctions are converted to disjunctions (and vice versa), but the negativity or positivity of the statement is unaltered. The theory is a very difficult one, and is intended to describe in symbolic terms the reasoning of the formal operational mind. It is not argued that subjects consciously reduce their thoughts to this symbolic process.

insecure/ambivalent *resistant and insecurely attached.*

insecure/detached *avoidant and insecurely attached.*

insecure/disorganized/disorientated Suggested additional 'insecurely attached' category in the *strange situation,* proposed by M Main, in which the child appears dazed and may simultaneously exhibit behaviours indicative of pleasure at seeing the parent and unease.

insecure/resistant *resistant and insecurely attached.*

insecurely attached Pertaining to children who appear to have an inappropriately weak *bond* with a parent or *caregiver.*

insensitive parent Parent who is relatively unresponsive to his/her child's needs. The opposite of *sensitive parent.*

insertion miscue Misreading an extra word into the text.

institutionalized behaviour Nebulous term for deleterious changes in some (but by no means all) individuals, resulting from a (usually lengthy) spell in an institution (e.g. hospital, children's home, etc.). Such afflicted individuals tend to have poor social skills, lack of 'individuality', lowered *IQ,* etc.

instructional reading level See *functional reading level*.

instrumental conditioning *operant conditioning*.

instrumental enrichment (IE) Term devised by Feuerstein for an instructional programme involving a sequence of mental (often non-verbal) exercises intended to stimulate and remediate. A key aim is *bridging*, in which pupils are encouraged to form links between the skills used in the exercises and other educational situations.

instrumental gesture Gesture designed to elicit a change in another person's behaviour and/or actions.

instrumental relativist orientation Stage 2 of *Kohlberg's theory of moral development*.

integrated avoidance response Reaction shown by infants to an object which they perceive is about to hit them (e.g. in the *approaching objects paradigm*). The head is thrown back, the hands cover the face, and a cry may be emitted.

integrated personality Personality type found in some older people – possessors are of three kinds: *reorganizers* (finding new things to do as old ones become impractical); *focused* (activities restricted to a small scope, but are rewarding); or *disengaged* (deliberately avoiding responsibility).

Intellectual Achievement Responsibility Scale (IARS) Questionnaire examining the degree to which a pupil attributes his/her academic achievements to him/herself, and how much s/he attributes to parents, teachers, etc.

intellectual impairment A rather nebulous term denoting impairment of intellectual functioning; may refer to e.g. *mental retardation*, to an acquired impairment following an accident, *learning difficulty* or *learning disability*.

intellectual operation In *Piagetian* theory, any mental *operation* dealing with logical relationships. See *infralogical operation*.

intellectual realism Term describing drawings or pictures in which the 'true' state of the objects is represented, rather than drawing what can actually be seen *(perceptual realism)*. The term is used particularly of young children's drawings. A common example is that in drawing two objects, one placed slightly behind the other so that not all of it can be seen, the children draw both objects in their entirety. Similarly, a cup with the handle placed away from the child (so that s/he cannot see it) will usually be drawn showing the handle. See *symbolism (children's drawing)*.

intelligence quotient (IQ) Often (erroneously) used as a synonym for 'intelligence'. The intelligence quotient denotes how intelligent a person is, in comparison with the rest of his or her *age cohort* (also known as the *deviation IQ*). Traditionally, a score of 100 has denoted a person of average intelligence for his/her age cohort – i.e. 50% of the group are cleverer, 50% are less clever then this person. A score of more than 130 indicates someone who is exceptionally bright for the group (i.e. there are few people in the age group with better scores) and a score of 70 or below indicates someone who is unusually ungifted. The older method of measuring IQ in children was by the formula of *mental age* divided by *chronological age*, multiplied by 100. The problem with this method is that it is useless for subjects aged over 18 years, because mental age is relatively stable in adulthood up to about 60 years of age. This means that the formula will cause their IQs to halve every 18 years they age. See *education quotient*.

interactionism Belief that the mind develops through an interaction between the person (possessing some *innate* predispositions) and the environment.

interactive compensatory reading (1) When coping with a non-standard text where there is a lack of information from one source, readers adjust by relying more heavily on other sources (e.g. in reading bad handwriting, one tends to rely heavily on context). (2) Readers of different abilities tend to have different relative strengths and weaknesses, and rely more heavily on their best skills.

interactive reading Any reading materials which involve interaction with the reader (e.g. children's books in which pressing a button or symbol produces a noise).

interchange Term for verbal exchanges between two or more speakers.

interest stage (of career choice) See *fantasy stage (career choice)*.

intermediate generation Adolescents are 'half way' between the ages of the children and their parents – hence the term.

internalized speech Thinking using words 'in the head'.

International Reading Association (IRA) Organization, principally of educationalists, dedicated to research on reading and its teaching.

interpersonal concordance of 'good boy–nice girl' orientation Stage 3 of *Kohlberg's theory of moral development*.

interpersonal problem-solving *Perspective-taking* with the added ability to see how some choices of actions by oneself or others are less or more desirable than the alternatives.

interpropositional thought *formal operations*.

intersensory coordination *intersensory perception*.

intersensory perception Coordination of different senses to perceive the same stimulus (e.g. turning the head to look for the source of a sound).

intersubjectivity Taking account of other people's thoughts, emotions and intentions in deciding what to do.

interval synchrony See *synchrony*.

intimacy versus isolation See *Erikson's theory of development*.

intonation pattern The rhythmic pattern and frequency fluctuations characteristic of speech. Infants typically demonstrate this prior to learning to talk.

intrafamilially adopted child Child adopted by a relative of one of the parents. This contrasts with the *extrafamilially adopted child*, adopted by a non-relative.

intraorganismic perspective The hypothesis that *attachment behaviours* are genetically inherited.

intrapropositional thought *concrete operational thought*.

intrauterine experience The experience of the *foetus*.

intrinsic reinforcement *Reinforcement* produced by feelings of internal satisfaction (as opposed to an external reward in *extrinsic reinforcement*).

intuitive thought (1) Thought using common sense/first principles. (2) *Piaget* sometimes used the phrase to refer to the (erroneous) thought processes of a child making errors in a *conservation* task.

invariances *invariants*.

invariants In *direct perception theory*, identifying an object as the same at many orientations and distances.

inverse element When used in connection with *Piagetian* theory – see *group*.

IP *information processing.*

IPAL Test *Inglis Paired Associate Learning (IPAL) Test.*

IQ *intelligence quotient.*

IRA *International Reading Association.*

IRI *informal reading inventory.*

Irlen Differential Perceptual Scale (IDPS) Measures various visual perceptual abilities, to identify the presence or absence of *scotopic sensitivity*, a perceptual problem resulting from an unbalanced perception of the spectrum. Irlen argues that this is a cause of *developmental dyslexia*, and advocates that dyslexic readers should wear tinted spectacles to redress the spectral balance and so remove scotopic sensitivity. The efficacy of these *Irlen lenses* has been disputed.

Irlen lenses See *Irlen Differential Perceptual Scale.*

IRM *innate releasing mechanism.*

irregular spelling A word whose logical pronunciation differs from the way it is supposed to be pronounced. Examples of irregular spelling abound in English – 'quay', 'misled', etc.

irregular word Word with an *irregular spelling.*

IS *Hachinski Ischaemic Score.*

Ischaemic Rating Scale *Hachinski Ischaemic Score.*

Isle of Wight hump P h e n o m e n o n found in a 1970s study of Isle of Wight schoolchildren, in which the proportion of subjects with *intelligence quotients* significantly higher than *reading quotients* (i.e. in effect suffering from *dyslexia*) was much higher than would be predicted by chance. For various reasons, this was taken as evidence for the 'qualitative' side of the *dyslexia – qualitative versus quantitative debate.* However, the 'hump' was later discovered to be a statistical artifact, and subsequent studies have largely failed to replicate it.

islets of intelligence See *idiots savants.*

isomorphism of measures An arithmetic process in which the answer is in the same units as one or more of the items in the sum (e.g. 2 penguins + 8 penguins = 10 penguins, not 10 aardvarks, etc.). See *product of measures.*

It Scale for Children Test in which the child is measured on preferences for toys and objects with a strong 'sex bias' (e.g. dolls, prams, etc.). Designed to test strength and direction of stereotypical sex roles in children.

i.t.a. *initial teaching alphabet.*

ITPA *Illinois Test of Psycholinguistic Abilities.*

J

James IV's experiment *Inchkeith experiment.*

JIIG-CAL A computerized career guidance package. The acronym stands for 'Job Ideas and Information Generator – Computer Assisted Learning'.

joint family Family grouping in which two or more adult siblings and their families live in the same household. Compare with *extended family* and *nuclear family.*

junior high school See *American school system.*

junior school See *British school system.*

K

K-ABC *Kaufman Assessment Battery for Children.*

K-TEA *Kaufman Test of Educational Achievement.*

Kanner's Syndrome *autism.*

Kaufman Assessment Battery for Children (K-ABC) Test battery for children aged 2–12 years. The battery is heavily influenced by the theories of the Russian neuropsychologist Luria, and, under his categorization scheme, measure the ability to perform sequential tasks and successive tasks. The measures are heavily biased towards non-verbal skills.

Kaufman Test of Educational Achievement (K-TEA) A battery of *achievement tests*, assessing mathematical, reading and spelling skills.

KDCT *Kendrick Digit Copying Test.*

Kendrick Battery for the Detection of Dementia in the Elderly Earlier version of the *Kendrick Cognitive Tests for the Elderly.*

Kendrick Cognitive Tests for the Elderly Test battery for identifying *dementia* in subjects aged 55 year and over. It consists of two tests. The *Kendrick Object Learning Test (KOLT)* is a memory test for arrays of pictures in varying numbers, and the time over which the memories must be retained. The *Kendrick Digit Copying Test (KDCT)* measures the speed at which the subject copies a set of 100 numbers.

Kendrick Digit Copying Test (KDCT) See *Kendrick Cognitive Tests for the Elderly.*

Kendrick Object Learning Test (KOLT) See *Kendrick Cognitive Tests for the Elderly.*

KeyMath test *Achievement test* of mathematical skills.

KFD *Kinetic Family Drawing.*

KGIS *Kuder General Interest Survey.*

kinaesthetic reading teaching Reading teaching method in which the child learns words by tracing over the pattern of the written word with his/her finger as s/he learns it.

Kinetic Family Drawing (KFD) *Projective* test in which the subject draws a picture of his/her family 'doing something'.

Kinetic School Drawing (KSD) *Projective* test in which the child subject draws a picture of him/herself performing an act at school.

Klinefelter's syndrome Possession of two X and one Y *chromosomes*, resulting in incomplete sexual development and *mental retardation.*

knowledge See *Bloom's taxonomy of educational objectives.*

Kohlberg's theory of moral development Lawrence Kohlberg (1927–1987), psychologist. His key study presented subjects with imaginary moral dilemmas. E.g. a man steals a drug to treat his sick wife, because the pharmacist was charging an extortionate fee – should the man have stolen? In a wartime scenario, who should be sent on a suicide mission which would ensure the survival of a company of soldiers – the unpopular troublemaker, or the diseased man who doesn't have long to live? Kohlberg analysed subjects' reasons for their answers rather than the answers themselves (e.g. whether they were 'yes' or 'no' or which man was chosen is relatively unimportant), and classified them into stages of moral development. Stage 1: the *punishment and obedience orientation* – subjects unquestioningly believe that something is wrong if a law or an authority figure prohibits it. Stage 2: the *instrumental relativist orientation* – the subject acknowledges that there may be two sides to an argument, and will tend to choose the one which provides the greater benefit. There is also a tendency to a 'tit for tat' philosophy of cooperation. Stage 3: the *interpersonal concordance of 'good boy-nice girl' orientation* – a justifiable action seems to be judged by whether it accords with accepted norms of 'good' or 'nice' behaviour (i.e. whether society would judge that someone's 'heart is in the right place', even if their actions contravene the letter of the law). Stage 4: the *law and order orientation* – subjects appreciate both arguments, but ultimately (and sometimes with great regret) side with whoever is more within the letter of the law. Stage 5: the *social contract legalistic orientation* – the subject can appreciate that some laws are wrong, and must be changed if there is a consensus in favour of this. None the less, even if a law is stupid, it must be obeyed until overturned by constitutional means. Stage 6: the *universal ethical principle* – the recognition that there are general rights and principles which transcend a country's statutes if the two are in disagreement. The six stages can be categorized into three levels – the *preconventional level* (stages 1 and 2); the *conventional level* (stages

3 and 4); and the *post-conventional level* (formed from stages 5 and 6; also known as the *autonomous level*, or the *principled level*). Kohlberg argued that subjects proceed through the stages in an invariant order, and that stages cannot be 'skipped'. Also, subjects are attracted to the stage of reasoning one above the one they presently hold. The preconventional level is the one most often held by children, who usually do not advance into the conventional level until their late childhood/early teens. The post-conventional level is not usually acquired until mid teens (if at all – the majority stay at a lower level, and a minority never advance beyond Stage 1). However, there is a considerable variability in the age of acquisition. Kohlberg's early work was criticized for being too vague, particularly in details of scoring. In reply, a standardized testing procedure was devised (note that Stage 6 is very rarely attained). Kohlberg's theory has been criticized – some of his findings are vague, and some commentators have questioned his admiration of some moral arguments. Kohlberg's theory is heavily influenced by *Piaget*, and in particular *Piaget's theory of moral development*. See *Defining Issues Test*.

Kohn Problem Checklist (KPC)
Measure of social and emotional functioning/dysfunctioning in children aged 3–5 years.

Kohn Social Competence Scale (KSC)
Measure of social skills and emotional expression in children aged 3–6 years.

KOIS *Kuder Occupational Interest Survey.*

KOLT *Kendrick Object Learning Test.*

Koluchova's twins Pair of Czechoslovakian twins who were *attic children*.

Korsakoff's syndrome (KS) Severe amnesia (particularly for new information), resulting from long term alcohol abuse coupled with vitamin deficiency through poor diet. Damage is particularly centred in the hippocampus. Korsakoff patients are sometimes used as a control group in studies of dementia.

KPC *Kohn Problem Checklist.*

Kreutzfeld-Jakob Disease
Creutzfeldt-Jakob Disease.

KS *Korsakoff's syndrome.*

KSC *Kohn Social Competence Scale.*

KSD *Kinetic School Drawing.*

Kuder General Interest Survey (KGIS) American test of general areas of interest (e.g. outdoor, scientific, etc.) for use in preliminary careers counselling in children in *grades* 6–12.

Kuder Occupational Interest Survey (KOIS) American measure of careers interests for use in careers counselling for pupils and subjects in *grades* 10–adult.

kwashiorkor *infantile marasmus.*

L

lacunar deficits The phenomenon, sometimes encountered in brain-damaged patients, whereby some intellectual functions are almost completely destroyed, while others remain relatively intact.

lacunar dementia (LD) Some (although not all) commentators argue that patients suffering from *multi-infarct dementia* and who exhibit *lacunar deficits*, should be reclassified as suffering from lacunar dementia.

LAD *language acquisition device.*

lag (1) Delayed relative to normal development. (2) *décalage.*

laissez-faire parents *permissive parents.*

laissez-faire teacher Teacher who allows pupils to make most or all of the decisions. Compare with *authoritarian teacher* and *democratic teacher.*

lalling Term used by some commentators (e.g. Lenneberg) to denote a baby's vocalizations at the stage (usually 6–8 months) where they are still not recognizable speech, but contain identifiable repetitions of sequences.

language acquisition device (LAD) See *deep structure.*

language delay In children, a delay in acquiring language or in progressing to an age-appropriate stage of linguistic development.

language dominance The language at which a bi- or multilingual person is most adept.

language experience programme Reading teaching scheme which integrates linguistic teaching experiences across a variety of domains (i.e. not just reading but also writing, speech, etc.).

LARR Test *Linguistic Awareness in Reading Readiness Test.*

late adult transition The period surrounding retirement, or retirement age. See *early adult transition (EAT).*

late paraphrenia Mental disorder of older people, whose symptoms are principally feelings of persecution and elaborate fantasies of the same. More common in women. Can have a variety of causes, including circulation problems and previous episodes of mental illness.

latency period See *Freud's theory of development.*

lattice In *Piaget's* theory, a set of elements in which for any two elements, one is entirely a subset of the other, or in which one has a larger value than the other. Hence a lattice is either a hierarchy of sets or a sequence of numerical values. The *least upper bound (l.u.b.)* describes a set which is the smallest which can possibly contain two smaller sets. The *greatest lower bound (g.l.b.)* is the largest set which two sets have in common. Within a lattice, any two sets have only one possible l.u.b. and one possible g.l.b. The concept is used by *Piaget* in discussions of intellectual development (see *concrete operations subperiod* and *16 binary operations*).

law and order orientation Stage 4 of *Kohlberg's theory of moral development.*

law of effect Rule devised by Thorndike which states that the likelihood of an action being repeated will increase if it has a positive outcome, and decrease if it is negative. See *law of practice.*

law of practice Rule devised by Thorndike that the more one rehearses a skill, the better it gets and the more likely it is to be repeated. See *law of effect.*

LC *locus of control.*

LD (1) *lacunar dementia.* (2) *learning disability.* (3) learning disabled.

LEA Local Education Authority.

learning curve The rate at which information about a topic is learnt. Typically (although not universally), this is a case of diminishing returns – a lot is learnt early in the study period, but progressively less new information is acquired the longer the person studies.

learning difficulty A rather nebulous term, often loosely used synonymously with *learning disability* and *learning disorder*, as well as to mean people with learning problems, regardless of origin.

learning disability (LD) (1) (UK) Profound problem in learning in the absence of a clear indication of brain damage and/or *deprivation.* (2) Many commentators add the caveat that the profound problem in learning originates in difficulties in using and/or comprehending language. The problem may be apparent in all aspects of learning (*general learning disability*) or in specific areas, such as reading (*specific learning disability*). (3) (USA/AUS) Used specifically to refer to problems relating to understanding and using language. Compare with *learning disor-der.* (4) Some commentators use the term to denote learning difficulties arising from neurological problems.

learning disorder Profound problem in learning, resulting from physical and/or mental disability, and/or emotional disturbance and/or socio-economic disadvantage. Compare with *learning disability.*

learning hierarchy Learning in stages which get increasingly difficult and/or build upon knowledge learnt in earlier stages.

Learning Potential Assessment Device (LPAD) 'Alternative' intelligence test, in which the child performs a *culture-fair test*, followed by training on problem-solving methods relevant to the test, followed by retesting.

Learning Process Questionnaire (LPQ) Questionnaire measuring study skills and motivation in secondary school pupils. See *Study Process Questionnaire.*

learning readiness The possession of the intellectual and other psychological skills necessary for learning a particular task.

learning set (1) The method by which an individual solves a problem, with the implication that he or she habitually uses this method. (2) Term used by Gagné to denote the set of skills a pupil possesses at a particular stage in learning a skill. (3) The mental state of readiness an individual creates when beginning a task (*Einstellung*).

learning structure The hierarchy of skills a pupil must necessarily possess to be capable of the target skill (e.g. being able to write a critique of 'Moby Dick' requires the underlying skills of reading, writing, high boredom threshold, etc.).

learning theory (1) General term for any theory which argues that children are best taught by *conditioning*. See *behaviourism*. (2) More generally, any theory which attempts to explain how learning occurs and/or is best accomplished.

learning versus memory distinction Generally, learning is defined as the formation of a piece of information, or the establishment of a connection between pieces of information. Memory is the retention and retrieval of such information.

least upper bound (l.u.b.) See *lattice*.

left brain skills Loose term for skills associated with the left *hemisphere* – chiefly linguistic and logical skills. This contrasts with **right brain skills**, which are said to be concerned with artistic and creative matters.

Leiter International Performance Scale Non-verbal intelligence measure for children.

Lesch-Nyham syndrome Rare *inherited* condition affecting only males, whose principal feature is a compulsive urge for self-mutilation.

letter strings Groups of letters which may or may not form real words.

Lewy body disease *Dementia* akin to demented forms of *Parkinson's Disease*, characterized by malformed neurons (Lewy bodies) in the cortex.

LH left handed.

licking reflex *Primitive reflex* – a pleasant taste may cause the infant to lick his/her lips and try to suck.

life crisis A set of profoundly negative feelings created by the transition from one *social age* to another (e.g. entering adolescence).

life expectancy How much longer an average person can expect to live. More accurately, the age by which 50 per cent of an *age cohort* will have died. Contrast with *lifespan*.

life satisfaction Degree of contentment with one's own lifestyle.

lifespan The maximum length of time a member of a species can be expected to live. Contrast with *life expectancy*.

lifespan development See *developmental psychology*.

linear development Development which is continuous and is shaped by the nature of earlier development.

linguistic awareness The conscious awareness of one's linguistic skills, and of how language is structured. See *morphemic awareness* and *phonemic awareness*.

Linguistic Awareness in Reading Readiness (LARR) Test Test of *linguistic awareness*, for beginning readers (e.g. tests ability to discriminate between pictures of reading and non-reading activities). Held by the test's authors to be a crucial determinant of whether the subject is ready to be taught to read.

liquid continuous quantity task See *conservation of quantity*.

literacy (1) The ability to read and write. Many authorities include a caveat that the skills must reach a certain level of competence (e.g. that commensurate with four year's schooling). This is an essentially arbitrary figure, and pragmatically, *functional literacy* may be a more useful measure. (2) More generally, a grasp of the essential skills for comprehending a particular task or medium. Hence, *computer literacy* and *television literacy*.

Little Albert See *Watson's theory of child rearing*.

Little Hans Case study by Freud, and the only one conducted on a child. The child had a fear of horses biting him (identified by Freud as a fear of his father castrating him), and a dream about giraffes (self-explanatory). Freud explained the case as primarily being an unresolved *Oedipus complex*.

living will Signed and witnessed declaration by a person that in the event of their becoming severely mentally and/or physically incapacitated, no effort will be made to prolong survival artificially.

L1 first language.

Locke's theory of human development John Locke (1632–1704), English philosopher. Locke argued that children were born with a mind like a *tabula rasa* (blank slate – note that the phrase was not his, but was later attributed to him), although he acknowledged that people differ in disposition, and capacity for learning. However, he argued that it is the environment which is the prime determinant of what is learnt and the (largely passively receiving) mind which is accordingly formed. To this end, Locke outlined a system of rewards and (non-physical) punishments which would form the basis of a teaching programme. Locke's work anticipates many of the basic tenets of modern learning theories, such as learning by association. See *Rousseau's theory of human development*.

locomotion development of infant *posture and locomotion development of infant.*

locus of control (LC) Degree to which an individual is in command of a situation, particularly his/her own destiny.

logicomathematical experience (1) Knowledge about properties of objects not directly derived from their physical nature and appearance (see *physical experience* for further explanation). The 'superior' thought process of *Piaget's* theory, which first appears in the the *concrete operations period*, and comes to fruition in the *formal operations period*. (2) Knowledge acquired through contemplation of one's own actions on objects.

LOGO Simple computer programming language. See *turtle graphics*.

London Reading Test Reading test for subjects aged 10–12 years. Consists of *cloze procedure* and comprehension tests.

longitudinal research/samples/study The experimental method of testing the same group of people at different ages. Contrast with *cross-sectional research/samples/study*. See *overlapping longitudinal study* and *sequential research design*. See *time-lag comparison*.

look-say (reading teaching) *whole word (reading teaching).*

looming experiment *approaching objects paradigm.*

Lordstown hypothesis The theory that older workers are more satisfied with working conditions than are young workers, because the older *cohort* has lower expectations. Named after the town in which the phenomenon was first observed.

Lorge formula *Readability* measure. Calculated by the formula: readability = 1.99 + (0.06 x mean no. words per sentence) + (0.10 x no. prepositional phrases per 100 words) + (0.10 x number of low frequency words not on Dale 769 section of the *Dale-Chall word list*). The result is expressed as the earliest *grade* in which an average child could answer half the questions on the text (to express the result as *reading age*, add five to the result). To find the *grade/* age at which the child can answer 75% of the questions, add 1.866 to the score.

loudness recruitment A physical complaint in which sounds in a particular frequency band (usually high) are (mis)interpreted as being louder then usual, sometimes to the point of being painful. Found in some older people with hearing difficulties.

love–hostility Scale for judging the degree of affection exhibited by a family.

love withdrawal Punishing a child by (temporarily) withdrawing affection.

low frequency words Words which occur very rarely in common usage.

LPAD *Learning Potential Assessment Device.*

LPQ *Learning Process Questionnaire.*

L2 second language.

l.u.b. *least upper bound.*

ludic Pertaining to play/make-believe.

ludic reading Reading for pleasure.

M

M-MAC *McDermott Multidimensional Assessment of Children.*

M power Term used by Pascual-Leone to denote the necessary intellectual 'power' to attain a particular stage of development.

MA *mental age.*

macrosystem See *microsystem.*

macular degeneration The degeneration and ultimate loss of the eye's 'yellow spot' or macula, which is responsible for the highest resolution of focusing in the eye. More common in older people.

mad cow disease See *bovine spongiform encephalopathy.*

mainstreaming American term for placement of children with physical disabilities and/or *mental retardation* in normal schools.

maintenance See *facilitation.*

maintenance of proximity to a discriminated figure by means of locomotion as well as signals Phase 3 of *Bowlby's theory of attachment.*

make-believe play See *play.*

manipulative latency (ML) The delay between an infant perceiving an object and beginning to play with it.

MAP test *Miller Assessment for Preschoolers.*

marble board test A measure used by some Gestalt psychologists to assess visuo-spatial skills. The apparatus is a board with an array of depressions arranged in a regular (usually 10x10) matrix. Marbles can be placed into the depressions. The subject's task is to place marbles onto the board to copy an array presented by the experimenter on an identical board.

Marianne Frostig Developmental Test of Visual Perception (DTVP) Test of perceptual skills presumed to underlie reading (e.g. hand–eye coordination, geometric figure identification, etc.). Designed for subjects aged 3–10 years. Can be used as part of *reading readiness* measures or as a diagnostic tool in assessing poor readers.

marking mothers Mothers whose verbal interaction with their infants tends to echo and comment on what is going on. See *non-marking mothers* and *passive mothers.*

MASI *Multilevel Academic Skills Inventory.*

Maslow's hierarchy of needs Theory by Maslow that humans have a hierarchy of needs, which can be symbolically represented as a pyramid. At the 'base' are physiological needs for food, shelter, etc. Above these are safety needs, followed by social needs (e.g. to form friendships, to fit into the social world, etc.). Above these are self-esteem, and at the top of the pyramid lies self-actualization (i.e. searching for and achieving 'higher' goals and fulfilling one's potential). Maslow argues that these stages are acquired through development, and the complete structure will take more than 30 years to complete.

MASP *Measure of Adolescent Social Performance.*

MAST *Multilevel Academic Survey Tests.*

mastery play See *play.*

Matching Familiar Figures Test
(MFF Test) Tests which assesses children's visual skills and the degree of their impulsiveness in making responses. The child has to find the drawing identical to the target from a range of very similar alternatives. The accuracy and speed of response are both recorded.

maternal deprivation Lack of adequate care by the mother or other *caregiver*. Can be considered in terms of *separation* and *deprivation of maternal care*. The former is any separation of mother/caregiver and child whether on a regular basis (e.g. the mother/caregiver goes to work) or occasional (e.g. hospital visits). The latter is where the mother/caregiver is present all the time, but inadequately looks after the child. NB – see caveat in *deprivation*. See also *cultural deprivation.*

maternal interaction Measure of how a mother (or other *caregiver*) interacts with a child.

maternal stress Stress suffered by the mother during pregnancy. In extreme cases, effects may be exhibited by the baby (e.g. premature birth, severe restlessness, etc.).

mathematics anxiety (Irrational) anxiety created by fear of studying or working on mathematical or arithmetical topics.

Matrix Analogies Test A measure of non-verbal intelligence for 5–17-year-olds.

matrix game *Gotkin Matrix Game.*

maturation (1) Growth, usually with the implication of development into the adult state. (2) See *Gessell's maturational theory* for specialist meaning.

maturationism Belief (first proposed in *Gessell's maturational theory*) that maturation (particularly in infancy) is governed by a genetically-controlled regulatory system.

maturity Any consideration of how well developed an individual is compared to his/her age average. However, the term is usually reserved for assessment of children's personality, social skills, and/or physical development.

maturity demands Parental pressure on children to behave/think in a more 'mature' manner (often at an inappropriately high level).

maturity test Measure of *maturity*, in which an individual's measure(s) can be compared against standardized age norms.

maximum life potential (MLP)
The maximum *lifespan* an accident- and disease-free and fit person can expect.

MBD *minimal brain dysfunction.*

MBI minimal brain injuries.

McCall-Crabbs Standard Test Lessons in Reading *Standard Test Lessons in Reading.*

McCarthy Scales of Children's Abilities (MSCA) Test battery of motor and intellectual development in children aged 3 years 6 months–8 years 6 months. Comprises eighteen sub-tests, yielding five scales of verbal, perceptual-performance, quantitative, memory, and motor skills.

McCarthy Screening Test Measure of potential learning difficulties, drawn from *McCarthy Scales of Children's Abilities.*

McDermott Multidimensional Assessment of Children (M-MAC) Computerized assessment programme. It comprises: Classification (interpretation of intellectual and academic abilities, and social skills and milieu); and Programme

Design (creation of appropriate remedial regimes/goal setting).

MCI *mild cognitive impairment.*

MD *molecular decomposition.*

MDI *Mental Development Index.*

ME *molar equivalence.*

ME-MD strategy See *molar equivalence (ME).*

mean length of utterance (MLU)
Average number of words in a single
spoken utterance – a quick method of
measuring speech development, since
MLU increases with maturity.

meaning blindness *formula blindness.*

**Measure of Adolescent Social Perform-
ance (MASP)** A self-report measure of
the eponymous skill.

mechanistic-functional approach See
organismic-structural approach.

mediation theory In developmental psychology, the term is sometimes used to
describe how thought can control (me-
diate) responses in *conditioning* experiments. Generally, the efficiency of the
mediation is held to improve with age.

melodic utterance Term used by some
commentators to denote the stage of
speech development (circa 9–18
months) where the child's vocalizations
begin to adopt a melody and rhythm,
and *proto-words* are produced.

memory versus learning distinction
learning versus memory distinction.

menarche Onset of menstruation.

mental age (MA) The level of mental
skills which is average for a particular
age group. See *dyslexia* and *intelligence
quotient.*

mental age matching C o m p a r i n g
groups with the same *mental ages.* Any
differences found cannot therefore be
attributed to mental age per se. See
chronological age matching.

mental capacity The limit on how much
information a mind can process at any
one time, and/or how quickly it can
process information. The term is a useful
conceptual notion, but producing an
objective, accurate measure is often impossible. It can be estimated, however,
and it is known that it differs between
individuals (generally, young adults can
process more information at a faster rate
than e.g. children and older people), and
within individuals across time (capacity
often declines in old age).

Mental Development Index (MDI)
Measure of mental development derived
from the *Bayley Scales of Infant Development. Mental age* can be extrapolated from
it.

mental retardation Intelligence level
well below normal, which is *congenital,*
or becomes apparent in childhood/ado-
lescence. Definitions vary, but most refer
to IQs of <80 at maximum. The DSM
classifies it as occurring when IQ is <70
(i.e. more than two standard deviations
below average on most IQ tests, which
puts the people concerned in the lowest
5% of the population). According to the
AAMD classification, there are several
grades of retardation – *profound mental
retardation* (IQ < 25), *severe mental
retardation* (25–39), *moderate mental
retardation* (40–54) and *mild mental
retardation* (55–69). The DSM has similar IQ values (<20, 20–34, 35–49, and
50–70 respectively). An earlier (and
now offensive) terminology classified
people of lower IQ into *idiots* (<30),
imbeciles (30–50), and *morons* (American) or *feeble minded* (British) (50–7.0).

mental retardation – the developmental versus the difference debate The *developmental view of mental retardation* is that subjects of the same *mental age*, but different *IQs* (e.g. a 12-year-old with a mental age of 6 and a 6-year-old with a mental age of 6) should have identical cognitive abilities. The *difference view of mental retardation* is that such individuals should be cognitively different.

Mental Status Questionnaire (MSQ) An assessment of a (usually *demented*) patient's intellectual status and degree of functional independence. See *Blessed Dementia Scale.*

mentally gifted Nebulous definition, but typically refers to individuals with *IQs* of 125 and over.

Merrill-Palmer Scales Battery of measures of intellectual, motor and linguistic skills for children aged 18 months–6 years. Available in 'standard' and 'extended' formats. The scales measure patterns of abilities, rather than producing a single general ability score.

mesosystem See *microsystem.*

meta- The prefix usually denotes an understanding of the mental process which forms the rest of the word. Usually it is implied that it is an understanding of how one's own mental skills work, rather than a more global understanding. See e.g. *metacognition.*

metacognition Knowledge of how one's cognitive abilities function.

metaknowledge What one knows about the state of one's own knowledge.

metalearning (1) study skills. (2) knowledge of how one learns and how learning can be optimized.

metalinguistic awareness Awareness of how the rules of a language operate.

metamemory Knowing the capabilities of one's own memory, and methods by which the memorization process can be optimized.

metaneeds In *Maslow's hierarchy of needs,* the 'higher' needs, rather than the more basic needs of survival, food, etc.

metapelet Professional *caregiver* for a small group of young children on a kibbutz.

metareading Knowing all the processes of reading (i.e. *linguistic awareness, morphemic awareness, phonemic awareness, pragmatic awareness, reading awareness, syllabic awareness,* etc.).

Metropolitan Diagnostic Tests Series of tests of scholastic attainment. See *Diagnostic Language Tests, Diagnostic Mathematics* and *Diagnostic Reading Tests.*

MFF Test *Matching Familiar Figures Test.*

MH mixed handed (i.e. ambidextrous).

MHV Test *Mill Hill Vocabulary Test.*

Michigan Picture Test – Revised (MPT-R) *Projective* test for subjects aged 7–15 years.

micropractice Procedure within a given culture for developing a particular skill.

microsystem Term devised by Bronfenbrenner in describing a hierarchy of influences on a child. The microsystem is the one whose effects are most immediately felt (e.g. a particular type of learning or social situation). Performance in different microsystems can be related (e.g. an *abused child* may also be a playground bully and be bad at classwork). These links comprise the *mesosystem.* The mesosystem can in turn be classified into various types. E.g. the *cross-sectional mesosystem* describes the mesosystems in two different situations encountered simultaneously, whilst the *transitional mesosystem* describes the transition from one situation to another. Impinging on the mesosystem is the *exosystem*, which is how factors affecting caregivers and teachers can have a 'knock-on' effect on the child. Finally, the exosystem in turn is influenced by the *macrosystem*, which (loosely) describes general social conditions.

MID *multi-infarct dementia.*

middle childhood The period between circa 6 and 11 years of age (note that commentators differ over the precise boundary ages).

midlife crisis Loose term for set of negative feelings in some middle-aged people, stemming from the realization that they are at the peak of their careers and affluence, and that ageing will result (in their eyes) in a decline.

midlife transitions (MLTs) Changes occurring in middle age (e.g. children leaving home, preparing for retirement, etc.). Negative changes can in some instances create a *midlife crisis*. See *early adult transition (EAT)* and *empty nest syndrome.*

mild cognitive impairment (MCI) Currently rather nebulous term for intellectual impairment associated with ageing, less than that experienced in *dementia*, though of greater severity than the relatively gentle intellectual loss normally found in old age (*normal cognitive ageing (NCA)*). Some commentators include impairment which others would classify as early stages of dementia.

mild learning difficulty (MLD) Nebulous term for a condition whose possessors usually have an *IQ* level commensurate with *mild mental retardation*, who are unlikely to thrive by conventional academic standards, but at the same time are not completely ineducable.

mild mental retardation See *mental retardation.*

Mill Hill Vocabulary (MHV) Test A measure of vocabulary, the test requires subjects to provide definitions of words whose obscurity increases as the test progresses (there is no time limit). Commonly used *crystallized intelligence* measure. Available in 2 formats: Junior (for children over 6 years and adults) and Senior (for children over 14 years and adults; especially individuals and groups likely to be of above-average ability).

Miller Assessment for Preschoolers (MAP) Test battery for children aged 2–6 years. Primarily intended to identify disability.

mimetic play *Play* consisting of a repetitious act, often with a principal purpose of practising a skill.

mind, theory of The understanding that other people have thoughts and feelings independent of one's own.

mind, theory of (autism) Theory that the principal deficit of *autistic* patients is a lack of a concept of mind. This in turn leads to a failure to perceive the independence of other people's minds and thoughts. See *autism.*

Mini Mental State Examination (MMS) Quickly administered test of intellectual abilities of older subjects (particularly those suspected of being in the early stages of *dementia*). Measures basic competence at everyday skills, level of wakefulness, ability to follow and remember simple instructions, perform elementary calculations, etc.

minimal brain dysfunction (MBD) (1) *attention deficit disorder.* (2) Some commentators define the condition as a disorder of learning and/or behaviour without *mental retardation*. Disorders of movement or *hyperactivity* may be present.

miscue Term used in reading research (particularly of beginning readers) to denote a misreading of a word. Intentionally, the term has a less derogatory meaning than 'mistake', because often the miscue maintains the text's meaning and may also physically resemble the word which should have been read. See *insertion miscue, non-response error/miscue* and *substitution miscue*.

miscue analysis Any experimental or diagnostic procedure which assesses the number and, more particularly, the nature of *miscues* in the subject's reading.

mismatch Learning the wrong word for an event or item. Sometimes occurs in infants' language acquisition.

ML *manipulative latency*.

MLD *mild learning difficulty*.

MLP *maximum life potential*.

MLT *midlife transition*.

MLU *mean length of utterance*.

MMS *Mini Mental State Examination*.

mneme Term devised by Vygotsky to denote methods of remembering with a hypothesized physical/genetic basis.

modelling Basing one's actions on those of others (i.e. modelling oneself on others). Several theories use modelling as a central method of learning (e.g. *Bandura's theory of social learning*).

moderate mental retardation See *mental retardation*.

modular development Development of separate skills which, once perfected, are combined to form more complex activities.

molar equivalence (ME) A *molar skill* is one which can be decomposed into a number of sub-skills *(molecular decomposition (MD))*. E.g. playing croquet is a molar skill, since it can be decomposed into sub-skills (e.g. planning of moves; aiming of mallet; strategic knowledge based on past experience, etc.). If a molar skill is performed equally well by groups of widely differing ages, then 'molar equivalence' is said to have occurred. If molar equivalence occurs even though some of the sub-skills can be shown to be worse in one of the age groups (e.g. older croquet players perhaps are less good at aiming the mallet) then a *ME-MD strategy* (or *compensation*) is said to have occurred (e.g. because the older players perhaps have a better strategic skill which compensates for other shortcomings).

molar skill See *molar equivalence*.

molecular decomposition (MD) See *molar equivalence*.

Mongolism Outmoded and racist term for *Down's Syndrome* (Down felt that European Down's Syndrome patients were 'arrested' at a 'Mongolic' stage of development because of a supposed physical resemblance).

monotropy Argument that a child has a tendency to attach him/herself to one person (usually the mother). Central tenet of *Bowlby's theory of attachment*.

monozygotic (MZ) From one egg. See *monozygotic twins*.

monozygotic (MZ) twins Twins formed from the same egg splitting soon after fertilization – i.e. identical twins. Compare with *dizygotic twins*.

Montessori educational method Based on *Montessori's theory of child development*. Children enter a Montessori school at

2 years 6 months upwards, and classes contain children from this age up to 6 years (i.e. there are no age divisions). Children are not rigidly supervised, and are left as free as possible to work with educational toys and apparatus of their choice (it is argued that they will choose items appropriate to their *sensitive period*). The teacher will only intervene if s/he feels that the moment is propitious gently to 'nudge' the child's mind towards discovering something new. Although teachers treat intellectual activities as passively as possible, social misbehaviour and/or damage to property is reprimanded. The Montessori method, in a diluted form, has influenced modern kindergarten and primary school teaching, so that children are usually no longer taught set tasks in regimented rows of seating.

Montessori's theory of child development Maria Montessori (1870–1952). Educationalist, originally a medical doctor. Central tenet of her theory is the concept of *sensitive periods*. These are akin to the *critical period*, and are time periods in a child's development when s/he is maximally responsive to learning about a particular aspect of him/herself and/or the environment (these range from a sensitive period for learning to use the hands to a sensitive period for language). The theory echoes *Rousseau's theory of human development* and *Piaget's*, and is the guiding philosophy of the *Montessori educational method*.

Mooney Problem Check List Test for subjects aged 12 years and over; there are different forms for different age groups. Measures problems with social life, relationship formation, etc.

moral absolutism The belief that a moral code is absolute and unalterable. See *Piaget's theory of moral development*.

moral development The development of a moral sense. See *Piaget's theory of moral development* and *Kohlberg's theory of moral development*.

moral precept An ideal code of morally correct behaviour.

moral realism See *Piaget's theory of moral development*.

morality of cooperation *Autonomy* stage in *Piaget's theory of moral development*.

morality of reciprocity *morality of cooperation*.

moratorium Taking time out from normal activity to investigate a particular situation with view to change. Used e.g. of adolescents contemplating future career, lifestyle, etc.

Moro reflex Type of *primitive reflex*. A loud noise or a sudden change in the position of the baby's head causes him/her to throw the arms outwards, arch the back, and bring the arms towards each other. The reflex disappears in humans at 6–7 months.

moron See *mental retardation*.

morpheme The smallest unit of a word whose addition or removal alters the word's meaning (e.g. 'illegible' contains two morphemes – 'il' and 'legible').

morphemic awareness A conscious awareness of the properties and structures of words. An aspect of *linguistic awareness*.

morphology Strictly speaking, the science of form. Also, an awareness of word meanings and word structure.

motherese Term for the language used by a parent in talking to pre-talking infants. Characterized by its simple structure, high pitched delivery, repetition, and exaggerated intonation.

motherese hypothesis Theory that *motherese* may determine the way in which an infant acquires language.

motion parallax The visual phenomenon whereby when one moves one's gaze, objects nearer to one appear to move further and more rapidly than those further away.

motor development Development of physical skills.

motor recognition See *sensori-motor stage 3*.

motor rules See *Piaget's theory of moral development*.

motor skills Ability to move and control bodily movements. *Fine motor skills* describes control of relatively delicate movements (e.g. manual dexterity, holding and manipulating small objects, etc.).

Movement ABC *Movement Assessment Battery for Children.*

Movement Assessment Battery for Children (ABC) *Test battery* assessing movement problems in children.

MPT-R *Michigan Picture Test – Revised.*

MS (1) multiple sclerosis. (2) mainstream (i.e. conventional – usually refers to schooling).

MSCA *McCarthy Scales of Children's Abilities.*

MSQ *Mental Status Questionnaire.*

Mugford chart A method of assessing *readability*. The procedure is detailed and requires charts – see an appropriate textbook for further information. Considered most reliable for texts aimed at beginning readers–13-year-olds.

multi-infarct dementia (MID) A form of *dementia*, caused by the brain suffering a large number of *infarcts*. Patients typically suffer a stepwise rather than gradual pattern of decline. Patients often have a history of cardiovascular problems. In the later stages of the illness, there may be very extreme swings of mood.

Multilevel Academic Skills Inventory (MASI) Measure of scholastic performance.

Multilevel Academic Survey Tests (MAST) Measure of the scholastic/academic performance of pupils with specific educational needs.

multiple mothering System of child rearing where it is shared between mothers, relatives and friends.

multiplicative relation The phenomenon whereby, whilst adding a value 'p' to any other number always produces the same change (i.e. p), multiplying any number by p produces a different result for every new number used (e.g. p=2; p+3=5, p+4=6: increase of 2 in both cases; px3=6, px4=8: increases of 3 and 4 respectively).

myelinization (-isation) The process of acquiring an insulating cover (myelin) over nerve fibres. Refers in particular to the first two years of life in which many nerves lack this coating and only relatively slowly acquire it. Myelinization greatly improves the efficiency with which the nerves conduct signals, and hence the amount of voluntary control the infant/child has over his/her body.

MZ *monozygotic.*

MZ twins *monozygotic twins.*

MZA twins *Monozygotic twins* reared apart (see *split twins study*).

MZT twins *Monozygotic twins* reared together (see *split twins study*).

N

NABC *Normative Adaptive Behaviour Checklist.*

nAch *need for achievement.*

NAPI test *Neurobehavioural Assessment of the Preterm Infant.*

NART *National Adult Reading Test.*

NATs *New Assessment Tests.*

National Adult Reading Test (NART) A list of words, most with *irregular spellings*, which the subjects are required to read out loud (i.e. pronounce). The more words correctly pronounced, the higher the test score.

National Child Development Study (NCDS) *Longitudinal study* of *cohort* of individuals born in mainland Britain between 3 and 9 March 1958, and tested at birth, and at 7, 11, 16 and 23 years of age.

national competency tests Tests used to assess academic attainment across the country. Also known in the USA as *Standard Assessment Tests (SATs)* and *New Assessment Tests (NATs).*

nativism Belief that psychological abilities are acquired primarily through genetic inheritance. Opposite of *empiricism*. See *hereditarian versus environmentalist theories of individual differences.*

nativist theory *hereditarian theory of individual differences.*

nature versus nurture *hereditarian versus environmentalist theories of individual differences.*

naughty teddy experiment See *conservation of number.*

NBAS *Neonatal Behavioural Assessment Scale.*

NBAS–K *Neonatal Behavioural Assessment Scale with Kansas Supplements.*

NBW *normal birth weight.*

NCA *normal cognitive ageing.*

NCDS *National Child Development Study.*

NCME National Council on Measurement in Education.

NDE *near-death experience.*

Neale Analysis of Reading Ability Reading test for subjects aged 7–11 years. Consists of passages of text which the subject reads aloud. S/he is marked for number of mistakes, reading speed, and comprehension of the passage. Additional diagnostic tests can be used to assess knowledge of *grapheme-to-phoneme correspondence rules*, ability to distinguish different word sounds, etc.

near-death experience (NDE) Subjective experience reported by some people who have been very close to death (e.g. when the heart has temporarily stopped). Common experiences include the impression of floating above the body and looking down on the action below, and of a great peace and stillness. A small number report travelling down a long tunnel towards 'heavenly lights', and then being pulled back, which has predictably raised media interest in the phenomenon. The most likely explanation of the experience is a temporary hallucination caused by pain killers, shaped by cultural stereotypes/expectations.

need for achievement (nAch) Measure of motivation to become a 'success'. Not necessarily synonymous with competitiveness.

need hierarchy *Maslow's hierarchy of needs.*

negative reinforcement Learning to perform an action because it removes an aversive stimulus. By extension, learning not to do something if this avoids punishment (the 'action' being the suppression of the urge to do the act).

negative social behaviour B e h a v i o u r which is disliked or punished by society. Opposite of *positive social behaviour.*

neglected child A child suffering *child neglect.* Compare with *abused child.*

neglecting parent (1) Parent responsible for *child neglect.* (2) In a slightly milder form, a parent who is incapable or unwilling to give adequate attention to his/her children. Compare with *permissive parent.*

neoconstructivism *Constructionist theory* with a greater emphasis on the specific effects of the situation in which a skill/piece of information is learnt.

neologism Made-up word.

neonatal Pertaining to the baby at birth and shortly after — see *postpartum.*

neonatal abstinence syndrome Behaviour pattern of infants of mothers addicted to drugs, alchohol etc. Such infants tend to be restless and fractious.

Neonatal Behavioural Assessment Scale (NBAS) *Brazelton Scale.*

Neonatal Behavioural Assessment Scale with Kansas Supplements (NBAS–K) See *Brazelton Scale.*

neonate Typically, the term refers to a baby aged less than one month, or more generally, to a newborn baby. However, individual commentators have extended this period. Also note that commentators differ over whether the period is post- the actual birth or (in the case of *premature* babies) the time period after the date when the baby would have been born in a *full-term* pregnancy (i.e. by this reckoning, premature babies will be neonates for longer than full-term babies).

neoPiagetian Collective term for research which has built upon *Piaget's* theory of development. There is no one unifying feature of neoPiagetian theories, though many have attempted to expand his model to include considerations of social and cultural forces, since Piaget tended to concentrate upon the logical state of the mind divorced from the social world.

neural noise Concept that neural signals lose some of their fidelity because of interfering signals from neighbouring neurons, and a general failure of insulation of neurons. This is assumed to make mental processing less efficient. Neural noise is held by many commentators to be inversely related to intelligence (i.e. the brighter the person, the less the noise), and to worsen in old age (due to a general worsening in the 'quality' of nervous tissue).

neuritic plaques *senile plaques.*

Neurobehavioural Assessment of the Preterm Infant (NAPI) Test battery measuring the developmental maturity of *preterm* infants.

neurofibrillary tangles Clumps of dead central nervous system neurons which under a microscope look like knotted string. Caused by abnormal protein metabolism, and found in the brains of many older people (and particularly in *demented* patients).

neurogenesis The growth and development of neurons (nerve cells).

neuroplasticity *plasticity.*

New Adult Reading Test Name given to an early version of the *National Adult Reading Test*.

New Assessment Tests (NATs) See *national competency tests*.

New Sucher-Allred Reading Placement Inventory Reading test for 4–15-year-olds.

New York longitudinal study *Longitudinal study* by Thomas and Chess in the 1950s and 1960s, assessing the development of temperament. Identified three types: *easy child* (essentially regular in habits, amenable); *difficult child* (irregular in habits, not very amenable); and *slow-to-warm-up child* (somewhere in between the easy and difficult child).

NFER Reading Test EH A battery of three reading tests for subjects aged 11–16: EH1 measures *sentence completion*, EH2 comprehension, and EH3 reading rate.

NFER Reading Tests A, AD and BD Reading tests which require subjects to complete unfinished sentences. 'A' is designed for subjects aged 6–8 years, 'AD', 8–10 years and 'BD', 7–10 years.

NFER Reading Tests SR-A and SR-B Reading tests, designed for subjects aged 7–12. Both consist of *sentence completion* problems.

NH normal hearing.

NIA (American) National Institute on Aging.

NICHD (American) National Institute of Child Health and Human Development.

NINCDS–ADRDA criteria A set of criteria for evaluating the probability that a patient is suffering from *dementia of the Alzheimer type*. The initials refer to the 'National Institute of Neurological and Communicative Disorders and Stroke' and the 'Alzheimer's Disease and Related Disorders Association of America', the two bodies who jointly devised the scheme. It provides a diagnosis of 'probable', 'possible' or 'definite'.

no-trial learning See *Bandura's theory of social learning*.

nocturnal enuresis bed-wetting.

'noise' in nervous system *neural noise*.

nominal A noun or noun-like word.

nominal realism Term by *Piaget* for children's mistaken concept that words possess the attributes of the object they refer to (e.g. the child will argue that 'snake' is a longer word than 'caterpillar').

non-alphabetic literacy See *alphabetic literacy*.

non-marking mothers Mothers whose verbal interactions with their infants tend to be shorter but more intense than for *marking mothers*. See *passive mothers*.

non-normative life development Measure of the effects of major events unique to an individual's life. See *normative age-graded development* and *normative history-graded development*.

Non-Reading Intelligence Tests (NRIT) Set of three standardized tests (Level 1 for ages 6 years 4 months–8 years 3 months, Level 2, 7:4–9:3; Level 3, 8:4–10.11) presented orally, and assessing linguistic and cognitive abilities.

non-response (NR) error/miscue A reading *miscue* where the reader halts in his/her reading because s/he does not recognize a word. A *non-response stage* in beginning reading is sometimes found, where a high proportion of miscues are of this type.

non-response stage See *non-response error/miscue*.

non-standard English (NSE) Any form of English other than *Standard English*. Term usually reserved for very extreme variants.

nonnutritive nipple sucking technique An experimental method in infant perception research. Babies cannot tell experimenters what they perceive. However, it is reasonable to assume that if a baby wants one item more than another, s/he prefers it. If a baby has a preference, then s/he can tell the difference between the stimuli. The baby is given a rubber nipple attached to electrical sensors to suck – if it sucks slowly it elicits one stimulus, and if it sucks quickly it gets another. If the baby consistently sucks either quickly or slowly, then it is reasonable to assume that the baby prefers the stimulus s/he is producing, and can tell the difference between the stimuli. E.g. in infant voice recognition experiments, it has been shown that very young babies (i.e. under 3 days old) will suck to produce the sound of their mother's voice in preference to that of a female stranger's. However, note that if the infant does not show a preference, this does not necessarily mean that s/he cannot tell the difference between the stimuli – it could be that s/he can tell the difference, but simply has no preference. See *habituation technique* and *preference study*.

nonshared environmental factors See *shared environmental factors*.

nonword Any group of letters which does not form a real word. The term often refers to letter groups which sound like real words when read out. The term can refer to children's spellings, or to letter strings devised by the experimenter to test the child's reading skills.

norm The typical standard(s) of a group or *population*.

norm referenced test Test for which the average scores for the population are known (and hence which may serve as a guide to the quality of the subjects' performance). See *domain referenced test*.

normal birth weight (NBW) Weight of infant at birth which falls within normal bounds, and accordingly is unlikely to signal problems. Compare *very low birth weight*.

normal cognitive ageing (NCA) See *mild cognitive impairment*.

normal pressure hydrocephalus Caused by the failure of cerebrospinal fluid (the fluid which surrounds the spinal cord and brain) to drain away, leading to a destructive pressure on brain tissue. The complaint can lead to *demented* symptoms.

Normative Adaptive Behaviour Checklist (NABC) Measure of adaptive skills, both intellectual and housekeeping for subjects aged 0–21 years.

normative age-graded development The basic developmental pattern one would expect to find in any average individual (e.g. in terms of *biological ageing*, the onset of puberty, in term of *social ageing*, the effects of retirement on behaviour and attitudes, etc.). See *normative history-graded development* and *non-normative life development*.

normative history-graded development Measure of the effects of historical events which would be normally experienced by the whole of an *age cohort* (e.g. experience of food rationing would be normal for most English people in their sixties, but would be unusual for people in their twenties). See *normative* *age-graded development* and *non-normative life development.*

novelty preference technique *habituation technique.*

Nowicki-Strickland Locus of Control Scale Measure of concept of self-assurance, designed for children and young adults.

NR error/miscue *non-response error/miscue.*

NRIT *Non-Reading Intelligence Tests.*

NSE *non-standard English.*

nuclear conflict See *Erikson's theory of development.*

nuclear family 'Traditional' family of parents and children. See *extended family* and *joint family.*

nurture group Remedial teaching scheme for young children (usually from deprived backgrounds) who lack the necessary skills of social cooperation, concentration, etc., to learn effectively. Consists of training in these skills.

O

Oakland Growth Study *Longitudinal study* begun in the 1930s on a sample of babies born in Oakland, U.S.A., and followed through to adulthood.

object-centred contact Early social interaction in infants, who come into contact because of a mutual interest in the same object (e.g. a toy).

object concept The knowledge that an object continues to exist even though it has disappeared from view. This is an apparently elementary piece of knowledge, but according to *Piaget's* theory of *sensori-motor development*, a baby spends the first 18 months learning this. In the archetypal experiment, Piaget allowed a baby to gaze at an attractive object (e.g. a toy). The object is then covered over with a cloth. Very young babies lose interest – it is as if the toy has ceased to exist, and Piaget inferred that the baby believes in the existence of an object only if it can be seen (literally, 'out of sight, out of mind'). At later stages of development, the baby will search for the object under the cover, though s/he can easily be fooled – e.g. if the baby has found the object at location A for several trials, and then the object is put under a cloth at B, the baby is still likely to search at A (the *A not B error*, occurring in *sensori-motor stage 4*). Efficient searching does not commence until circa 18 months. See *sensori-motor development*, and *sensori-motor stages 2* to *6* for a fuller explanation. Piaget's theory has been heavily criticized, not least because of his research methodology. For example, if a young

baby genuinely has an attitude of 'out of sight out of mind', then why will s/he not search for an object when a cloth is put over it, but will search when e.g. the object is made invisible by the room lighting being switched off? The debate is still vigorous and far from settled. The term 'object concept' is, pedantically speaking, more 'correct' than *object permanence*, but in reality, the two are interchangeable. See *drawbridge experiments*.

object constancy Ability to recognize an object as the same even though it may change its visual appearance (e.g. getting smaller by being further away, changing shape when seen from a different angle, etc).

object counting Counting items to determine their *cardinal number*. See *abstract counting*.

Object Memory Evaluation (OME) Measure of memory for objects. The subject is presented with a set of everyday objects, and is asked to recall them at short (30 or 60 second) and long (5 minute) intervals. Five learning trials are given, and measures are taken of which items are recalled on which trial and which are not.

object permanence See *object concept*.

objective group When used in connection with *Piagetian* theory, particularly of *sensori-motor development* – see *group*.

objective self See *subjective self*.

oblique décalage *Piagetian* term for the refinement of a skill which prepares the child to move from one stage of development to the next. Compare with *horizontal décalage* and particularly with *vertical décalage*.

observational learning Learning by observing and copying others. See *Bandura's theory of social learning*.

observed score *raw score*.

observer memory The phenomenon whereby one's distant *autobiographical memories* are usually recalled as if one were a bystander.

observer rotation task Measure of *position constancy* in infants/young children. Typically, the subject is seated in a room, is shown how to find a target item, and is then seated (usually) 180° round from the first location, and is asked to find the target. The principal interest is usually whether the subject adjusts to the shift in position. If s/he has done, then s/he should perform actions opposite to the ones performed before the shift. E.g. if the subject learns that from among a range of boxes in front of him/her, a toy is hidden in the box furthest away, when s/he is moved to the opposite side of the display, s/he should search in the nearest box. If the child repeats the action which previously was rewarded (e.g. in the example, choosing the furthest box after the shift in position), then s/he is said to be *egocentric*. See *display rotation task*.

Observing Pupils and Teachers in Classrooms (OPTIC) An observation schedule for assessing the positivity and/or negativity of teachers' responses to pupils (Section A), and the degree to which pupils are attending to the lesson's set tasks (Section B).

obsolescence effect Theory that some of the 'deterioration' in old age may be because older people's mental strategies are no longer in tune with the modern world (i.e. are obsolescent), rather than that they have decayed per se. I.e., ageing changes may be due to qualitative changes in mental strategies.

occluded Hidden from view.

odd man out test See *Assessing Reading Difficulties*.

Oedipus complex See *Freud's theory of development*.

OKN *optokinetic nystagmus*.

old age dependency ratio The number of people aged 60 and over divided by the number aged 20–64 in a given population. This gives an indication of how many people are working and hence helping to support pensions and other welfare provisions for older people.

old elderly Most commonly defined as those individuals aged over 75 years (although commentators differ over this figure). See also *young elderly*.

OME *Object Memory Evaluation*.

ondansetron Drug whose effects include the enhanced release of acetyl choline (a key neurotransmitter in the brain – see *cholinergic hypothesis*). Has been cited as a possible treatment for patients suffering from *dementia*. See *ganglioside* and *tacrine*.

onlooker play Watching others play.

ontogenesis Can be synonym for *ontogeny*, but can also refer to growth of a particular aspect or part of the individual.

ontogeny The growth of the individual. See *ontogenesis*, *phylogeny* and *recapitulation theory*.

OPC *orthography-to-phonology conversion*.

open classroom Teaching method where the pupils are relatively free to pursue activities, with minimal formal guidance. Contrast with *traditional classroom*.

open education General term for the sort of education which takes place in an *open classroom*. See *Montessori educational method.*

open family Family fairly open to 'outsiders' and outside assistance. Opposite of *closed family.*

open word See *pivot word.*

operant conditioning Broadly, the training of a subject to perform a particular act by rewarding him/her for doing it or to stop an act by punishing him/her. Central research tool of *behaviourism.*

operation (1) In *Piagetian* theory, a mental action which can only exist as part of a *group* or *grouping* of related mental actions. See *infralogical operation* and *intellectual operation.* (2) More loosely, a mental processing of ideas which can be carried out in reverse.

operation learning Learning directed at the surface structure of the problem/situation. This contrasts with *comprehension learning*, which concentrates on the deeper underlying structure.

operational thought *operative thought.*

operations to the second power *formal operations.*

operative thought In *Piagetian* theory, the manipulation of facts stored in *figurative thought*. The manipulative processes used are called *schemes*. Operative thought generally describes the more sophisticated thought processes of the *concrete operations subperiod* and beyond. See *scheme.*

OPTIC *Observing Pupils and Teachers in Classrooms.*

optimal ageing *successful ageing.*

optimal performance level See *developmental range.*

optokinetic nystagmus (OKN) The phenomenon whereby in watching a moving display, the eye moves forward with the flow of the movement, and then makes sudden involuntary backwards movements across the display.

optokinetic nystagmus (OKN) technique Method of assessing *visual acuity* in infants. Infants watch a moving pattern of lines, which get progressively narrower until they blur into a uniform grey (and hence the display appears to stop moving). At this point, the infants' eyes cease to display *optokinetic nystagmus*, and thus a measure can be made of the smallest pattern the infant can accurately identify. See *preference study.*

oral reading Reading aloud (e.g. pupil reading to the teacher, experimenter, etc.).

oral stage See *Freud's theory of development.*

ordinal number The concept that numbers have a fixed order of size (e.g. two is always bigger than one but smaller than three). See *cardinal number.*

organismic-structural approach View of psychological development in terms of biological development, with stress upon genetically-inherited factors. This is in contrast to the *mechanistic-functional approach*, which treats psychological development in terms of the functioning of a machine, which can only change by having pieces added to it (i.e. it develops through environmental input, rather than genetically-controlled change).

organization (-isation) In *Piagetian* theory, 'the accord of thought with itself' – the structure of mental processes and their relationship to each other. These are created from *adaptations*, with which they are inexorably linked.

organized play See *play.*

orientation and signals directed towards one (or more) discriminated figure(s) Phase 2 of *Bowlby's theory of attachment.*

orientation and signals without discrimination of figure Phase 1 of *Bowlby's theory of attachment.*

Orleans-Hanna test Test of potential ability at algebra – the test measures ability to process symbolic representations.

orthogenetic principle The principle which states that development advances from the general to the specific (e.g. there is initially a general ability which progresses to a set of more specialized skills).

orthographic reading *visual reading.*

orthography Writing system (e.g. European alphabet, Chinese script, etc.). The term is loosely used by many commentators to describe any aspect of print or, more loosely, spelling.

orthography-to-phonology (OPC) conversion More sophisticated version of *grapheme–phoneme conversion.* Although some words are converted into sound at the graphemic level, most are processed in larger units, such as 'ing', 'ave', etc.

ossification Hardening of the bones. Not usually complete until puberty.

other-centred relationship Any familial relationship with a child described from the adult's viewpoint (e.g. daughter, grandchild, etc.). See *child-centred relationship.*

other-initiated repair Linguistic term for the listener correcting or initiating a correction made by the speaker (e.g. by asking 'pardon?'). Compare with *self-initiated repair.*

overconstancy Overestimating the area in the 'background' of a visual perception. E.g., if asked to draw a horizontal line across a picture so that equal areas are represented below the line (i.e. the foreground) and above the line (i.e. the background), subjects tend to draw the line too high up (making the area represented by the background too small). Perhaps surprisingly, the error is made more often by older children and adults than by younger children.

overcontrolled behaviour Behavioural problem in children, in which apprehension about an event, person, etc., controls their lives to the point of creating anxiety and/or depression.

overextension Using a word to refer to too wide a range of items and concepts. Typically found in infants learning to speak (e.g. the archetypal example is calling all men 'daddy'). Compare with *underextension.*

overgeneralization (-isation) *overregularization.*

overlapping longitudinal study An attempt to overcome the pitfalls of the *cross-sectional research* and *longitudinal research* methods. Different age groups of subjects are tested and compared, and then retested some time (usually years) later. At each testing, the different age groups can be compared, as in a cross-sectional study (e.g. a group of 40-year-old subjects can be compared with a group of 60-year-old subjects). Also, however, the same *age cohort's* scores can be compared across test periods (e.g. the scores of a group of subjects who were 40 on the first test session and 60 on the next can be compared). This enables researchers to keep a check on possible *cohort effects.* E.g. suppose that on retesting, the 40-year-old subjects have scores

20% higher than the 60-year-old sub-jects. This might seem to indicate an age decline. However, suppose it is found that the scores of the 60-year-old group, when they were 40, were only 5% higher. This indicates that a principal cause of the difference is not ageing per se, but rather that the two age groups have been reared differently.

overregularization (-isation) Error by children learning to speak who make 'exception words' obey a more common grammatical rule (e.g. 'goed' instead of 'went').

overt curriculum That which is officially taught in the school curriculum. See *covert curriculum*.

P

paediatric psychology The study of psychological aspects of childhood health care.

paediatrics The medical study and treatment of childhood illnesses.

paedography Any writing system intended to aid in the teaching of reading (e.g. *initial teaching alphabet*).

paired associate learning Any learning task in which the subject is required to recognize which item has previously been encountered in the company of another item. In a typical design, a subject is presented with items A and B simultaneously. Subsequently, s/he is shown only item A, and is asked to select B from a range of choices. Often the alternatives to B will resemble B in some manner, thereby making the choice harder.

paired reading (1) Reading in which a beginning reader reads aloud, under the supervision of a teacher or other experienced reader. (2) A more specific method, whereby the beginning reader and teacher read in unison. The beginner then reads for him/herself until s/he reaches a word s/he cannot read, whereupon the teacher begins to read in unison again until the beginner requests otherwise. The scheme is claimed to reduce stress and the feeling of being tested.

parallel play *Play* in which two or more children play in the same space, often sharing the same toys, but without much or any coordination of their activities. Held by *Piaget* to indicate a failure to integrate socially through failure to *accommodate* the other children, or to *decentre*. Middle stage between *solitary play* and *cooperative play*.

Parallel Spelling Tests (PST) Spelling test for children aged 6–13 years. The test uses blocks of sentences drawn from a large set, and by using different combinations, a wide variety of test blocks can be created.

parent aspiration Level of academic attainment that parents expect their child to achieve.

parent orientation The degree to which a child agrees with and follows the wishes and edicts of his/her parents. In mid-adolescence, there is usually a switch to a greater emphasis on *peer orientation.*

parental style Any measure of how parents elect to bring up their children. There are numerous methods of doing this, but most include assessments of the degree of autonomy permitted to the children and the amount of affection shown by the parents.

Parkinsonian dementia Any *dementia* in which symptoms of *Parkinsonism* are present.

Parkinsonism A set of symptoms, including a shuffling gait and trembling hands, typically found in *Parkinson's Disease* (hence its name), but also in other illnesses (e.g. *dementia of the Alzheimer type*).

Parkinson's Disease (PD) Illness caused by a lack of dopamine (a chemical transmitter used in some sections of the brain) whose characteristic symptoms have the group description of *Parkinsonism*.

partial reinforcement Not rewarding/punishing behaviour on every occasion it occurs.

partially occluded Partly hidden from view.

passive–dependent personality Personality type found in some older people – possessors rely on others to help them (*succourant seeking*) or withdraw from human interaction as much as possible (*apathetic*).

passive euthanasia Allowing someone to die by not administering life-saving or life-prolonging treatment.

passive mothers Mothers who tend not to indulge in verbal interaction with their infant while the infant is engaged in an activity. See *marking mothers* and *non-marking mothers*.

passive vocabulary Total set of words an individual can understand. Almost always larger than his/her *active vocabulary*.

pathological fixation Part of the *Strauss Syndrome*, the phenomenon whereby some (particularly brain-damaged) children will persevere at a (usually trivial) task for an abnormally long time.

patient cohort A group of people with not only illness in common, but also a set of attitudes (e.g. feeling 'unhealthy'). Compare with *cohort* and *disease cohort*.

patterners Children who, when playing, use toys to form patterns. Compare with *dramatists*.

PB words *phonetically balanced words.*

PBCs *pregnancy and birth complications.*

PBK words *phonetically balanced kindergarten words.*

PBKs *phonetically balanced kindergarten words.*

PBs *phonetically balanced words.*

PCC *Portage Classroom Curriculum.*

PD *Parkinson's Disease.*

Peabody Individual Achievement Test (PIAT) *Achievement test* principally assessing mathematics, reading and spelling skills.

Peabody Picture Vocabulary Scale See *British Picture Vocabulary Scale.*

peek-a-boo Game played with infants/very young children, in which the adult (usually the mother) hides her face from the infant, and then re-appears, saying 'peek-a-boo' or something similar. Inexplicably, to an adult layperson, the infant loves this. The game is sometimes integrated into psychological experiments (e.g. as a reward). Called *guck-guck da-da* in German.

peer orientation The degree to which a child agrees with and follows the wishes and edicts of his/her *peers*. In mid-adolescence, usually becomes a greater influence than *parent orientation*.

peers Members of one's own *cohort* (usually *age cohort*).

pendulum problem Test by *Piaget* to assess *formal operations* in older children and teenagers. The subjects are given a pendulum, which can be varied in length and weight, and are asked to discover what determines the speed of its swing. A subject possessing formal operations would typically systematically vary the length and weight to see what happened under different conditions. A subject in the *concrete operational sub-period* would be more haphazard in his/her approach.

penis envy See *Freud's theory of development.*

Perceived Competence Scale for Children
Measure of children's assessment of their own abilities at intellectual, social and physical skills, plus a measure of general self-esteem.

perceptive deafness Deafness due to damage to connecting nervous tissue of the inner ear. A cause of deafness in infants whose mothers contracted *rubella* in the early stages of pregnancy.

perceptual pregnance The degree to which a child will be prone to *perceptual seduction*.

perceptual realism Term describing a drawing or painting which represents what can be seen from one fixed viewpoint (i.e. a conventional picture). The method of pictorial representation which children develop after an earlier phase of *intellectual realism*.

perceptual seduction In a *conservation* task, the phenomenon whereby a *preoperational* child may be 'seduced' by a purely visual change in an item into (erroneously) presuming that other features of the item have also changed. See *perceptual pregnance*.

Performance scales (WAIS) See *Wechsler Adult Intelligence Scale*.

performance tests (1) Measures of (usually complex) motor skills (often with a vocational relevance). (2) A non-verbal test (usually of non-verbal intelligence). (3) Measure of ability at a practical skill.

perinatal Around the time of birth.

perinatal stress Stress surrounding the birth.

permissive-demanding dimension
Term devised by Baumrind to denote the degree to which parents may be regarded as *permissive parents*.

permissive parents Parents who exert relatively little control over their chil-

dren. Compare with *authoritarian parents, authoritative parents* and *neglecting parents*.

perseverations When referring to linguistic errors in *demented* subjects – the inappropriate and immediate repetition of a phrase.

person-orientated language See *restricted code*.

person permanence Akin to *object concept*, except that it refers specifically to perceptual knowledge of people, rather than objects.

personal distress *empathic distress*.

perspective-taking Adopting the viewpoint and/or emotions of another person or persons.

phallic stage See *Freud's theory of development*.

phenomenalism In the *sensori-motor period*, the infant's erroneous belief that because two events occur close together in time, that there must be a causal link between them.

phenotype The physical appearance of an organism. See *genotype*.

phenylketonuria (PKU) *Innate* metabolic disorder, resulting in failure to process phenylalanine, a chemical found in many foodstuffs; unless the affected person is given a diet which omits this substance, *mental retardation* results.

PHI *profound hearing impairment*.

Phoenecian readers and spellers
People who rely heavily on *phonic mediation* in reading and spelling. Applies to average readers, but the symptoms in extremis resemble those of *surface dyslexia*. Compare with *Chinese readers and spellers*.

phonation stage Term given by some commentators to the vocalizations present in the first two months of life. See *speech development stages*.

phoneme The smallest unit of speech whose substitution or removal from a word causes a change in the word's sound. More loosely, the basic sounds which make up words (and even more loosely, the verbal equivalent of letters).

phoneme constancy The ability to perceive the identity of a *phoneme* across a wide variety of pronunciation styles.

phoneme deletion task C o m m o n method of testing *phonemic awareness* – subject is asked to calculate what a word would sound like if a *phoneme* was removed from it (e.g. 'what would "cat" sound like if the "c" was removed?'). See also *phonemic segmentation*.

phonemic awareness The conscious realization that words are composed of phonemes, and that all words can be constructed from a limited set of phonemes. Compare with *syllabic awareness*.

phonemic buffer The temporary memory store for *phonemes* in a word retrieved from memory, prior to its pronunciation. Compare with *graphemic buffer*.

phonemic segmentation (1) A popular method of assessing *phonemic awareness* – the subject is required to break down a word into its constituent *phonemes*. See also *phoneme deletion task*. (2) The ability to perform the task described in (1). See also *syllabic segmentation*.

phonetically balanced kindergarten (PBK) words Word lists containing phonemes in proportion to their incidence in young children's speech.

phonetically balanced (PB) words Word lists containing phonemes in proportion to their incidence in everyday speech.

phonic mediation Pronouncing (usually new or nonsense) words by calculating the sound of each letter and stringing the sounds together to form a coherent pronunciation (akin to children learning to read). Compare with *reading by analogy*.

phonics (reading teaching) Method of reading teaching which emphasizes the use of *phonic mediation*. See also *whole word (reading teaching)*.

phonological Pertaining to *phonemes*.

phonological confusability Mistaking a letter or word for another because they sound similar (e.g. 'B' and 'D').

phonological dyslexia An *acquired dyslexia* – the patient is incapable of reading nonsense words, indicating a failure to translate letters into their oral representations.

phonological lag hypothesis See *structural lag (reading)*.

phonological loop See *working memory*.

phonology Strictly speaking, the study of phonetics. Also, an awareness of phonological structure.

phrenoblysis theory Theory that stages of childhood development are linked to periods of physical brain development.

phylogenesis *phylogeny*.

phylogeny The growth and development (in evolutionary terms) of the species. See *ontogeny* and *recapitulation theory*.

physical experience Deceptively obvious term by *Piaget* for experiencing (and hence learning about) the physical properties of an object. However, note that he was only talking of the properties inherent in the object. Any discovery which extrapolates beyond the immediate properties to a more abstract level of knowledge is an example of *logico-mathematical experience*. E.g., to use Piaget's examples, learning that bigger objects are usually heavier is a physical experience. However, learning that counting a row of pebbles from left to right yields the same answer as does counting from right to left is logico-mathematical experience. The latter discovery is not reliant on the specific physical properties of the objects being studied (e.g. the same effect could be obtained by counting a row of sleeping sheep), whilst the former is.

physiological age *Biological age* expressed through the state of the body's physiological processes (e.g. metabolic rate). See *anatomical age*.

Piaget Jean Piaget (1896–1980). Swiss born; he spent his early career in France before settling in Geneva (see *Genevan School*). It is justifiable to claim that he was the single most important developmental psychologist. Certainly he was paramount in creating developmental psychology as a specialism with its own identity. This is ironic, because he trained as a zoologist, and entered psychology (originally in Binet's Paris laboratory) as a means of pursuing his aim of unifying biology and logic. Piaget developed a complex theory of human development, of which the best known facet is his theory of cognitive development, consisting of *sensori-motor development* (concerning infants), the *concrete operational period* (concerning post-infancy–circa 11 years) and the *formal operations period* (11 years and over). Several tenets underpin Piaget's theories, most derived from his zoological background: *accommodation, assimilation* (which, when in balance, constitute *adaptation*), *decentration, equilibrium, organization* and *structure d'ensemble*; and underlying all this was his belief in *genetic epistemology*. Piaget argued that developmental change is gradual (although broad stages of development –

which are fixed in order and are never 'skipped' – can be seen within this). Although much of his work – especially his experimental methods – has been criticized, Piaget's position of eminence is firmly secured, not least because of the thoroughness and accuracy of his observations of children in naturalistic settings (many of his studies were of his own three children – Lucienne, Jacqueline, and Laurent). It is important to note that Piaget's theories are exceedingly complex (and often well nigh unreadable, especially in some of the less adroit translations). The popular presentations of Piaget's work are very simplified – e.g. consider the entries on *grouping* to see what is usually glossed over. Piaget's experiments, particularly those concerned with the concrete operational period, have been criticized for making the tasks unnecessarily difficult for the child subjects. Certainly, when given easier-to-comprehend instructions, children can successfully perform tasks at a younger age than did the children in Piaget's own studies. However, Piaget argued that it is not simply when the child can perform a task which matters, but when s/he can explain the reason for his/her actions (i.e. when the child can provide unequivocal evidence that s/he understands what s/he is doing). Performing an action without providing evidence of understanding its purpose is an example of *functional thought* (an uninterpreted recollection of facts), which Piaget felt was inferior to *operative thought* (knowing how and why to do something). Piaget supported many of his experimental findings with transcripts of discussions with children expressing their thoughts about the task in question, a procedure which few of

Piaget's critics have emulated. See *neoPiagetian*.

Piagetian Adjective derived from *Piaget*.

Piagetian experiment/task Any task which was invented by *Piaget* or is a variant on one of his basic themes.

Piaget's 'kidnapping' Anecdote of *Piaget's* which demonstrates the fallibility of *autobiographical memory*. Piaget had a distinct memory of a kidnap attempt on himself when he was aged 2 years, which his nurse successfully repulsed. As an adolescent, Piaget discovered that the nurse had made up the whole episode, and accordingly, his memory was an elaboration of her story, rather than of a real event.

Piaget's theory of moral development
The theory is closely allied to *Piaget's* theory of cognitive development (see *sensori-motor development* and *concrete operational period*). Four major themes are observable, concerning the development of concepts of rules, right and wrong, lying, and justice. Underlying these is the basic concept of the transfer from *heteronomy* (blind obedience to an authority figure) to *autonomy* (developing a moral code of one's own). Rules: Piaget observed children at play (the most often cited example is marbles), and identified several stages. *Motor rules* (less than 2 years) – the child plays without any obvious rules beyond those imposed by physical limitations. *Egocentric rules* (2–6 years) – the child imitates the play of older children, but lacks an understanding of the social interaction of true game playing (see *parallel play*). *Cooperation rules* (7–10 years) – the child obeys the rules, which are viewed as unchangeable and necessary. Play now involves genuine social interaction. *Codification rules* (10 years

and over) – the child recognizes that rules can be altered by mutual consent of the players to suit particular situations. In tandem with this, the developing child changes his/her concept of the purpose of rules. In the earliest stage (less than 2 years) the child is only aware that play is not a compulsory activity. Subsequently (2–8 years) s/he regards rules as sacred (sometimes literally God-given) and inviolate, before (at 8 years and over) recognizing that rules can be adapted to suit the mutual consent of the players. Right and wrong: Piaget argued that children begin in a state of *moral realism* – a belief that the letter rather than the spirit of the law is paramount, and that a person's behaviour must be judged by its consequences rather than its intentions. Piaget supported this by citing experiments in which subjects were given stories in which e.g. a child doing a good deed accidentally broke many things, while a naughty child doing something bad only broke a small item. Children under 7 years usually argued that the former child was naughtier, because the effects of his/her actions were worse. Children over 7 years tended to argue the opposite. Lying: there are several stages in the development of the concept of 'a lie'. (i) Less than 5 years – a 'naughty' word; (ii) 5–7 years – anything untrue (including accidental errors); (iii) 8–10 years – anything untrue (excluding accidental errors); (iv) 10 years and over – a deliberate intent to deceive. Moral realism again plays a role. Children possessing the trait tend to judge a lie by its effects. Hence, they find an act where unintentional misinformation is given and major difficulties arise to be more reprehensible than a deliberate lie whose consequences are relatively minor. Moral realism maintains a stronger hold in the development of the concept of lying than in the concept of right and wrong, and it is not until 10 years and over that it is fully shaken off. Justice: there are three main stages in the development of the concept of this idea. (i) Less than 8 years – a just decision or command is one given by an authority figure. (ii) 8–12 years – reward/punishment should be divided equally between all deserving it; no individual should have more nor less than his/her fair share. (iii) 12 years and over – the child assesses each case on its own terms. Piaget measured this by observing children's judgments on a series of stories in which a child receives extra work from an authority figure, because another child has not done his/her allotted share. Like many of his other theories, Piaget's moral development work has had its critics. However, it has also been very influential, not least in providing an impetus to *Kohlberg's theory of moral development*.

Piaget's theory of play See *Piaget's theory of moral development* and *play*.

PIAT *Peabody Individual Achievement Test.*

Pick's bodies Damaged neurons, found in the brains of *Pick's Disease* patients, which have a characteristic swollen appearance under a microscope.

Pick's Disease Named after its discoverer, a form of *dementia* characterized by a progressive deterioration of brain tissue commencing in the 'front' of the brain (more accurately, the frontal lobes) and progressing backwards. Psychologically, there are often disturbances in personality before any intellectual changes manifest themselves (unlike other dementias, memory loss is usually one of the last symptoms to appear).

Piers-Harris Children's Self-Concept Scale Measure of children's self-esteem.

PIP Developmental Charts *Behavioural checklist* assessing the key developmental 'milestone' of pre-school children.

PIPS *Preschool Interpersonal Problem Solving Test.*

pivot grammar See *pivot word*.

pivot word Complex concept used by some researchers of language development to describe a small set of words which are used in nearly all early two word utterances (e.g. 'gone', 'run', etc.) to describe the action performed on or by the second word in the phrase, called the *open word* (e.g. open word = 'dog'; pivot word = 'run'; phrase = 'dog run'). The rules governing the joining of pivot and open words form *pivot grammar*.

PKU See *phenylketonuria*.

PL technique *preferential looking technique.*

plasticity Refers to the ease with which the nervous system (particularly the brain) can adapt to change. This can be divided into several related concepts: (i) *Cortical thickening*. (ii) The ease with which new synapses and neural interconnections can be formed and, by extension, (iii) the ease with which new information and concepts can be grasped. (iv) The phenomenon whereby if an area of the brain is 'unused', surrounding areas will take it over. For example, if an animal is born blind in one eye (or more sinisterly, the eyelid is sutured by experimenters), then the visual cortex representing that eye will be 'taken over' by other areas of the brain. If the animal now has sight restored in that eye, then it is effectively blind in it, because the area of the brain capable of interpreting what it sees has been taken over. The time period in which the area must receive information or else be 'taken over' is called the *critical period* (NB – the term has other meanings). Plasticity is sometimes referred to by the slang term *soft wired*.

play A diversionary and/or pleasurable exercise with no intrinsic aim of improving one's material well-being. Play which is structured with rules (e.g. as in some games) is called **organized play**. *Piaget* defined three types of play in children: (i) **mastery play** (where the child is 'mastering' a concept – e.g. language games, making models, etc.); (ii) **play with rules (organized play)**; (iii) **make-believe play** (e.g. 'let's pretend'-type games). See *cooperative play, cathartic play, creative play, deep play, diversive play, dramatists, exploratory play, functional play, mimetic play, parallel play, patterners, pretend play, reality play, sensori-motor play, serious play, solitary play* and *symbolic play*.

play with rules See *play*.

pleasure principle See *Freud's theory of development*.

pleitrophy Dual function of some genes, which cause development of some factors in youth, and their decline in old age (e.g. reproductive organs in women).

PMA Test *Primary Mental Abilities (PMA) Test.*

PMAs *primary mental abilities.*

point size The standard measure of *print size*. It is defined as the distance between the baselines (the lines on which the letters 'sit') of two lines of type when the type is set out for single spaced printing. Measurement is in units called points (1 point = 1/72 inches). People with impaired eyesight (e.g. many older people) may require a point size of 20 to be able to read comfortably. Beginning readers usually perform optimally with type in the 14–18 point range. By comparison, normal adult readers read most efficiently with 11–12 point type (although type as small as 8 point can be read for reasonably long periods).

point synchrony See *synchrony*.

policeman experiment Study by Hughes which attempted to make the problem presented in the *three mountains experiment* easier to understand, whilst requiring subjects to exercise the same level of logical thought. The child is shown a set of toy walls arranged in the shape of a cross. A policeman doll is placed at the end of one arm of the cross, and the child is asked to hide a doll behind one of the walls so that it could not be 'seen' by the policeman (e.g. if the policeman is standing at the end of the 'north' wall, then either the SE or the SW segment is the correct choice). A subsequent test places two policemen at the end of adjacent arms, and the child is asked to hide the doll so neither policeman could see it (e.g. if the policemen are at the end of the N and W walls, then the correct choice is the SE segment). Approximately 90% of children aged 3 years 6 months upwards could perform the tests correctly, which indicates that they could *decentre*, and assume the view of one or even two other individuals (the policemen). Piaget argued that children usually have to be 8 years old or older before they can decentre. Arguably, this suggests that failure on the three mountains task was because the test was too difficult, and not because the children were *egocentric*.

polyadic Between many subjects. See *dyadic*.

Portage Classroom Curriculum (PCC)
Behavioural checklist for assessing the psychological and motor development of children aged 2–6 years.

position constancy Knowledge of one's spatial position despite changes in orientation and/or visual landmarks.

position-orientated language
See *restricted code*.

positive reinforcement Rewarding a subject for performing the behaviour which s/he is being taught.

positive social behaviour Behaviour which is accepted or praised by society. Opposite of *negative social behaviour*.

post-conventional level Highest level in *Kohlberg's theory of moral development*.

post-developmental ageing Term devised by Bromley to stress that 'development' in older people is largely negative.

post-formal thought Theory that in adulthood subjects develop the ability to combine subjective and objective criteria in resolving a problem. The term refers to the fact that it is felt to develop after *formal operations* (although it is not intended to imply that it is automatically 'superior').

post-habituation In the *habituation technique*, the stage when subjects are presented with a new stimulus to look at.

post-natal depression State of depression which occurs in some mothers shortly after giving birth. Symptoms also include feelings of inadequacy and hopelessness.

postpartum The state of the mother after birth and the return to a fertile state. See *neonatal*.

posture and locomotion development of infants The list cited by many researchers was provided by Shirley's work on American babies in the 1930s, and other scales generally accord with its findings. It is a guide for the average infant – there is a considerable variance between individuals and some stages may be skipped. In addition, some cultural practices may accelerate development of certain skills (e.g. walking appears earlier in many African babies). Newborn – *foetal* posture (i.e. curled up); 1 month – raises chin; 2 months – raises chin and chest; 3 months – reaching movements with hands and arms; 4 months – sits when supported; 5 months – sits on lap, and can grasp 'easy-to-grasp' objects; 6 months – grasps dangling objects and can sit in chair; 7 months – sits alone; 8 months – 'sits up' unaided, and can stand with help; 9 months – stands if holding on to support; 10 months – crawls; 11–· 12 months – walks if supported; 13 months – climbs stairs; 15 months – walks unaided. See *Ganda infants study*.

potential concept stage See *vague syncretic stage*.

Powers-Sumner-Kearl formula
Readability measure, which is a revised version of the *Flesch formula reading ease* measure. Calculated by the formula: readability = $-2.209 + (0.0778 \times$ mean number of words per sentence) + $(0.0455 \times$ mean number of syllables per 100 words of text). Considered most reliable for texts aimed at beginning readers–9 year olds.

PQRST method Method of studying materials to be learnt. The initials stand for stages in the operation – preview (attain an overview of the topic); question (assess the main themes); read (study the topic in detail); self-recitation (recall the main themes and ideas); test (assess oneself on ones work).

practical group When used in connection with *Piagetian* theory, particularly of *sensori-motor development* – see *group*.

practical reversibility In *Piaget's* theory of *sensori-motor development* –the infant's conservation of sensations derived from an object which has changed its appearance (i.e. the infant is aware that it will still provide the same sensations). This, however, is different from the *conservation* which occurs in older children.

pragmatic awareness Awareness of the pragmatic forces in an utterance or text. I.e. that what is intended by the speaker or writer is not necessarily conveyed in the surface appearance of the message (e.g. satirical or sarcastic comments). See *pragmatics*.

pragmatics Study of the intentions expressed in utterances, rather than their explicit meaning (e.g. the classic English euphemism, 'would you like to wash your hands?'). By extension, the understanding of intent in utterances.

pre-delinquent Child whose behaviour patterns indicate a danger of him/her becoming a *delinquent*.

pre-morbid IQ The *IQ* level (usually estimated) of a person before the onset of an illness (usually one which has affected the intellect – e.g. *dementia*).

Pre-School Behaviour Checklist *Behavioural checklist* for assessing the development of children aged 2–5 years.

pre-senile dementia *Dementia* whose onset occurs before the patient's sixtieth birthday. It was once felt to be qualitatively distinct from *senile dementia*, but this division is now disputed.

precocious development Development which is faster than average. The term often denotes a disadvantageous state (akin to the lay derogatory sense of the term) or abnormal ageing (e.g. *progeria*).

preconcepts *Piagetian* term describing faulty concepts (usually containing illogical groupings of ideas) found in the *preoperational subperiod.*

preconventional level Lowest of the three levels in *Kohlberg's theory of moral development.*

predeterminism The belief that psychological skills follow a predetermined, inherited, sequence and pattern.

Predictive Screening Test of Articulation (PSTA) Test which assesses a child's articulation defects, and also predicts whether the child will automatically 'grow out of them'.

preference study An experimental method in infant perception (usually visual) research. Obviously, babies cannot tell experimenters what they perceive. However, it is reasonable to assume that if a baby looks at one object more than another, then s/he prefers it, and that if a baby shows a preference, then s/he can tell the difference between the stimuli. E.g. in infant *visual acuity* research – it is known that given a choice between looking at a display of black and white stripes or plain grey, the baby will choose the former (see *complexity preference*). Over successive trials, the stripes can be made progressively finer until the baby looks equally at the stripes and the grey. This is held to indicate that the baby cannot see the stripes and that they have blurred into an overall grey (i.e. the two displays look the same). Thus, the experimenter can find the smallest pattern a baby can see, and hence his/her visual acuity. Note that there is a logical problem with the preference technique – if an infant shows a preference, then s/he can obviously discriminate between the stimuli. However, an absence of a preference may mean that the infant cannot tell them apart, or it could mean that the infant can tell them apart, but does not have a preference. Whilst this is implausible, it is nonetheless logically correct, and is a potentially serious flaw in the technique. See *forced choice preferential looking technique, habituation technique, nonnutritive nipple sucking technique* and *optokinetic nystagmus (OKN) technique.*

preferential looking (PL) technique *preference study.*

preformationism The belief that children are qualitatively identical to adults, and have only to acquire knowledge and pass through puberty to be like them. Accordingly, the belief that the structures of psychological abilities are inherited. The most integrated refutation came from *Piaget.* In an extreme form, preformationism was the doctrine (active from the fifth century BC to the eighteenth century) that the sperm or ovum consisted of a ready-made miniature human being.

pregnancy and birth complications (PBC) Essentially, any non-genetic problems with birth or pregnancy (e.g. *anoxia*).

preliminary grouping of equalities In *Piaget's* theory of *grouping,* a special grouping for coping with adding groups together where the members of each group are equal.

prelingual stage Stage of speech development prior to the production of recognizable words.

prelinguistic Prior to the onset of speech. The term can describe the mental processes prior to speaking, or the stage of infant development prior to the production of recognizable words.

prelinguistic knowledge Knowledge an infant has gained about the world before s/he begins to talk, which may be used to shape his/her comprehension and word production.

premature baby Baby born before the 38th week of pregnancy and weighing under five pounds (approximately).

prenatal development Development of the *foetus* prior to birth.

preoperational period *preoperational subperiod.*

preoperational stage *preoperational subperiod.*

preoperational subperiod Stage of the *concrete operational period (Piaget)* lasting from approximately 18 months to 7 years (although most work has concentrated on 4–7 year olds). Essentially, children in the subperiod are characterized by a failure to see sufficient aspects of problems to solve them accurately. Either they fail to look at all the information presented in a problem, or they presume that everyone else has the same knowledge and perceptions of a situation as themselves. By the end of the subperiod, children have become more flexible, and are able to consider several facets of a problem or situation simultaneously (i.e. they have learnt to *decentre*). The transition to this state is gradual – in the interim period, the child may decentre at one time in one task, but not at other times or other tasks – Piaget terms these occurrences *regulations.* Preoperational thought is primarily examined through the concepts of *conservation* and *egocentrism.*

prep school See *British school system.*

preparatory school See *British school system.*

preponent perceptual feature *perceptual pregnance.*

preretirement education Instructional materials/courses designed to prepare people for retirement.

presbycusis Hearing loss characterized by a relatively greater difficulty in perceiving high frequency sounds. Often found in older people suffering from hearing loss.

Preschool Interpersonal Problem Solving Test (PIPS) A test which presents subjects with pictures of various social problems, to which they must provide as many solutions as possible.

preserved differentiation The theory that some intellectual skills are relatively better preserved than others in old age, because they have always been better (i.e. the same difference would have been found in youth, although the absolute size of the scores might have been higher). E.g. a group of professional musicians may have a better preserved level of manual dexterity. This could be due to practice which enables them to maintain this *(differential preservation)*, or because they have always had better manual dexterity (preserved differentiation). See *age x treatment interaction.*

pretend play (1) *make-believe play.* (2) *Play* in which the child pretends to perform 'real' actions.

preterm Born prematurely. Hence, 'preterm infant', etc.

prewired *hard wired.*

Preyer's theory of developmental psychology Wilhelm Preyer (1841–1897), biologist. He analysed development in terms of the sense, the will, and the intellect. The work has a very heavy bias towards embryology and developmental biology. The majority of Preyer's theories are now very dated, but he is credited with being one of the first of the modern developmental psychologists.

primary ageing Age changes to the body (e.g. wrinkling skin, more brittle bones, etc.). See *secondary ageing,* and *universal ageing.*

primary circular reaction See *sensorimotor stage 2.*

primary class When used in *Piagetian* theory – see *grouping I.*

primary mental abilities (PMAs) The most basic mental skills, held to underlie all mental processes. Often classified as verbal, numerical, and visuo-spatial, but many researchers cite Thurstone's wider calculation of seven primary mental abilities (memory, numerical, perceptual, reasoning, space, verbal, and word fluency). See *Primary Mental Abilities (PMA) Test.*

Primary Mental Abilities (PMA) Test Intelligence test battery assessing ability at Thurstone's seven *primary mental abilities.*

primary process thought See *Freud's theory of development.*

Primary Reading Test (PRT) Reading test for subjects aged 6–12. The test is in two 'Levels': Level 1, for 6–10 year olds, and Level 2, for 7–12 year olds. Both consist of word-picture matching and *sentence completion* tasks.

primary school See *British school system.*

primitive reflexes Found in babies, they usually vanish by the end of the first twelve months. Sometimes called *subcortical reflexes,* after the brain areas controlling them. Traditionally, it has been argued that primitive reflexes are often useful survival aids, which are replaced by similar but more sophisticated learnt behaviours. However, more recent theories have suggested that they are adaptations to life in the womb, which are lost because they are of no use once born (e.g. see *stepping reflex*). See *Babinski reflex, grasping reflex, licking reflex, Moro reflex, pursing reflex, rooting reflex, stepping reflex, sucking reflex* and *swimming reflex*.

principle learning See *signal learning.*

principle of least effort The principle that in any intellectual task, the mental processes requiring least mental labour will be sought.

principled level *post-conventional level.*

print literacy *literacy*, definition (1).

print size See *point size.*

prion disease (Speculative) group term for a range of degenerative brain diseases such as *bovine spongiform encephalopathy* and *Creutzfeldt-Jakob Disease*, which some commentators believe to be due to an abnormal protein metabolism. 'Prion' is an abbreviation of 'proteinaceous infectious particle'.

privation See *deprivation.*

probabilistic ageing Aspects of ageing likely to affect most (but by no means all) who reach old age (e.g. arthritis). Similar to *secondary ageing.* See *universal ageing.*

probabilistic epigenesis The likely direction in which an individual's development, shaped by *epigenesis*, will be directed.

problem-focused coping Dealing with a life crisis by trying to solve the problems created by it. See *appraisal-focused coping* and *emotion-focused coping.*

problem isomorphs Intellectual problems in two or more settings which require the same symbolic solution.

problem solving (1) solving problems. (2) See *signal learning.*

process intelligence (Ps) *fluid intelligence.*

processing limitation hypothesis See *structural lag (reading).*

processing resources theory of ageing Any theory which argues that changes in ageing intellectual skills are attributable to a lowered capacity for mental calculations (e.g. of *working memory*), lowered speed of processing, etc.

product intelligence (Pt) *crystallized intelligence.*

product of measures An arithmetic process in which the answer is in different units from those of the sum (e.g. 2 inches x 3 inches = 6 square inches). See *isomorphism of measures.*

productive ageing *successful ageing.*

profound hearing impairment (PHI) *Hearing impairment* of less than 90dB.

profound mental retardation See *mental retardation.*

progeria Disease in which the patients appear to age from babyhood at an abnormally fast rate, usually dying in their teens. Although sharing many of the features of normal ageing, the illness is not simply accelerated normal ageing. Compare with *Werner syndrome.*

programmed instruction See *Skinner's theory of child rearing.*

programmed neuronal death Phenomenon that neurons (nerve cells) die in large numbers during early development, apparently because they are surplus to requirements (the surviving neurons having made connections with other surviving neurons).

programmed senescence The belief that the body is genetically programmed to age.

Progressive Matrices Test *Raven's Progressive Matrices.*

progressive supranuclear palsy (PSP) An illness characterized by disturbances of motor function and mild to moderate *dementia.*

projective test Personality measure in which the subject is required to make up stories or other descriptive passages based upon a picture or other object. The technique supposedly reveals details of the subject's personality. It is favoured most strongly by some branches of psychoanalysis – the opinions of experimental psychology have generally been less complimentary.

propositional thought See *formal operations.*

prosocial behaviour Behaviour which helps others.

protest In discussion of *maternal deprivation* – see *Bowlby's theory of attachment.*

protest, despair and detachment See *Bowlby's theory of attachment.*

proto-word Relatively stable sound pattern indicating a particular intent or expression, but which is not a recognized word in mature language. Proto-words are exhibited by infants in the post-*babbling* stage, when they are beginning to learn adult language.

prototype theory of language acquisition Theory that an infant decides on a word's meaning from a prototypical example. Items or events which share one or more characteristics with the prototype are named using the word. If the prototype is too specific, then *underextension* results, while too broad set of criteria create *overextension.* As the infant acquires more information, the prototype becomes more exact, thereby decreasing naming errors.

proverb interpretation Specialist tests, such as the *Gorham Proverb Interpretation Test,* and several other studies, assess subjects' abilities to provide meanings of proverbs. Patients in the early stages of *dementia* may give very literal interpretations of well-known proverbs (e.g. 'people in glass houses...' may be literally interpreted as advice to greenhouse owners).

provoked correspondence (number conservation) *Conservation of number task* in which the items used in the two rows should force the child to compare them on a one-to-one basis (e.g. a row of eggs and a row of egg cups).

proximal ageing effects Ageing changes directly attributable to changes in another process (e.g. a *stroke,* due to an ageing cardiovascular system). See *distal ageing effects.*

proximal development (zone of) See *Vygotsky's theory of development.*

proximodistal development See *cephalocaudal development.*

PRT *Primary Reading Test.*

Ps intelligence *process intelligence.*

pseudo-conservation Phenomenon whereby children can often give the correct responses in a *conservation* task if the results of the transformation are hidden from view. E.g. in a *liquid continuous quantity task,* if the child does not see the shape of the container the liquid is poured into (because it is hidden by a screen), s/he may be willing to accept that the hidden container has the same quantity of liquid as before. However, when the whole operation is open to view, then s/he will argue that the quantity has changed.

pseudo-dialogue Interaction in which only one of the participants is effectively communicating. Term used to describe early parent–child interaction.

pseudodementia A side-effect of depression in some older people – a lowering in intellectual abilities, which in turn masquerades as *dementia*.

pseudohermaphrodism See *hermaphrodism*.

pseudomutuality (1) Term describing how families of remarried parents may strive to prevent or hide disharmony to an unrealistic (and possibly damaging) extent, rather than risk another marital break-up. (2) More generally, any false portrayal or delusion of an intimate, harmonious relationship.

PSP *progressive supranuclear palsy*.

PST *Parallel Spelling Tests*.

PSTA *Predictive Screening Test of Articulation*.

psychic energy See *Freud's theory of development*.

psychoeducation Term for the application of psychological theories and methods to educational practices.

psychogenic mortality Psychological factors leading to physical symptoms which in turn cause death.

psychological age A person's psychological state compared to that of an average person of the same *chronological age*.

psychological autopsy Discussion of psychological factors surrounding a patient's death.

psychological moratorium See *Erikson's theory of development*.

psychologically available space In children's early drawings, the phenomenon whereby body parts tend not to overlap each other, even though this produces rather odd anatomical representations.

psychosexual development General term for development of sexual behaviour. Particularly applied to *Freud's theory of development*.

psychosis with cerebral arteriosclerosis *multi-infarct dementia*.

psychosocial development (1) Essentially, any aspect of social development. (2) Often used to refer to *Erikson's theory of development*.

Pt intelligence *product intelligence*.

public school (1) In America, a non-feepaying school. (2) In Britain, the opposite.

puerperal Adjective relating to childbirth and the period shortly after.

pugilistic dementia *Dementia*-type symptoms resulting from blows to the head. The precise symptoms vary, but usually include disturbances of movement as well as intellectual impairment. The symptoms are permanent, unlike the colloquial notion of being 'punch drunk', which can be relatively short-lived. Most often encountered in boxers (hence the name), but also can occur as a result of other violent activities or accidents.

punishment and obedience orientation Stage 1 of *Kohlberg's theory of moral development*.

Pupil Rating Scale – Revised Measure of pupils who appear to have normal abilities but who have learning disabilities.

pupil subcultures Groups of pupils within a school, linked by a particular set of values, perceived ethnic and/or social background, etc., which they or others perceive as making them different from the rest of the school.

pursing reflex *Primitive reflex* – the infant may purse his/her lips when confronted with an unpleasant taste.

Pygmalion in the Classroom
Phenomenon whereby the brighter the teacher thinks the child is, the better his/her subsequent scholastic performance.

pyramidal society Society in which there are far more young than old people. The population can be envisioned as a pyramid with the youngest age groups at the bottom, supporting increasingly small blocks of older age groups. See *rectangular society*.

Q

qualitative development (1) *stage theory of development*. Often presented as the opposite of *quantitative development*. (2) Development in which a skill or attribute changes in structure (and usually also in efficiency).

quantitative development (1) Any theory with leanings towards *preformationism*. Often presented as the opposite of *qualitative development*. (2) Also, improvement in the performance of a skill within a stage of development. (3) Any development in which the skill retains essentially the same structure as the efficiency with which it is executed improves.

Quick Test Measure of *receptive vocabulary*, for subjects aged 2 years and over.

R

RA (1) *reading age.* (2) *request for action.*

RAGS *Relatives' Assessment of Global Symptomatology.*

Raven's Progressive Matrices IQ test in which subjects have to find from a multiple choice the item (a figure or pattern) which follows the same rules as some given examples. The test items, whilst maintaining the same format, get progressively harder (hence the name). The test is available in three forms: *Coloured Progressive Matrices (CPM)* for children and intellectually compromised adults; *Standard Progressive Matrices (SPM)* for children over 6 years and adults; and *Advanced Progressive Matrices (APM)* for children over 11 years and adults (and particularly intended for assessing groups likely to be of above-average ability).

raw score A score as it is first recorded. In some instances, the raw score is the one which is subsequently analysed, but in others, the raw score has to be manipulated before it is of use to the experimenter (a raw score, after it has been adjusted, becomes a *derived score*). E.g. given the same test, a 7-year-old might get 10 answers correct, compared with a 16-year-old's 20. In terms of raw score, the 16-year-old is obviously better. However, there is also a great disparity in their ages. To allow for this, it would be more sensible to see how the two subjects fare compared to their age peers. When this is done, it might transpire that a score of 10 is better than 95% of other 7-year-olds can manage, whilst a score of 20 might be below average for a 16-year-old. However, in comparing older and younger adults, it is often the raw scores which are important, and not how well people of different age perform relative to their age peers – see *efficiency quotient.*

RDLS *Reynell Developmental Language Scale.*

RE *reading ease.* See *Flesch formula.*

re-engagement theory *activity theory.*

readability Any measure of the ease with which a passage of text may be read. Typically, a mathematical formula (for the mathematically minded, a regression equation) derived from characteristics of a sample of the text in question is used. Examples of such formulae include the *Botel formula, Dale-Chall formula, Devereaux formula, Farr-Jenkins-Paterson formula, Flesch formula, FOG formula, FORCAST formula, Fry graph, Lorge formula, Mugford chart, Powers-Sumner-Kearl formula, SMOG formula,* and the *Spache formula.* In these formulae, readability is expressed in terms of the minimum age at which an average person could read the text in question. The measures produced are usually reasonably accurate, though they can make erroneous judgements about non-standard texts (e.g. selected sections of James Joyce). Readability is usually used to assess if instructional and recreational texts can be comprehended by the target audience (usually schoolchildren), but researchers have also used it as an objective measure of text difficulty.

readiness General term for any measure of how prepared a child is to learn a particular skill (e.g. *reading readiness*).

reading age (RA) The level of reading attainment which is average for a particular age group. A person's reading age is only revealing of his/her abilities when compared with other 'age' measures (e.g. a 12-year-old with a reading age of 12 is average, whilst a 7-year-old with a reading age of 12 is very advanced for his/her years). See *dyslexia*.

reading awareness Knowledge of what reading is. Usually seen at a fairly basic level of being able to distinguish between activities which involve reading and activities which do not. A more sophisticated insight into reading processes is usually labelled as *metareading*.

reading by analogy Pronouncing (usually new or nonsense) words in a similar manner to words whose pronunciation is known which look similar (e.g. pronouncing 'zant' to rhyme with 'pant'). Compare with *phonic mediation*.

reading by phonological buildup *phonic mediation*.

reading ease Measure of how easily a passage of text can be read. See *Flesch formula*.

reading level Level of difficulty of a text, usually expressed in terms of *reading age*, or the school *grade*/class at which an average reader should first be able to read it with ease.

Reading Miscues Inventory Test for assessing *miscues*. For subjects of any age.

reading quotient (RQ) Calculated as for *intelligence quotient*, except that reading development, rather than general intellectual development, is calculated. Thus, a child's reading ability relative to his/her peers can be assessed.

reading readiness Measure of how cognitively and linguistically prepared a child is for learning to read.

Reading Vocabulary Tests Reading test for subjects aged 6–12 years. Consists of *sentence completion* problems.

'real books' method Reading teaching scheme which provides children with a relatively free choice of reading materials and emphasizes the need to see reading as enjoyable and a means of communication, as opposed to the more traditional *basal reading* schemes, which emphasize a gradual build-up of basic skills, with communication and enjoyment of stories gradually assuming emphasis.

realism Term sometimes used by *Piaget* to denote a child's erroneous belief that his/her perceptions are shared by others (in this sense the term is synonymous with *egocentrism*), as are his/her thoughts and dreams.

reality play *functional play*.

reality principle See *Freud's theory of development*.

reality testing Assessing whether something is or could plausibly be real.

rebus Writing system in which pictures of objects or events represent words (e.g. a picture of an eye represents 'I').

recapitulation theory The argument that development of the individual *(ontogeny)* echoes the development of the individual's species' evolutionary development *(phylogeny)*.

recasting Parental method of correcting a child's language whilst keeping the conversation going. Involves recasting the child's statement or question into more mature language as part of the reply (e.g. 'allgone dinner' – 'where has all the dinner gone?').

Received Pronunciation (RP) The pronunciation of *Standard English* – i.e. the most socially 'correct' pronunciation of British english.

receptive language (1) Language which can be understood. (2) *receptive vocabulary*.

receptive play See *functional play*.

receptive vocabulary The total range of language which can be understood.

recessive gene See *genetic dominance*.

reciprocal determinism In *Bandura's theory of social learning*, the interaction between the subject's personality, behaviour, and environment.

reciprocal interweaving See *Gessell's maturational theory*.

reciprocal roles Any situation (usually in play) where the individuals can exchange roles (e.g. cricketers/baseball players can alternately bat and field).

reciprocity Cognitive skills acquired, according to *Piaget*, in the *formal operations* period. The subject learns that two or more substances can be directly compared if all other aspects of them are made equal. E.g., comparing types of wax in candles is relatively meaningless unless reciprocity is observed, and the types of wax are made into candles of the same size, using the same wicks, etc.

recognition assimilation In infants, performing an action which indicates that they recognize an object by using it (e.g. squeezing a squeaky toy).

rectangular society (1) Future society in which the *age cohorts'* survival rates would follow *rectangular survival curves*. (2) Society in which there are roughly equal numbers of people alive in each age decade (i.e. equal numbers of 0–9-year-olds, 10–19-year-olds, etc.). A histogram plotting numbers against age decade would appear like a rectangle. See *pyramidal society*.

rectangular survival curve Hypothesized graph of percentage of *survivors* in an *age cohort* in a future of very effective medical care. By this reckoning, very few people will die until their *lifespan* is reached, when most will die within a few years of each other. A graph of the percentage of the age cohort alive at different ages (with percentage on the vertical axis, and age on the horizontal) would thus look rectangular – an almost horizontal line going from left to right, joined to an almost vertical line going downwards when the lifespan mark is reached on the horizontal axis.

redevelopment In *Piagetian* theory, the learning of mental representations during the *concrete operational period* of physical transformations already acquired in the *sensori-motor period*.

reductionism Belief that a complex skill/behaviour is formed from a set of simple skills/behaviours.

reduplicated babbling Babbling characterized by the repeated use of a limited set of sounds (e.g. 'mamamama').

referential language style A tendency to refer to real objects. See *expressive language style*.

reflective abstraction In *Piagetian* theory, abstracting information on an attribute of an item, and then transposing the information to another 'level' of thought.

reflex A response which does not require conscious thought and which is typically automatic and hard or impossible consciously to control. Often a reflex is *innate*. See *survival reflex* and *primitive reflex*.

reflex exercise The progressive improvement in the ease with which actions (particularly reflexes) are performed as *sensori-motor stage 1 progresses.*

refrigerator parent Parent with a 'cold', unemotional personality, who may also be ambitious for his/her children.

regression hypothesis Theory that the linguistic or other skills of older people revert to the qualitative state of a child's.

regulations See *preoperational subperiod.*

reinforcement The strengthening of a belief or behaviour.

relation In *Piagetian* theory – refers to how one item is related to another (see *group, grouping* and *lattice*).

relational control structures See *sensori-motor control structures.*

Relatives' Assessment of Global Symptomatology (RAGS) Questionnaire measure of symptoms of the patient observed by his/her *caregivers.*

reminiscence peak The phenomenon whereby the bulk of *autobiographical memories* stem from the period between 10 and 30 years of age.

remote grandmother See *apportioned grandmother.*

remote memory Memory for non-autobiographical events which have occurred during a subject's lifetime. A frequent proviso is that these events must not include very famous ones, which are seen as part of common general knowledge, and are thus more properly classified as part of semantic memory.

reorganizers See *integrated personality.*

repression See *Freud's theory of development.*

reproductive assimilation The process of repeating mental representations, so that they become more memorable.

request for action (RA) A verbal request for something. See *desired act.*

resistant and insecurely attached See *strange situation.*

resorption When used in *Piagetian* theory – see *grouping I.*

response-sensitive instruction Teaching in which the teacher's questions and instructions are responses to the way in which the pupil has just answered. Obviously only practical for one-to-one teaching, but can be replicated in *computer aided instruction* programmes.

responsive parenting Descriptive of parents who respond to child's requests and in are generally sensitive to the child's needs.

restricted code Term devised by Bernstein to denote language principally characterized by shorter, less complex sentences, a relative absence of abstract images or formal phrases, and a higher proportion of redundant fillers such as 'you know?', as if agreement/reassurance were being sought. The code, it was argued, was more typical of children from lower socio-economic *(SES)* groups. The *elaborated code* of middle class children was held to be the reverse of this, and accordingly was more complex, better suited to formal argument, and seemed more confident, through greater use of the word 'I'. In addition, the middle class children used *person-orientated language*, which was on a more personal level than the rather more remote *position-orientated language* of the working class children. These factors, it was argued, place the child from a low SES background at a disadvantage, because formal education is largely conducted in elaborated code. The theory has been heavily debated.

restricting parenting Parenting style which places limits on what a child may do.

restructuring See *complex learning*.

retrolental fibroplasia (RLF) Blindness resulting from (often premature) babies receiving too much oxygen in incubators. The condition was relatively common when incubator nursing was first introduced, but is now very rare.

reversibility The ability to imagine a sequence of events in both forward and reverse directions. Used extensively in *Piagetian* theory of the *concrete operational period*. See *group* for a more formal definition.

Reynell Developmental Language Scale (RDLS) Test battery measuring the development of a variety of linguistic skills (comprehension, expression, etc.).

RH right handed.

rhesus baby Second or subsequent baby with rhesus positive blood born to a mother with rhesus negative blood who has given birth to a first baby with rhesus positive blood. The first baby is unaffected, but the mother's immune system is changed by this first pregnancy so that it reacts to the second or subsequent foetuses as 'infections' if they possess rhesus positive blood. This can have a variety of effects, including miscarriage and *mental retardation*. Can be easily prevented with drug treatment.

Rhett's disorder A decline in head size and psychological, motor and/or social skills after conventional development of 5 months – 4 years.

rhyme sensitivity The degree to which a subject can detect that words end with the same sound – is a good indicator of ability to process *phonemes*, and thus of

phonic mediation ability. See *alliteration sensitivity*.

rhythmicity The regularity/predictability of a subject's behaviour.

Ribot's hypothesis The theory that in damaged or decaying minds, memories for recent events should be worse than memories for remote ones.

Richmond Test of Basic Skills Reading and study skills test battery for subjects aged 8–14 years. Includes measures of vocabulary, comprehension, spelling and punctuation, as well as maths and map and chart reading.

right brain skills See *left brain skills*.

rigidity General term for any relative inability to change an aspect of personality or a skill. Sometimes used of older people in comparison with the young.

Rivermead Behavioural Memory Test A set of memory tasks analogous to everyday situations where memory is required (e.g. face recognition, remembering a route set out by the experimenter, etc.). The test is intended for adults of all ages with memory problems, and it is used for assessing *demented* patients.

RLF *retrolental fibroplasia*.

rocking chair personality *dependent personality*.

role cycling The attempts by parents in a *dual career family* to integrate the cycle of activity of their careers with the cycle of activity in their home life.

rooting reflex *Primitive reflex* – if a baby is touched on the cheek, it turns its head in the direction of the touch (useful in targeting mouth to nipple). See *sucking reflex*.

rotation task See *display rotation task* and *observer rotation task*.

roughness discrimination test *Reading readiness* test devised by Nolan and Morris to determine if a blind child has sufficient touch sensitivity to learn to read *Braille*. Consists of being able to distinguish between very finely differentiated grades of sandpaper.

Rousseau's theory of human development Jean Jacques Rousseau (1712–1778), French philosopher. He disagreed with the *tabula rasa* argument of *Locke's theory of human development*, and argued that children possess a set of *innate* values and predispositions, which differ from those of adults. Children proceed through four stages of development, vaguely reminiscent of *Piaget's* theory: infancy (experienced through the senses); childhood (the child's thoughts are concrete, and exhibit his/her innate understanding of concepts such as motions of objects, etc.); late childhood (more advanced concrete thoughts); and finally, adolescence (the advent of abstract thought and the increased need for social interaction). Rousseau argued that historical development reflects human development, and that more 'primitive' societies had lived in a world akin to the pre-adolescent state. In his early work, this was held to be a preferable, but now permanently lost state of being (the phrase 'noble savage' is derived from this, although Rousseau later rejected much of the argument). Much of Rousseau's theory is contained in *'Emile'*, the story of the education of an imaginary boy.

RP *Received Pronunciation.*

Rp level thought Thought confined to describing a situation. This contrasts with *A level thought*, in which subjects are capable of abstracting information, such as causality and general themes.

RQ *reading quotient.*

rubella German measles – usually harmless (if annoying), unless the patient is a woman in the early stages of pregnancy, where the illness can afflict the *foetus* with physical disabilities (including blindness) and *mental retardation*. See *perceptive deafness*.

rule awareness The awareness of the need for rules and how they operate. The growth of rule awareness has been examined by several researchers (e.g. see *Piaget's theory of moral development*).

Rutter B(2) Questionnaire *Teacher Rating Scale B(2).*

S

S-R theory *Learning theory* – the 'S-R' stands for 'stimulus–response', the basic unit of learning.

SA *spelling age.*

Salford Sentence Reading Test Reading test for subjects aged 6–11 years. Similar in format to the *Holborn Reading Scale.* Subjects are given a series of sentences of increasing difficulty to read. The test terminates when a set number of errors has been made.

Sally–Anne task See *autism.* The experiment has also been used on non-autistic children. See *Smarties task.*

saltatory growth Growth in fits and spurts.

SAMI *Sequential Assessment of Mathematics Inventories.*

SAT *Scholastic Aptitude Test.*

SATs *Standard Assessment Tests.*

scaffolded performance level See *developmental range.*

Scales of Independent Behaviour Measure of adaptive behaviour (i.e. how well subjects can adapt to their surroundings) for subjects of any age.

scanners See *selection strategies.*

Schachtel's theory of development Ernest Schachtel (1903–1975), psychologist. He argued that infantile perceptions are primarily through the *autocentric* senses (perceived within or on the body – smell, taste, etc.), before a shift of emphasis to the *allocentric* senses (perceived outside the body – i.e. sight and hearing). Cognitive development and social interaction require one to label events and items with names. Whilst this is convenient, it trivializes the richness of sensory experiences, and it is argued that too much is lost in the process. Schachtel also argued that child rearing practices stifle curiosity.

Schedule of Growing Skills (SGS) Measure of skills and behaviours which assesses the development of children aged 0–5 years and assesses their growth relative to *age norms.*

schema (1) A collection of memories about an event or item which enable one to plan responses and to interpret information surrounding the said event or item. For example, if one is asked to dinner at an expensive restaurant, one's schema for expensive restaurants will indicate that turning up in jeans and a t-shirt would not be a good idea. (2) In *Piaget's* theory, a package of ideas in *figurative thought.* There is an important distinction between 'schema' and 'scheme' – see *scheme.*

schematic learning Learning which is shaped by an existing *schema,* or learning with the intent to create a schema. Generally used to denote learning in an interpretive fashion, as opposed to blind rote-learning.

scheme (1) In much of the writing about *Piaget,* and some translations of his work, the word 'scheme' is used interchangeably with *schema.* Strictly speaking, 'schema' describes groupings of facts (in *figurative thought*) and 'scheme' describes groupings of mental processes for manipulating information (in *operative* *thought*). However, the blurring together of the two terms through incorrect usage is now almost complete, and to perpetuate the distinction is probably a forlorn task. (2) The term was also used in *Baldwin's theory of developmental psychology*, rather more loosely.

scholastic aptitude test Any test which measures skills taught in the classroom, or skills which are felt to impinge directly upon scholastic abilities. Often used to predict a pupil's likely scholastic performance. When the term has capital letters – i.e. the *Scholastic Aptitude Test* – then a specific test is implied.

Scholastic Aptitude Test (SAT) Test used by American College Entrance Examination Board, which tests basic scholastic aptitude in university/college entrants. Not to be confused with *scholastic aptitude test*, which is a generic term for any test of scholastic skills.

Schonell Graded Word Reading Test Reading test for subjects aged 6–12 years. Consists of a list of words (most with *irregular spellings*) which the subject has to pronounce. Words increase in difficulty as the test progresses. Testing ceases when the subject has incorrectly pronounced a set number of words.

Schonell Graded Word Spelling Test Spelling test for subjects aged 5–15 years. Subjects spell words which increase in difficulty as the test progresses. Testing ceases when the subject has made a set number of errors.

school adjustment The degree to which a pupil can cope with the demands of school life.

school phobia A phobia (irrational fear) of school, and not simply of leaving home to go to school. See *school refusal*.

school psychology In America and some other countries, the implementation of psychological testing and treatment within a school. Most practitioners have a teaching qualification and have then specialized.

school readiness The degree to which a child has attained the necessary psychological prerequisites to commence schooling.

school refusal A refusal to go to school. The term may be synonymous with *school phobia*, but can also describe a reluctance to leave home per se.

schools, U.K. *British school system.*

schools, U.S.A. *American school system.*

Science Lesson Analysis System (SLAS) Score sheet of activities and objectives in school science classes. Includes measures of both verbal interaction between pupil and teacher and non-verbal interaction with the lesson materials.

scotopic sensitivity See *Irlen Differential Perceptual Scale*.

SDAT *senile dementia of the Alzheimer type.*

SDMT *Stanford Diagnostic Mathematics Test.*

SDRT *Stanford Diagnostic Reading Test.*

SE *Standard English.*

second age See *first age*.

second degree operations *formal operations*.

secondary ageing Age changes which are associated with, but not necessarily an inevitable consequence of, ageing (e.g. arthritis, cataracts, etc.). See *primary ageing* and *probabilistic ageing*.

secondary circular reaction See *sensorimotor stage 3*.

secondary class When used in *Piagetian* theory – see *grouping I*.

secondary education Education which is provided by a *secondary school*.

secondary modern school See *grammar school.*

secondary process thought See *Freud's theory of development.*

secondary school See *British school system.*

secure attachment (1) Descriptive of child who finds comfort and consolation in presence of parent of *caregiver* after separation or other aversive event. (2) See *strange situation.*

segmented drawing Drawing in which parts (e.g. of the body) are clearly demarked.

SEH *seriously emotionally handicapped.*

selection strategies General term employed by Bruner to denote methods of concept formation. There are several of these: (i) *conservation focusing* is the process of deciding which attributes are part of a concept and which are not (e.g. in judging which animals are mammals, one might consider number of legs, presence of fur, rearing of young, etc.). A series of attributes are processed one at a time to see which fit in, and which are either unnecessary (e.g. must have four limbs on the ground) or exclude an item from membership (e.g. has scales). (ii) *focus gambling* is like conservation focusing, except that two or more attributes are considered at once. This is obviously a more risky and less informative strategy, but it is also faster. (iii) *simultaneous scanning* involves the formation of several hypotheses about a concept, and then using the evidence to find which hypothesis gives the best explanation. (iv) *successive scanning* is akin to simultaneous scanning, except that a single hypothesis is tested at a time. The theory can be extended to categorizing individuals into *scanners* and *focusers.* The former tend to collect (too much) evidence before making a

hypothesis, while the latter (often rashly) make a hypothesis, and then search for evidence to support their theory.

selective optimization (-isation) with compensation (SOC) *compensation.*

self-bias *egocentrism.*

self-efficacy Belief in one's own abilities.

self-hatred personality Personality type found in some older people – possessors (unrealistically) blame themselves for all their misfortunes.

self-initiated repair Linguistic term for the speaker correcting his/her own mistake. Compare with *other-initiated repair.*

self-referent In terms of spatial processing, encoding or expressing a spatial location by reference to one's own spatial position (e.g. 'the coffee jar is in front of me, to my left, and at my head height').

self-regulation (1) See Gessell's *maturational theory.* (2) Generally, an infant's developing ability to fit in with other people's needs (e.g. waiting to be fed at regular feeding times, sleeping all night, etc.). (3) Ability to regulate one's own behaviour.

selves See *Allport's theory of personality development.*

semi-structured interview See *structured interview.*

senescence Old age, usually with the implication of normal ageing.

senescing Ageing, particularly in terms of *biological age.*

senile Medical term for 'old'. The term is not synonymous with *demented.*

senile dementia *Dementia* whose onset occurs after the patient's sixtieth birthday. It was once felt to be qualitatively distinct from *pre-senile dementia,* but this division is now disputed.

senile dementia of the Alzheimer type (SDAT) See *dementia of the Alzheimer type*.

senile plaques Amorphous clumps of dead neurones, found in the brains of all older people, but particularly prevalent in *demented* individuals.

senile psychosis Misleading synonym for *dementia*. Although some demented patients do have feelings of persecution in the early stages of the illness (a common feature of psychosis), this is far from universal.

senior student American final year student.

sensitive parent Parent who is responsive to his/her child's needs. Contrast with *insensitive parent*.

sensitive period (1) Period of development during which the subject is most sensitive to a particular type of experience. The term is sometimes used as a synonym of *critical period*, though this has a more specialized meaning. (2) The term has another specialized meaning in *Montessori's theory of child development*.

sensori-motor development In *Piagetian* theory, the period from birth to circa 18 months when an infant learns to develop and coordinate the sensory and the motor systems. Many of the changes are argued to result from the processes of *adaptation, organization* and *decentration*. The baby begins life believing that the world is a product of his/her own perceptions, and what cannot be perceived (initially orally, and subsequently with the other senses) cannot exist. Gradually, s/he learns that s/he is a unit within a world governed by logical rather than perceptual rules, and that other people and objects have separate existences and can produce their own effects on the environment. This is particularly well demonstrated by the development of the *object concept*. Piaget argued that the infant progressed through six stages of sensori-motor development (see *sensori-motor stages 1,2,3,4,5,* and *6* for more details). These follow each other in an unvarying order, with no stage being skipped over. The transition from one stage to the next is gradual. Piaget's theory was originally based on the observations of only three children. Accordingly, the age of onset of each stage should only be taken as approximate. The sensori-motor stage progresses in the *preoperational subperiod* of the *concrete operational period*. See *practical reversibility* and *group*.

sensori-motor play *Play* involving the manipulation of objects and an examination of their physical properties.

sensori-motor stage 1 (0–1 months) The baby is born with a repertoire of *reflexes* and nothing else. S/he first learns about the environment through reflexes (e.g. a reflexive action brings him/her into contact with an object). Furthermore, s/he may begin attempts to tie new behaviours onto the reflexes (e.g. by sucking more vigorously at a nonnutritive source, such as a thumb or a dummy, when hungry).

sensori-motor stage 2 (1–4 months) The first habits are formed, by means of the **primary circular reaction**: the baby by chance performs a pleasurable body movement, and then repeats it until it becomes a habit, done for its own sake. The baby begins to anticipate events (e.g. by making sucking movements before being placed near the nipple). The baby shows curiosity – new items are likely to be stared at. The baby begins to imitate other people, but only if their action resembles one already in the baby's repertoire. (Note that Piaget argues that these actions show the precursors of intelligence, but not intellectual behaviour itself – the baby does not 'plan' or interpret in an adult sense.) *Object concept* is poor – if a baby is gazing at an object, which is then covered over, s/he may look at the space where it was for a few seconds before losing interest. It is as if the object has ceased to exist in the baby's mind.

sensori-motor stage 3 (4–10 months) The baby develops the ***secondary circular reaction***. This is the formation of a habit in a manner akin to the *primary circular reaction*, but now producing a definite goal. This often involves an external object (e.g. shaking a rattle), although the infant does not recognize objects as existing except in conjunction with actions. For example, the baby appears to recognize familiar objects through the appearance of ***motor recognition***. This is making a truncated form of a movement associated with an object when the said object is seen (e.g. Piaget observed his own daughter making a swinging movement of her arms when she saw a doll – she normally played with the doll by swinging it). Imitation also improves (although it is still best when familiar patterns of actions are involved). *Object concept* develops to the point where the baby will briefly search for an object if s/he has caused it to disappear (though this searching is really only a continuation of arm and hand movements already being performed). If anyone else hides the object, then the baby does not search.

sensori-motor stage 4 (10–12 months) The baby now recognizes an object as a goal, and will attempt to gain it, using a definite set of movements (as opposed to movements in the general direction of the object) indicating purposive behaviour (and thus intelligent thought). The baby will remove or push aside objects standing between him/her and the goal, indicating an understanding of rudimentary planning and spatial relationships. The baby begins to understand that other people can initiate actions. *Object concept* improves – s/he can search for a hidden object, although s/he is prone to the *A not B error*. The baby, having seen an object hidden in location A, tends to search at A on subsequent trials, even though s/he has seen the object hidden at the new location of B. The baby can (poorly) imitate novel (as opposed to familiar) actions of other people. Novel objects appear to be explored more thoroughly than before, and for their own properties rather than how they feel.

sensori-motor stage 5 (12–18 months) This stage is characterized by attempts to produce novel actions, rather than to reproduce old actions which had (usually accidentally) produced serendipitous results. The interest in novelty and in novel objects is called the ***tertiary circular reaction***. This incorporates a systematic exploration of objects (e.g. Piaget cites his infant son Laurent dropping his soap dish from different heights, and then comparing the effect with that of dropping a toy swan). The baby will produce actions which apparently best suit the object being dealt with. In *object concept*, the *A not B error* is overcome only if the baby sees the object moved (e.g. if the baby sees the object at B, then s/he will search at B). However, if s/he cannot see the object being hidden at B (e.g. the object is moved in a clenched fist), then the baby searches at A. The baby will also produce the error if the object is placed under too many layers of covering material. The baby becomes more competent at imitating other people's actions.

sensori-motor stage 6 (18 months and over) The problems posed by the sensori-motor period are now overcome. In *object concept*, the baby can now search systematically, and mentally 'fill in' missing movements, so that the A not B error does not occur when the baby has not seen the object moved, or when s/he has to search through several layers of covering. S/he can also imitate people's actions when they are no longer present (*deferred imitation*). Piaget argues that at this stage the infant possesses symbolic mental images, as opposed to literal perceptions, of the world. The stage progresses in the *pre-operational subperiod* of the *concrete operational period.*

sensorimotor Alternative spelling of 'sensori-motor'. See *sensori-motor development.*

sensorimotor control structures F i r s t stage of development (0–18 months) in a model devised by Case. It is akin to *Piaget's sensori-motor development*, in that thought is very much linked with learned physical actions. Subsequent stages include: *relational control structures* (18 months–5 years) – the discovery of relationships between items and events; *dimensional control structures* (5–11 years) – the discovery of how differences and similarities can be measured; and *abstract control structures* (11 years and over) – the development of abstract thought.

sensory-motor Alternative spelling of 'sensori-motor'. See *sensori-motor development.*

sentence completion *sentence frame completion.*

sentence frame completion (1) Akin to *cloze procedure*, the subject must complete a sentence. It is used to test reading/comprehension skills. (2) A *projective test* where the completed sentence reflects the subject's own feelings.

sentential grouping Linking items because they fit together in a sentence (e.g. 'the bunny ate the carrot'), rather than for reasons of more conventional grouping logic.

separation See *maternal deprivation.*

separation anxiety Anxiety displayed by young children and infants on being separated from their parent(s). See *maternal deprivation, strange situation* and *stranger anxiety.*

separation protest *Protest* phase in *protest, despair and detachment* – see *Bowlby's theory of attachment.*

Sequenced Inventory of Communication Development (SICD) Test battery of measures of linguistic skills in infants/young children.

Sequential Assessment of Mathematics Inventories (SAMI) Test battery of measures of mathematical skills.

sequential design *sequential research design.*

sequential research design *Longitudinal study* in which different *age cohorts* are tested at intervals over several years. In addition, age cross-sections of the population are also tested in tandem with the longitudinal test panel, to gain an insight into possible *cohort effects.*

serialist student Student who gradually builds up knowledge of a topic from basic principles. Contrast with *holist student.*

seriation In *Piaget's* theory of cognitive development, the ability to arrange items in order (e.g. of height, weight, etc.).

serious play *Play* with a directed purpose.

seriously emotionally handicapped (SEH) General term (principally American) for children with severe emotional/mental health problems, who are not *mentally retarded*, nor are they inadequately socialized.

SES Socio-economic status – i.e. social class and income bracket.

severe hearing impairment (SHI) *Hearing impairment* of 70–90 dB.

severe mental retardation See *mental retardation*.

sex chromosomes See *chromosomes*.

sex identity *gender identity*.

sex-linked disorder A disorder (e.g. some forms of colour blindness and haemophilia) which is carried on a *sex chromosome*.

sex role *gender role*.

sex role identity The feeling of how one's behaviour defines one as 'masculine' or 'feminine'. Compare with *gender identity* and *sex role preference*.

sex role preference The attributes a person would like to possess to strengthen his/her *sex role identity* (e.g. a thin man might want bigger muscles). Compare with *sexual preference*.

sex role transcendent personality *androgynous personality*.

sex typing The process of instilling into a child the concept that s/he is male or female. The term is often used censoriously, since the process usually involves reinforcing cultural stereotypes of 'masculine' or 'feminine' behaviours and beliefs.

sexual preference Preferred gender of sexual partner. Compare with *sex role preference*.

SFD *small for date*.

SGA *small for gestational age*.

SGS *Schedule of Growing Skills*.

shape constancy The knowledge that a shape remains the same, even though its retinal image changes when viewed from different angles. This can only be done if a person can extrapolate a three-dimensional image from the two-dimensional image falling on the retina. E.g. a circle tilted on one axis, strictly speaking, appears as an ellipse, yet we are capable of recognizing it as a circle receding away from us. There is some experimental evidence that newborn babies possess shape constancy. See *size constancy*.

shared environmental factor Effects of the environment in which the child is raised which are shared with the other children in question. In contrast, *non-shared environmental factors* are unique to an individual (e.g. accidents, birthdays).

shared meaning Quality of a baby's early utterances whereby, although they are meaningless to strangers, s/he and his/her parents understand that they have a specific meaning (e.g. 'ba' may mean 'bottle', 'uh' a particular toy, etc.).

SHI *severe hearing impairment*.

Shirley's stages of motor development See *posture and locomotion development of infant*.

Shortened Edinburgh Reading Test Truncated form of the *Edinburgh Reading Test*. Consists of three sub-scales which measure vocabulary, syntax and comprehension.

sibling order *birth order*.

SICD *Sequenced Inventory of Communication Development.*

sight-word reading *whole word (reading teaching).*

sign In *Vygotsky's theory of development,* any social signal/method of communication which can be internalized and converted into a tool of thought.

signal learning Term devised by Gagné to denote learning to expect a particular consequence of a stimulus. Terms used in the same taxonomy include: *stimulus–response learning* – learning to give a particular response when given a certain stimulus; *chaining* – learning to join several responses together to make a longer sequence of actions; *verbal association* – learning labels for items; *discrimination learning* – learning to differentiate between two or more items; *concept learning* – learning to classify items into superordinate groups; *principle learning* – learning the explanations for previously unexplained phenomena; and *problem solving* – learning to solve problems.

signs (Piagetian theory) See *index (Piagetian theory).*

silent reading The ability to read and comprehend a text without saying the words out loud. In reading development, usually indicates the onset of a more 'mature' reading style.

simultaneous scanning See *selection strategies.*

single adult executive Family in which one parent makes all the major decisions. Compare with *adult executive* and *family executive.*

six hour retarded child American term for child who appears *mentally retarded* when at school (for six hours each day), but who successfully adapts to non-school life.

16 binary operations Term describing *Piaget's* concept that there are sixteen possible states which describe all possible occasions where two variables can be true and/or false. Using this knowledge enables a subject in the *formal operations* period to methodically work through all possible methods of addressing a problem in which there are two variables. (Note that Piaget does not argue that subjects consciously do this, but that their thought processes can be represented using this symbolism.) These range from the simple ('if p is true, then so is q', or, 'if p is true, then q is false', or vice versa) to the complex (e.g. 'if p is true, then so is q, provided that there is not a state where q can be false when p is true, p can be false and q true, and both p and q can be false simultaneously'). The sixteen states form a *lattice* – every one of the statements has only one *least upper bound (l.u.b.)* and *greatest lower bound (g.u.b.)* which is another member of the lattice.

sixth form British school classes for pupils aged over 16 (who are in their sixth year or above at *secondary school,* and twelve to thirteenth year of their total school attendance).

sixth form college British state school for pupils aged circa 16 years and over. Teaching is principally of 'A' level exam syllabi (possession of 'A' level grades is a usual prerequisite for entrance into tertiary education and many training schemes). Unlike the *comprehensive school,* pupils may be required to have attained certain minimum scholastic standards.

size constancy The knowledge that objects in the distance may look smaller, but their actual size remains the same (e.g. if we see a person walking away from us, we don't assume that s/he is shrinking). See *shape constancy.*

Skinner box Test apparatus for training animals (usually rats). Basically consists of a lever/button to press in response to a stimulus (often a light placed adjacent to the lever/button, although e.g. a sound or tactile stimulation have also been used). The action is usually met with a reward (typically a food pellet dropped into a food hopper in the cage). Widely used in *operant conditioning.*

Skinner's cradle A type of baby's crib invented by Skinner (see *Skinner's theory of child rearing*). Nothing particularly unusual about its features, and not, as some commentators have supposed, a type of *Skinner box* for babies.

Skinner's theory of child rearing Skinner (1904–1990), psychologist and staunch *behaviourist.* Believed, like Watson before him (see *Watson's theory of child rearing*) that children's (and indeed adults') behaviour and learning could be shaped by *conditioning* techniques. *'Walden Two'*, a novel (1948), describes how an ideal community can be created by these methods. In education, Skinner advocated ***programmed instruction*** – the pupil reviews a piece of information, answers questions about it, and proceeds to a more advanced task if s/he is correct. Learning is thus incremental, with the child acquiring knowledge in comfortable 'bites'. The work has been criticized for being too harsh and mechanistic, although it can be argued that the basic principles of conditioning are used in all forms of education – only the thickness of the sugar coating differs.

SLAS *Science Lesson Analysis System.*

SLD (1) *specific learning difficulties* (alternative: *SPLD.*) (2) severe learning difficulty.

Slee 13+ Reading Test Reading test for subjects aged 13–14 years. It tests comprehension of short passages of prose.

sleeper effect Any effect of a treatment which takes some time to become apparent.

SLI specific language impairment.

Slingerland Screening Tests Set of measures for assessing children (age range 5–12 years) with language difficulties.

Slosson Intelligence Test General intelligence test for subjects aged 1 month–27 years.

slow learners Pupils who are just above the level of *mental retardation*, but who, relative to pupils of average intelligence, may be slow to grasp new concepts. The term may also imply poor motivation/behaviour. See *slow starter.*

slow starter Rather nebulous term for pupil who at first makes slow academic progress, but who subsequently catches up to or exceeds his/her *age norm.* See *slow learner.*

slow-to-warm-up child See *New York longitudinal study.*

slow virus A very slow-acting infection which may account for some forms of *mental retardation.*

slowing Term denoting the general decline in the intellectual skills of many older people (e.g. as witnessed by a slowing in the speed of processing).

small for date (SFD) *small for gestational age.*

small for gestational age (SGA) Babies who are underdeveloped compared with the average for the same *gestational age.*

Smarties task Test of children's abilities to perceive other people's concepts of the same situation, akin to the *Sally–Anne task*. The child is shown a tube of 'Smarties' (a popular British children's confection akin to 'M & M's', sold in cardboard tube containers). The child is asked what is in the Smarties tube, to which the child (logically) responds 'Smarties'. The child is then shown that the tube in fact contains a pencil. S/he is then asked what s/he thinks the next child to be tested will say is in the tube when s/he is first asked the question (i.e. before s/he has seen what is actually inside it). *Autistic* children (and many pre-school children) incorrectly answer 'a pencil', apparently indicating that they cannot conceive that the next child can have a different frame of mind from their own. However, it is worth noting that the effect, like many developmental psychology experiments, is very dependent on the manner in which the question is phrased.

SMOG formula *Readability* formula. The number of polysyllabic words which occur in thirty sentences of the text are counted, and this number is called P. Readability = 3 + P. This provides the earliest *grade* in which the average child could read the text. To express the result as *reading age*, add five to the result.

SOC *selective optimization with compensation.*

social age A set of behaviours and attitudes considered to be socially appropriate for the *chronological age* of the individual (i.e. what is colloquially known as 'acting one's age'). See *eldering*.

social clock A hypothesized mechanism which an individual 'consults' to determine the most appropriate behaviour for his/her *social age.*

social cognition (1) The comprehension of social situations, relationships, etc. (2) *social learning.*

social comparison standard Comparing one's performance against that of one's peers to assess the level of one's achievement. Compare with *autonomous standard.*

social contract legalistic orientation Stage 5 of *Kohlberg's theory of moral development.*

social learning See *Bandura's theory of social learning.*

social perspective taking The ability to understand other people's emotions and motivations.

social preadaption The concept that babies have *innate* behaviours which facilitate the formation of *bonds* and social contacts in general.

social referencing Using feedback from others to determine how one should respond to a particular situation.

social smiling Smiling at a person expressing recognition, or as a socially positive response. Begins to be reliably exhibited by infants at 2–3 months.

socialization (-isation) agent Any person or event involved in teaching social skills, acceptable social behaviour, etc.

socialized conduct disorder See *conduct disorder.*

socially blind child Child who tends to ignore other children.

socially dependent child Child with strong drive to mix with other children.

socially independent child Child who is aware of other children, but seeks to play by him/herself.

socio-dramatic play Play in which children assume roles from adult life or stories.

sociocultural retardation Moderate *mental retardation*, not usually apparent until the child encounters difficulties in learning at school. Compare with *clinical retardation*.

soft wired Psychological slang (derived from electronics/computing) for a mental system which is relatively flexible (i.e. demonstrating *plasticity*). See *hard wired*.

solid continuous quantity task See *conservation of quantity*.

solitary play *Play* in which the child plays totally by him/herself, to the total exclusion of other children. Subsequent stages are *parallel play* and *cooperative play*.

SOLO taxonomy *Structure of the Observed Learning Outcome (SOLO) Taxonomy.*

somatic mutation theory of ageing Theory that as cells are lost through natural 'wear and tear' they are replaced by cells which are increasingly likely to contain genetic 'errors' (i.e. are mutations), and are less likely to function efficiently. Accordingly, the ageing body progressively deteriorates. See *autoimmune theory of ageing, disposable soma theory of ageing, free radical theory of ageing* and *Hayflick phenomenon*.

sophomore Second year American student.

SP *switching pause.*

space, psychologically available *psychologically available space.*

Spache formula *Readability* measure. Calculated by the formula: readability = (0.121 x mean no. of words per sentence) + (0.082 x percentage of unfamiliar words) + 0.659. The result is expressed as the earliest *grade* in which the text could be read by an average child. To express the result as *reading age*, add five to the result. The rules governing what constitutes an 'unfamiliar' word are straightforward but lengthy – consult an appropriate textbook for further information. Considered most reliable for texts aimed at beginning readers–13-year-olds.

Spadafore Reading Scale American reading test battery, including measures of silent reading, reading aloud, comprehension, and fluency. The test is applicable for an age range up to (American) college level.

SPAR *Spelling and Reading Tests.*

special identities When used in *Piagetian* theory – see *grouping I.*

specific developmental disorder An isolated problem arising during development which is not attributable to general ill-health and/or general *mental retardation*.

specific learning difficulties (SLD) *specific learning disability.*

specific learning disability See *learning disability.*

specific learning skill Ability to learn a specific skill, and by implication, the recognition that some skills can be learnt more easily than others. The concept can be used to compare individuals or species. Compare with *general learning skill*.

specific reading difficulties (SRD) *developmental dyslexia.*

specific reading retardation (SRR) *developmental dyslexia.*

speech act Minimal length of utterance needed to convey a meaning (depending on the context, this can vary from a single word to a sentence).

speech development stages Typically: 0–4 months – range of crying sounds (depending on nature of pain/need) and pleasure sounds; 4–9 months – phonemes and phoneme-type sounds (see *babbling*); 9–18 months – simple conjunctions of phonemes, first words; 18 months–2 years 6 months – vocabulary explosion, simple phrases, expressions of wishes and thoughts (not just labelling); 2 years 6 months–6 years – acquisition of syntax and emergence of adult-type speech patterns. This would be the pattern for a 'typical' child, but there is enormous variability between individuals. Note also that different researchers use different terms and boundary ages – the above is a general guide. A simpler definition is that as a rule of thumb, an infant/child should be speaking his/her first words by 15 months, have some command of syntax by 30 months, and be reasonably easy to comprehend by 3 years.

speed hypothesis Theory that intellectual decline in old age can be attributed to a general slowing in the speed of nervous functions and in the speed and efficiency of mental processes in general.

spelling age (SA) The level of spelling attainment which is average for a particular age group. A person's spelling age is only revealing of his/her abilities when compared with other 'age' measures (e.g. a 12-year-old with a spelling age of 12 is average, whilst a 7-year-old with a spelling age of 12 is very advanced for his/her years). See *dysphasia*.

Spelling and Reading (SPAR) Tests Reading and spelling test battery. Reading test has same format as *Group Reading Test*. Spelling is to dictation from the experimenter.

spelling-to-sound rules *grapheme-to-phoneme correspondence rules.*

spina bifida Physical paralysis and (sometimes) *mental retardation* resulting from incomplete development of the brain and spine in the developing *foetus.*

spiral curriculum Revisiting the same topic at several stages of the curriculum. The level of complexity with which the topic is treated is increased on each revisitation, commensurate with the pupils' level of knowledge and intellectual skills.

SPLD (alternative: *SLD*) *specific learning difficulties.*

split twins study A research tool in the *hereditarian versus environmentalist theories of individual differences* debate. Identical (*monozygotic*) twins have identical genes. On rare occasions, such twins may be raised separately (i.e. in different environments). If, after separation, their *IQs* are highly correlated, then this strongly supports the *hereditarian theory of individual differences*, because people with the same genes have been reared in different environments, and have developed in the same manner. Such studies have typically found high correlations, but the results have been hotly contested (e.g. about how separate and distinct the environments were), and the fact that one study (conducted by the late Sir Cyril Burt) was allegedly fraudulent has not enhanced their case.

SPM *Standard Progressive Matrices.*

spontaneous drawing Drawing without anything to copy being present at the time of the drawing.

spontaneous visual preference technique *preference study.*

SPQ *Study Process Questionnaire.*

SQ3R *PQRST method* – the initials refer to 'survey, question, read, recite and review', and to the same processes as the PQRST processes.

squint *strabismus.*

SRD *specific reading difficulties.*

SRR *specific reading retardation.*

SSA *Survey of School Attitudes.*

SSHA *Survey of Study Habits and Attitudes.*

stage 4 search error *A not B error.* See *sensori-motor stage 4.*

stage model of development *stage theory.*

Stage 1 grammar Early grammatical constructions of infant speech, characterized by short, simple two or three word phrases, usually devoid of mature grammatical inflections.

Stage Ia children (conservation) See *conservation.*

Stage Ib children (conservation) See *conservation.*

stage theory Any theory which argues that development is a sequence of qualitatively different stages. Most often used to describe *Piaget's* theories of development.

stage theory of development *stage theory.*

Stage III children (conservation) See *conservation.*

Stage IIa children (conservation) See *conservation.*

Stage IIb children (conservation) See *conservation.*

stand line *ground line.*

Standard Assessment Tests (SATs) See *national competency tests.*

Standard English (SE) A form of British English whose rules of syntax and semantics are considered to be most socially 'correct'. This is not as snobbish as it at first sounds – most national and regional variants may be regarded as deviations from Standard English, and accordingly it is the most useful baseline from which to work and teach. See *Received Pronunciation.*

Standard Progressive Matrices (SPM) See *Raven's Progressive Matrices.*

Standard Reading Tests Test battery of reading ability and potential reading problems. Ability is assessed by a sentence reading task. Possible problems are examined with a variety of measures assessing e.g. visual perceptual skills, phonological skills, etc.

Standard Test Lessons in Reading Collection of texts of various (standardized) levels of difficulty. A reading test, but has also been employed to assess accuracy of *readability* formulae.

standardized test A test which is either *domain referenced* or *norm referenced*, and which is reliable, in that different testers should produce identical findings given the same set of subjects. Such tests have well-established procedures for administration and scoring.

Stanford–Binet Scale/Test *IQ* test – the first to be standardized. Based on original work by Binet, standardized by Terman at Stanford University. Revised several times, and still in common use. See *Cattell Infant Intelligence Scale.*

Stanford Diagnostic Mathematics Test (SDMT) Mathematics test battery.

Stanford Diagnostic Reading Test (SDRT) Reading test battery, concentrating on comprehension, decoding, vocabulary, and reading rate.

Stanley Hall's theory of developmental psychology Stanley Hall (1844–1924), psychologist. An early pioneer of psychology (trivia: first American PhD in the subject, and first professor of psychology, in 1884). His theories in developmental psychology concentrated particularly on adolescence, and to a modern reader appear over-moralistic and 'Victorian'. Hall's probable principal influence on developmental psychology was to inspire others to enter the field.

status offences Acts which are only illegal if conducted by an under-age person (e.g. drinking alcohol).

stepping reflex A form of *primitive reflex*. Young babies held upright with their feet just touching the ground will attempt stepping motions. The reflex disappears at circa 2 months unless it is practised. It has been suggested that the reflex is used in the womb when moving through the *amniotic fluid*.

stepping stone theory See *gateway drugs*.

stimulus–response learning (1) Type of learning associated with *behaviourism* – the stimulus given to the subject and the response made to the stimulus are measured, but no assumption is made about the subject's thought processes in making the response. (2) See *signal learning*.

strabismus *Squint* – where the two eyes' 'lines of sight' are not parallel. When one eye points inwards relative to the other, then *convergent strabismus* is said to occur, and *divergent strabismus* occurs when one eye points outwards.

strange situation Measure, devised by Ainsworth, of the level of attachment of a child to his/her parent. It consists of a series of episodes in which: (i) the parent and child enter a room; (ii) a stranger enters; (iii) the parent leaves, leaving the child with the stranger; (iv) the parent returns, and the stranger leaves; (v) the parent leaves, the stranger returns; (vi) the parent returns, the

stranger leaves. The child's reaction to each stage is observed. Three common types of response are observed. A *Group B child*, who has *secure attachment*, protests mildly when the parent leaves, and is comforted by his/her return. A *Group C child*, who shows exaggerated responses (e.g. bawls his/her head off, and clings to the returning parent), is said to be *resistant and insecurely attached* . *A Group A child*, who appears relatively unaffected by the events, and generally avoids the parent upon reunion, is *avoidant and insecurely attached*.

stranger anxiety Distress or wariness shown by a young child or infant upon meeting a stranger. Several researchers have identified a particularly pronounced period of such behaviour in infants aged 9–15 months. See *separation anxiety* and *strange situation*.

stranger reaction The reaction to a stranger – the term is particularly used of young children (where e.g. an extreme display of fright can be indicative of problems).

Strauss Syndrome Named after its author, a collection of behaviours felt to be typical of certain types of brain-damaged children: *hyperactivity*, a failure of *configurational organization, forced responsiveness to stimuli* and *pathological fixation*.

streaming The placement of pupils in classes with other pupils of the same ability level. This is an attempt to overcome some of the problems of *age grading* (i.e. unusually bright or dull pupils can be treated at a level appropriate to their abilities, rather than being frustrated by being taught in the same manner as average pupils). However, this creates the problem that such children feel they are being made an exception of, and hence are in some sense social outcasts.

street mathematics The skill of street vendors at calculating charges for multiple items, change, etc., with a high degree of accuracy. This is contrasted with their poor ability when the same sums are presented in a more formal mathematics test. Many of these studies have concentrated on individuals in developing countries, where the vendors are often children.

strephosymbolia A distortion of symbolic information. Found in e.g. many forms of *developmental dyslexia*.

stroke Damage to brain tissue caused by the cessation of its blood supply. The psychological effect of the stroke very much depends upon the location of the injury. The term is usually reserved for a relatively large scale haemorrhage, in contrast with the *infarct*.

structural lag (reading) The hypothesis that beginning readers need sufficiently mature spoken linguistic and cognitive skills to be able to read properly (see *reading readiness*), and that if their development is retarded, then reading will be faulty. Often identified by a more specific deficit – e.g. *phonological lag* (retarded phonological speech processing), *syntactic lag* (retarded syntactic speech processing), *processing limitation* (retarded memory – particularly *working memory*).

structuralism Any study of the underlying structure of a subject. Most often associated with linguistics and literary studies, but occasionally used in connection with the study of the structure of knowledge and thought (e.g. *Piaget*).

structure d'ensemble (1) In *Piaget's* theory, the state within a stage of development where the various skills have

reached *equilibrium*, and in effect the particular stage is working optimally and characteristically. (2) The simultaneous development of several different skills based on the same underlying ability.

Structure of the Observed Learning Outcome (SOLO) Taxonomy method of classifying older pupils'/students' understanding of the structure and aims of a piece of instruction. Students are asked to describe 'what the course was about', and answers are classified according to how many aspects of the course are mentioned and the degree to which interrelationships between them are identified.

structured interview Interview technique in which the questions and their rder of presentation is fixed. Subjects' responses to questions are not followed up with further questions, although in the *semi-structured interview* they are. In an *unstructured interview*, there may be an initial plan of topics to be covered, but no set order is pre-arranged, and the interview is allowed to find its own course.

Study Process Questionnaire (SPQ) Questionnaire measuring study skills and motivation in older pupils/students. See *Learning Process Questionnaire*.

stuttering Speech impediment characterized by an abnormal and involuntary repetition or elongation of a phoneme or syllable. Has a variety of causes and treatments.

Style 1 language A tendency to concentrate on specifics and a heavy use of single words. See *Style 2 language*.

Style 2 language A tendency to take a wider view, and use of strings of words. See *Style 1 language*.

sub-cortical dementias *Dementias* whose principal focus of damage is not in the *cortex*. Compare with *cortical dementias*.

sub-cortical reflex *primitive reflex*.

subdural haematoma Blood clot in the brain. See *cerebral haemorrhage*.

subitizing Directly perceiving a quantity without counting the items or using another form of calculation.

subjective group When used in connection with *Piagetian* theory, particularly of *sensori-motor development* – see *group*.

subjective reading inventory O l d e r (and now outmoded) term for *informal reading inventory*.

subjective self In developing self-awareness, the discovery in early infancy of one's own existence. This is followed by the acquisition of the ***objective self*** – an awareness that a description of oneself places one in categories shared by others (e.g. name, sex, etc).

substitute pretend play *make-believe play*.

substitution miscue M i s r e a d i n g   o n e word for another.

successful ageing A rather nebulous term. (1) Describes older people whose lifestyles are successful, or at least trouble-free, by cultural standards. (2) More specifically, describes individuals whose psychological skills have retained their youthful levels of performance.

successive scanning See *selection strategies*.

succorant-seeking See *passive–dependent personality*.

sucking reflex *Primitive reflex* – anything placed in the mouth is sucked (useful in getting a baby to suck at the nipple). See *rooting reflex*.

sundown syndrome The phenomenon observed in some *demented* patients, who get up during the night and wander about without apparent regard for the propriety of the time or place.

superego See *Freud's theory of development*.

supernormal ageing *successful ageing*.

supraordinate element When used in *Piagetian* theory – see *grouping I*.

surface approach (learning) See *deep approach (learning)*.

surface dyslexia An *acquired dyslexia* – the patient shows a complex set of symptoms, which most closely resemble a child learning to read. Some words are immediately correctly read, but others have to be 'sounded out', or are pronounced as a word which looks like the to-be-read word.

surface study reading Reading for facts and key ideas. Contrast with *deep study reading*.

Survey of School Attitudes (SSA) Measure of pupils' attitudes to their education.

Survey of Study Habits and Attitudes (SSHA) Measure of study skills and pupils' attitudes to their eduction.

survival reflex A *reflex* which is *innate* and essential to survival, principally to prevent death or serious injury – e.g. breathing, blinking, pupillary (the contraction of the pupil in strong light), and swallowing reflexes.

survivor (1) A person in a particular age group who is still alive (e.g. there are relatively few survivors from the group of people born in 1900, whilst there are a lot from 1984). (2) An individual who has experienced traumatic events.

Swansea Test of Phonic Skills Test of phonological skills, for subjects aged under 7 years.

swimming reflex A type of *primitive reflex*. If a young baby falls into water, then s/he will hold his/her breath and make paddling movements with arms and legs. The reflex disappears at 4–6 months. (Readers are advised not to test this reflex for themselves).

switching pause (SP) The gap between speaker's turns at speaking in a conversation.

syllabic awareness The conscious realization that words are composed of *syllables*, and that different words can have syllables in common. Compare with *phonemic awareness*.

syllabic reading teaching Teaching to read emphasizing an analysis of words into their constituent *syllables*.

syllabic segmentation (1) A popular method of assessing *syllabic awareness* – the subject is required to break down a word into its constituent *syllables*. (2) The ability to perform the task described in (1). See also *phonemic segmentation*.

syllabic writing system Writing system in which symbols represent the *syllables* of the language.

syllable The smallest unit of a word whose pronunciation forms a rhythmic break when spoken (e.g. 'transubstantiation' is a six-syllable word, 'yes' is a one-syllable word).

syllogism Statement about the relationship between two items, inferred from separate statements about the relationships between the two items and other items with which they can be compared. E.g. 'A is a subset of B, B is a subset of C, therefore A is a subset of C: all dogs (A) are mammals (B); all mammals (B) are animals (C); therefore, all dogs (A) are animals (C)'. See *three term series problem* and *transitive inference*.

syllogistic reasoning Ability to solve *syllogisms*.

symbolic deficit theory Theory that a primary deficit in *autism* is an inability to create and use symbolic thought.

symbolic expression Over-wide term for any expression involving symbolic communication (e.g. language, play, drawing and painting, etc.).

symbolic gesture *enactive gesture*.

symbolic grandmother See *apportioned grandmother*.

symbolic parenting Parental response to an infant which indicates by means of verbal and non-verbal communication that something is about to be done to the infant. The **functional parenting** response is simply to do it without preliminaries.

symbolic play *make-believe play*.

symbolic thought See *enactive thought*.

symbolism (children's drawing) Expressing the general properties of the class to which the to-be-drawn object belongs. E.g., a cup with the handle occluded from view may be drawn with a handle because the child knows that cups usually possess handles. This contrasts with *intellectual realism* theory, which argues that the child draws the handle because s/he knows that the cup in question possesses a handle. Evidence for the two viewpoints is mixed.

symbols (Piagetian theory) See *index (Piagetian theory)*.

synaptogenesis The growth and development of synapses (the points of communication between nerve cells).

synchrony The degree to which *décalage* is avoided when acquiring a new skill and/or piece of knowledge. In **point synchrony**, the skill/knowledge is acquired in all its permutations at the same point in time, whilst in *interval syn-chrony*, the acquisition is over a relatively small time period.

syncretic thought The erroneous grouping of disparate and unrelated concepts. Argued by *Piaget* to be a feature of the *preoperational subperiod.*

syntactic competence The mature mastery of syntactic skills.

syntactic lag hypothesis See *structural lag (reading).*

syntactic speech Term used by some commentators (e.g. Lenneberg) to denote stage of speech acquisition (typically 2 years–2 years 6 months) characterized by early use of two word phrases.

synthesis See *Bloom's taxonomy of educational objectives.*

syphilis Venereal disease, which if untreated can (many years after the initial infection) damage the central nervous system, causing *dementia*-like symptoms.

T

tabula rasa Latin for 'blank slate'. Term used by early theorists to describe what they thought was the completely blank and unprepared mind of the new-born infant (see *Locke's theory of human development*). It is now known that babies arrive armed with at least *survival reflexes* and *primitive reflexes*.

tacrine Drug whose effects include the enhanced release of acetyl choline (a key neurotransmitter in the brain – see *cholinergic hypothesis*). It has been cited as a possible treatment for patients suffering from *dementia*. See *ondansetron* and *ganglioside*.

tactile evoked potential See *evoked potential*.

tadpole figure Characteristic early stage of children's drawing, in which the torso and face are represented as one 'blob', with a pair of spindly legs projecting underneath. The overall resemblance is of an anthropomorphic tadpole.

tag question Question formed from a statement with the question section tagged on the end (e.g. 'this is a good programme, isn't it?').

talk engagement Any occasion when talking occurs.

talking doll experiment Experimental technique using a doll (or cuddly toy) with a concealed speaker through which the (hidden) experimenter communicates with the child.

TAP *Test of Academic Progress.*

TAS *Test Anxiety Scale.*

task-related talk In educational theory, verbal interactions relating to the lesson.

tautology When used in *Piagetian* theory – see *grouping I*.

Tay-Sachs disease An *innate* lack of the enzyme hexoseaminidase-A, which results in a failure to process certain fats. This in turn leads to severe physical handicap and *mental retardation*. The patient usually dies before school age.

teacher burnout Exhaustion of teachers' intellect and motivation through stressful classroom and teaching experiences.

Teacher Rating Scale B(2) Twenty-six-item questionnaire eliciting teacher's rating of a pupil's behaviour and aptitude.

technical school See *grammar school.*

telegraphic speech Condensed language, characteristic of telegraph senders and infants learning to talk (e.g. 'hit dog', 'all gone dinner', etc.).

television literacy Understanding the stylistic conventions of television programmes (e.g. fading out one scene and fading in another denoting the passage of time, etc.). See *literacy.*

temperament theory Any theory of development which emphasizes the role of fairly fixed (usually genetically-or-dained) personality traits.

tentative choice stage (of career choice) See *fantasy stage (career choice).*

teratogen General term for any substance or process affecting *foetal* development.

Terman-Merrill tests Revised versions of the original intelligence test by *Binet.*

terminal drop model A theory that older individuals maintain the same level of intellectual functioning until a sudden and precipitous decline a few months/years before their death. See *critical loss.*

terminal phase (of dying) See *acute crisis phase.*

terrible twos Slang term for the onset of 'unreasonable' behaviour (temper tantrums, etc) in many children aged circa two years.

tertiary ageing A phase of rapid deterioration during dying.

tertiary circular reaction See *sensori-motor stage 5.*

tertiary memory *remote memory.*

Test Anxiety Scale (TAS) Early version of the *Achievement Anxiety Test.*

test bias Flaw in the construction of a psychological (usually *IQ*) test, which favours some groups of subjects more than others. E.g., some researchers argue that many IQ tests unfairly favour subjects from a white middle class background.

Test of Academic Progress (TAP) Test battery of scholastic attainment in maths, reading and spelling (plus subtests of writing speed and composition).

Test of Motor Impairment – Henderson Revision (TOMI) Test assessing motor skills (e.g. peg board, catching, hopping, etc.) for children aged 5–11 years.

Test of Reception of Grammar (TROG) Test assessing comprehension of various grammatical forms. Subjects are shown a set of four pictures, and are asked to point to the picture which best describes a sentence read out by the tester. The sentences increase in grammatical complexity as the test progresses. It is designed for use with children (particularly those with suspected language problems), but norms are also available for older, low *IQ* subjects.

test savvy subjects *test wise subjects.*

test smart subjects *test wise subjects.*

test wise subjects Subjects who have been given so many psychology tests that they score higher marks than would be predicted on any further tests, because they are used to the general procedures and wiles of psychologists and their testing procedures.

thanatology The study of death and dying.

theory of mind *mind, theory of.*

theory of mind (autism) *mind, theory of (autism).*

third age See *first age.*

'Thought and Language' See *Vygotsky's theory of development.*

three mountains experiment Test by *Piaget* to demonstrate *egocentrism* in children in the *preoperational subperiod*. The child is placed in front of a model of three mountains, and asked to select a photo showing the view s/he can see, from a set of alternatives. The child does this correctly, indicating that s/he understands the concept involved. A doll is placed at a position different from the child's, and the child is asked to select the photo which represents the doll's view. Children under 8 years are poor at this task (and those aged under 6 years are likely to select a picture of their own view). Analogous results are found if the child is given cardboard models of the mountains and asked to reconstruct the doll's view. The experiment has been criticized for being unnecessarily complicated and confusing for the child – see the *Policeman experiment.*

three Rs Stands for 'reading, 'riting, and 'rithmetic' (i.e. reading, writing and arithmetic). The acronym obviously relies on bad spelling yet, ironically, remains the rallying cry of the *back to basics* educational movement, which stresses the need, among other things, for an increased emphasis on good spelling skills.

three term series problem *Syllogism* with three terms (e.g. A>B, B>C, A?C).

threshold age The *chronological age* which (usually fairly arbitrarily) denotes the start of a particular age group (e.g. 'adulthood', 'old age', etc.).

threshold model of dementia The theory that individuals have a genetically-fixed predisposition to develop *dementia*, but that it requires an environmental cause to push the person past a particular point so that the onset of the illness becomes inevitable. In people with a low predisposition, a large environmental input is required, and vice versa.

tilted cup experiment Ingenious study by *Piaget*. Children were given a drawing of a tilted cup, and asked to draw a line indicating the surface of the liquid in the cup. The correct solution is to draw a line parallel to the true horizontal. However, most children draw a line parallel to the cup's base. The study is an example of how children construct concepts through faulty logic – the error cannot be one of faulty memory, because children can never have seen liquid behave in the way they draw it. (Some (disputed) studies have found the same error in some university students).

time-lag comparison Comparing different *age cohorts'* performance at the same age in a *longitudinal study*.

time-lag effect *cohort effect*.

time on task (TOT) Time spent engaged in the target activity (e.g. in education, the amount of time the pupil spends attending to the lesson versus staring out of the window, etc.).

time-sequential design A curious 'extended' *cross-sectional study* design now no longer practised. Two or more age groups are compared at one time period, and then several years later, different subjects are tested, who are the same ages as the subjects were in the first experiment when they were tested. E.g., a group of 30-year-olds and a group of 40-year-olds are tested in 1970, and then new groups of 30- and 40-year-olds are tested in 1985.

tinnitus A hearing complaint in which the sufferer is afflicted by a (usually permanent) irritating noise (sometimes painful) which interferes with normal hearing. The noise can take many forms, but one of the most common is a high pitched 'ringing in the ears' and hence its lay term.

TMR *trainable mentally retarded*.

t.o. *traditional orthography*.

token economy *Behaviourism*-based method of shaping behaviour/learning by means of reward. Dismissed by many as too mechanistic for 'normal' people, the method has found greatest favour in the training of the mentally ill and retarded. Basically involves giving subjects tokens as a reward for good behaviour/performance (e.g. not hitting other people). When sufficient tokens have been earned, they can be exchanged for a reward (e.g. sweets).

Token Test Assesses comprehension of verbal commands of varying levels of complexity, and short-term verbal memory. Used to measure *acquired aphasia* (in brain damaged and *demented* patients).

Subjects are shown a set of tokens of varying shapes, colours and sizes, and are asked to perform actions with them (e.g. 'put the yellow circle on the blue circle', etc.).

TOMI test *Test of Motor Impairment – Henderson Revision.*

tonic neck reflex Discovered by Gessell (see *Gessell's maturational theory*). A young baby will tend to lie with the head turned to one side, with the arm on that side stretched out, and the other arm bent up, the hand level with the head. Sometimes called the *fencing posture*, because the baby's upper torso and head resemble a fencer in the 'en guard' position.

topic sharing The sharing of an item or belief in common around which a dialogue takes place. The term is sometimes used of mother–infant interaction, in which both parties attend to the same item or event.

TOT *time on task.*

traditional classroom Teaching method where the pupils receive the majority, if not all of, their instruction from the teacher, are set reading tasks and other exercises, desks are arranged in rows, etc. Compare with *open classroom*.

traditional orthography (t.o.) Writing system which uses the conventional letters of the alphabet. Compare with *initial teaching alphabet (i.t.a).*

trainable mentally retarded (TMR) American term – refers to person of very low *IQ* (<50), who can nonetheless be trained to perform very basic tasks. Compare with *educable mentally retarded (EMR).*

trajectory, dying *dying trajectory.*

transductive *Piagetian* term for the linking of *preconcepts* by children in the *preoperational subperiod.*

transductive reasoning Assuming (possibly erroneously) that because two events occur in conjunction, one causes the other.

transfer test Academic or other measure to assess the type of institution to which a candidate should transfer (e.g. *eleven plus*).

transformational-generative grammar *transformational grammar.*

transformational grammar Theory devised by Noam Chomsky, that utterances, although phrased in different ways, derive from the same underlying mental structure (e.g. 'the boy kicked the ball', and 'the ball was kicked by the boy' mean the same thing). It is argued that some of these structures are *innate*, and accordingly, that one is predisposed to learn language in a particular way. See *deep structure.*

transient ischaemic attack *Stroke* whose effects are relatively trivial, and are gone within twenty-four hours.

transition cycle The typical sequence of life events experienced by an individual as s/he progresses through his/her life.

transitional mesosystem See *microsystem.*

transitive When used in *Piagetian* theory – see *grouping V.*

transitive inference In the *Piagetian* theory of cognitive development (particularly the *concrete operations period*), the understanding that the relationship between two items which cannot be compared directly can be inferred by reference to one or more intermediary items. For example, the relationship between A and D can be calculated if one knows that A>B, B>C, and C>D – namely, A>D. See *syllogism*.

transitivity *transitive inference.*

transmitted difficulty (reading) Hypothesis that difficulties with a relatively simple process (e.g. word recognition) may cause problems with more complex skills further down the processing chain (e.g. story comprehension). Explains why beginning readers who cannot master the 'basic' skill of *phonic mediation* are usually bad at other reading skills as well.

transposition problem The subject (a young child) is shown two boxes, A and B, where B is larger than A. S/he learns that B always contains the reward. S/he is then presented with box B and a new box, C, which is larger than B in the same proportion that B is larger than A. The subject should learn to look in C, because the rule the experimenter wants him/her to learn is to always look in the larger of the two boxes. Children of about 5 years and over can do this, but younger children have great difficulty, and persist in looking in B, even though this does not get rewarded. It is argued that this indicates that they cannot transpose the relationship, when the sizes increase, and/or have learnt to respond to the absolute value of B (i.e. they simply look for the same size box).

triad of impairments Term used by Wing & Gould to describe characteristic *autistic* behaviour – impairment of social relationships, social communication and social understanding and imagination.

triarchic theory of intelligence Theory by Sternberg which argues that intelligence is composed of three factors: *componential intelligence* (roughly akin to *fluid intelligence*); *contextual intelligence* (the ability to adapt to and live in one's environment); and *experiential intelligence* (intellectual skills derived from experience).

trichotillomania (TTM) Compulsive hair-pulling.

trichromacy Normal colour vision (i.e. there are the usual three types of colour receptors in the eye). See *dichromacy*.

trimester A period of three months – sometimes used to divide the course of a pregnancy into three stages.

tripod grip The 'traditional' way of holding a pen/pencil, i.e. between the thumb and first and second fingers.

trisomy 21 Most common form of *Down's Syndrome*, in which the patients have an extra chromosome 21.

TROG *Test of Reception of Grammar.*

true speech Term used by some commentators (e.g. Lenneberg) to denote stage of speech acquisition (usually 15–24 months) where vocabulary moves from simple labelling to issuing commands.

TS teaching style.

TTM *trichotillomania.*

tuning See *complex learning.*

Turner's syndrome Genetic abnormality found in females – the patients possess only one *X chromosome* (sometime represented symbolically as XO). Although possessing the external appearance of being female, they lack reproductive organs. Other symptoms include stunted growth and *mental retardation*.

turtle graphics Computer programming exercise for children (using the *LOGO* programming language). The child's commands control the movements of a model or an on-screen turtle.

Twenty Statements Test Measure of adolescent self-perception. Subjects are asked to make a series of statements about themselves. Generally, the older the subject, the fewer responses which sound like replies to a census form (e.g. precise age, full name and address, etc.), and the more about aims, ideals, career hopes, etc.

U

UCLSQ *University College London Study Questionnaire.*

UKRA *United Kingdom Reading Association.*

ultrasound Method of measuring the internal state of certain parts of the body, including, in the case of pregnant women, the state of *foetal* development. Very high frequency sounds are directed through the body and the reflected sound waves are measured, electronically interpreted, and presented as an image on a visual display unit. Can be used to identify some developmental disorders.

Ulverscroft large print series Series of reprints of popular books in large *point size*, for the visually handicapped. Traditional market is older patrons of public libraries.

unconditioned response A response which is habitually and 'naturally' given (e.g. salivating when seeing food). The stimulus causing this is the **unconditioned stimulus.**

unconditioned stimulus See *unconditioned response.*

underextension Using a word to refer to too narrow a range of items and concepts. Typically found in infants learning to speak (e.g. using 'dog' only to refer to the family pet). Compare with *overextension.*

undersocialized conduct disorder See *conduct disorder.*

undifferentiated sex role identity Personality type whose possessors have low scores on measures of both stereo-typically 'masculine' and 'feminine' behaviours. Compare with *androgynous personality.*

unidimensional model of development Theory that all individuals develop in the same sequence of stages.

United Kingdom Reading Association (UKRA) British organization (principally of teachers and educationalists) dedicated to research on reading and reading teaching.

universal ageing Aspects of ageing held to affect everyone who reaches old age (e.g. wrinkling skin). Similar to primary ageing. See *probabilistic ageing.*

universal ethical principle Stage 6 of *Kohlberg's theory of moral development.*

universal processes Mental attributes and operations held to be possessed by all normal individuals, regardless of their environment.

University College London Study Questionnaire (UCLSQ) Measure generating eight sub-scales of personality attributes relevant to study (e.g. motivation, obsessionality, etc.).

unstructured interview See *structured interview.*

Uzgiris-Hunt Scale Test battery of infant development, based on *Piagetian* theory of *sensori-motor development.* Measures include assessment of motor skills, *object concept,* etc.

V

vague syncretic stage In *Vygotsky's theory of development*, proceeding by trial and error. This is followed by the *complexes stage*, in which strategies are used, although not necessarily with great insight. In the *potential concept stage*, the child can only cope with some aspects of a concept at a time, until in the final, mature, stage, s/he can simultaneously manipulate several attributes.

Vai tribe A Liberian tribe who use four different writing systems, depending upon the function of the text. There is some evidence that use of the different systems influences performance at certain intellectual tasks.

variegated babbling *Babbling* in which the there is a switching of consonants and vowels.

vascular dementia *multi-infarct dementia.*

VCA verbal comprehension age.

VEP *visual evoked potential.*

verbal association See *signal learning.*

verbal fluency measure Any measure which assesses the ease with which a subject can produce verbal information. A typical test might be to see how many words beginning with a particular letter can be produced within a time limit, or how many words can be formed out of the letters in another word.

verbal mediation hypothesis Theory that a mental verbal code is used to solve some forms of problem.

veridical perception Perception of the world as it is, without the 'biasing' effect of interpretation.

Vernon-Miller Graded Arithmetic-Mathematics Test A test of mathematical and arithmetical skills. There are two formats, for junior and senior schools.

vertical décalage *Piagetian* term for the changes in a skill when the child moves from one stage of development to the next. Compare with *horizontal décalage* and particularly with *oblique décalage.*

vertical growth The ability successfully to perform tasks of increasing difficulty. Compare with *horizontal growth.*

vertical relationship Relationship with a person at a different level of a hierarchy (e.g. social, knowledge) such as that between a parent and child. In contrast, a *horizontal relationship* is one between two people at the same level.

very low birth weight (VLBW) infant Baby weighing under 1500 grams. Such a low weight carries a significantly heightened mortality risk.

vicariances Also known as *complimentary substitutions.* See *grouping II.*

vicarious reinforcement See *Bandura's theory of social learning.*

Victor See *Wild Boy of Aveyron.*

view from the bridge Title of a play by Arthur Miller. Also, used by some theorists to denote the desired state in old age where older people have come to terms with their past.

Vineland Social Maturity Scale (VSMS) Measure of how capably a child can fend for him/herself. Consists of a checklist of skills (e.g. can button up coat, can use knife and fork, etc.).

visual acuity The ability to focus. At birth, acuity is fairly fixed – babies can focus clearly 9 inches from the face, and can see less clearly at 10–20 inches (9 inches is the approximated distance between the baby's and mother's faces during breastfeeding). The ability to focus at varied distances does not arise until circa 6 months.

visual acuity – measurement Methods of measuring visual acuity vary, but are often expressed as the fraction x:y, where x is the distance from which the subject can accurately identify certain items on the eyesight chart, and y the distance from which a normally-sighted person can see the same items. In normal vision, x and y are equal (hence the well-known expression '20:20 vision'). However, for subjects with poor eyesight, the larger the value of y and/or the smaller the value of x, the worse the acuity. E.g. a subject with 20:80 vision can only see from 20 feet what a normally-sighted person can see from 80. Typically, the ratio is expressed with x having the value of 20, until y exceeds 200; thereafter the value of x is lowered (e.g. what the subject can see from 10 or even 5 feet is tested).

visual cliff Ingenious method for studying depth perception in infants, invented by Gibson and Walk. The apparatus essentially consists of a glass-topped table; the glass is non-reflective. Under one half (the 'solid half') is a checkerboard pattern flush with the underside of the glass. On the floor under the other half of the table (the 'drop' half) is the same checkerboard pattern. Looked at from above (i.e. when the child is on the apparatus), the 'solid' half looks safe to stand on, while the 'drop' half looks to be several feet below the level of the 'solid' half. There have been many permutations of this experiment, but in the original version, a baby old enough to crawl was placed on the 'solid' half, while the baby's mother stood at the end of the 'drop' half and encouraged the baby to crawl to her. Babies would crawl to the edge of the 'solid' half, but would usually refuse to crawl on to the 'drop' half (although in reality it would be perfectly safe to do so). This indicates that the baby can perceive (and fear) depth from visual information alone, and acted against a variety of contemporary theories which argued that babies this young could not do this. A problem with the original design was that babies had to be capable of moving themselves, limiting the study to older babies. Later studies overcame this by moving babies belly down across the apparatus using a trolley, and measuring the babies' physiological reactions (i.e. fear, surprise, etc.).

visual evoked potential (VEP) See *evoked potential*.

visual literacy General term for the ability to interpret visual displays. The term thus describes the ability to interpret conventions of films, television, pictures, etc., to denote concepts (e.g. thought bubbles in cartoons).

visual reading Reading words by their visual appearance rather than by *phonic mediation*. It is an invaluable strategy in reading *irregular spellings* (e.g. 'quay' can only be correctly pronounced using visual reading). For obvious reasons, visual reading can only be used on words already encountered, and accordingly, cannot be used to read new or nonsense words.

visual reading error Misreading a word for one which looks similar (e.g. 'cabbage' for 'cribbage').

visuo-spatial scratchpad See *working memory*.

VLBW *very low birth weight.*

vocalization Any sound made with the vocal chords, whether real words or not.

Von Recklinghausen NF1 Genetic abnormality resulting in a variety of physical ailments and *mental retardation.*

VSMS *Vineland Social Maturity Scale.*

vulnerable period Period of development when the organism is particularly sensitive to certain forms of damage and/or is most likely to show negative results if deprived of certain forms of input.

vulnerability Term used by F Horowitz and others to denote *inherited* problems likely to mar development.

Vygotsky's theory of development Vygotsky (1896–1934), Russian developmental psychologist. Relatively little of his work has been translated from Russian until recently, but what little has been made available (notably his book, *'Thought and Language'*, translated into English in 1962) has been hugely influential, notably on *Piaget* and Bruner. Vygotsky died young (of tuberculosis) but left behind an impressive collection of work (over one hundred research papers alone) although without, alas, a cohesive overview. However, a central theme in his work is the role of language. Vygotsky argued that a child begins to use language purely as a means of communication, and by means of requests, etc., s/he is able to exert some control over his/her environment. However, s/he can also be controlled by speech (e.g. through pa-

rental requests). The child then begins to use speech as a means of controlling his/her own actions, witnessed by the characteristic phase in development when young children talk to themselves while performing an action (e.g. 'I'll put the red brick on top of the blue brick' etc.). This speech eventually becomes internalized into *inner speech*, and becomes a tool of thought (in Vygotsky's view, a higher level of thought than is available without language). Since language is acquired through social interaction, Vygotsky placed a greater emphasis on socialization and instruction than other contemporaries (e.g. Piaget). He devised a *general law of cultural development,* which stated that a skill first appears in a social context, before developing as a psychological skill. He also argued that there is a gap between what a child knows and what s/he can be taught, called the *zone of proximal development.* Vygotsky argued that children differ in the size of their zones (the larger the zone, the more the child is capable of learning). Such an emphasis on the social aspects of learning should be placed against Vygotsky's background in post-Revolutionary USSR. See *vague syncretic stage.*

W

WAIS *Wechsler Adult Intelligence Scale.*

WAIS-R[NI] *Wechsler Adult Intelligence Scale – Revised as a Neuropsychological Instrument.*

'Walden Two' See *Skinner's theory of child rearing.*

Walker Problem Identification Checklist Checklist for teachers, assessing personality problems in their pupils.

warm teacher Teacher who expresses a degree of emotionality to the students (e.g. smiling and being obviously pleased with good work). Opposite of *impersonal teacher.*

warmth versus hostility Scale used for grading the level of emotional content in interactions between family members.

water level problem (1) *tilted cup experiment.* (2) a *conservation of volume* experiment.

Watson's theory of child rearing J o h n Watson (1878–1958), psychologist and journalist. He emphasized a rigid timetable of the 'correct' times when a baby should be fed, bathed, put in the cot, etc. A staunch advocate of *behaviourism*, he argued that children's behaviour and attitudes could be shaped by conditioning. The (in)famous example is the case of ***Little Albert***, a child who was conditioned into fearing a white rat by a loud frightening noise being sounded every time he was shown the rat. Albert subsequently feared not only the rat but many other white furry things. Albert was an orphan, and was adopted and moved away before deconditioning could take place. Not one of psychology's greater achievements.

Watts Vernon (WV) Test Reading test comprising thirty-five *sentence completion* questions.

WCST *Wisconsin Card Sorting Task.*

wear and tear theory Theory of ageing which argues that parts of the body gradually 'wear out' with use. Compare with *cytologic theory.*

Wechsler Adult Intelligence Scale (WAIS) An adult (16–74 years) intelligence test battery covering all commonly assessed areas of intelligence. The tests can be subdivided into those which test verbal skills, and those which have no strong verbal element (the ***Performance scales***). See *WISC.*

Wechsler Adult Intelligence Scale – Revised as a Neuropsychological Instrument (WAIS-R[NI]) Adaptation of the *WAIS* with revised and new tests, designed for assessment of patients with compromised intellectual/linguistic abilities.

Wechsler Deterioration Quotient (DQ) *deterioration quotient.*

Wechsler Individual Achievement Test (WIAT) Manual giving *standardised* procedure for combining scores on *WOLD, WOND* and *WORD* tests to form a composite measure of individual academic achievement. A truncated and faster to administer version – *WIAT-Quicktest* – is also available.

Wechsler Intelligence Scale for Children (WISC) The *WAIS* adapted for older children (7–16 years). The tests can be subdivided into those which test verbal skills, and those which have no strong verbal element (the *Performance scales*). See *Bannatyne-WISC categories* and *Wechsler Preschool and Primary Scale of Intelligence.*

Wechsler Memory Scale (WMS) Memory test battery for adults (16–74 years).

Wechsler Objective Language Dimensions (WOLD) *Test battery* of linguistic skills (listening comprehension, written and oral expression) for children aged 6 years – 16 years 11 months.

Wechsler Objective Numerical Dimensions (WOND) *Test battery* of numerical skills (mathematics reasoning and basic arithmetic skills) for children aged 6 years – 16 years 11 months.

Wechsler Objective Reading Dimensions (WORD) Reading (word recognition and prose comprehension) and spelling *test battery* for children aged 6–16 years. Cross-linked with *WISC, WPPSI* and *WAIS.*

Wechsler Preschool and Primary Scale of Intelligence (WPPSI) Intelligence test battery, derived from the *WAIS,* for young children (3–7 years). See *Wechsler Intelligence Scale for Children.*

Wechsler test suffixes Often a Wechsler test (see e.g. preceding entries) carries a suffix, denoting the particular form or edition. A common suffix is 'R', denoting a 'revised' version (though this does not necessarily mean it is the most recent revised version). A number (in Roman numerals) denotes the edition. A suffix of initials denotes the country for which the test is *standardized* (e.g. 'UK' denotes United Kingdom). At the time of writing, the most current versions (for the UK) are: *WAIS:* WAIS-R (1986); *WAIS-R^{NI}:* WAIS-R^{NI} (1991); *WISC:* WISC-

III (1992); *WMS:* WMS-R (1987); *WOLD:* WOLD (1995); *WOND:* WOND (1995); *WIAT:* WIAT (1995); *WORD:* WORD (1993).

Werner syndrome An illness akin to *progeria* in its effects, but whose onset is in the late teens, rather than at birth. Patients display signs of ageing at a faster rate than normal, and usually die in their forties.

Wernicke's dementia *Dementia* caused by vitamin deficiency (particularly Vitamin B). Often there is an associated motor impairment.

whole word (reading teaching) Method of teaching reading which emphasizes the use of *visual reading* strategies. Compare with *phonics (reading teaching).*

why not? conservation *pseudo-conservation.*

WIAT *Wechsler Individual Achievement Test.*

WIAT-Quicktest See *Wechsler Individual Achievement Test.*

Wide Range Achievement Test (WRAT) Test battery assessing basic reading, maths, and spelling skills.

Wide-span Reading Test Reading test for subjects aged 7–15 years. A type of *cloze procedure* test – the required word is presented in the sentence preceding the test sentence.

Wild Boy of Aveyron *Feral child,* discovered when he was 7–8 years old, in 1800. Some suggestion that he was *autistic,* which may have caused his initial abandonment. First described by JMG Itard, who called him *Victor.*

WIPI Test *Word Intelligibility Picture Identification Test.*

WISC *Wechsler Intelligence Scale for Children.*

Wisconsin Card Sorting Task (WCST) Measure of hypothesis formation and the ability to reject or not persevere with an invalid one. Subjects must discover the correct rule for matching up cards of differing patterns and colours (e.g. a yellow card must always be matched with a red card, etc.). Once they have discovered the correct rule, the experimenter changes the rule; the speed at which the subject stops using the old rule and searches for the new one is measured, as well as how quickly s/he solves the new problem. The test is used with average subjects and patients of all ages, but is of considerable use in research on older people.

WM *working memory.*

WMS *Wechsler Memory Scale.*

WOLD *Wechsler Objective Language Dimensions.*

WOND *Wechsler Objective Numerical Dimensions.*

Woodcock-Johnson Psycho-Educational Battery Test battery assessing intellectual skills in children. The battery broadly assesses intelligence, achievement and general interests.

WORD *Wechsler Objective Reading Dimensions.*

word blindness The best literal synonym is *alexia*, but the term is often used interchangeably with *dyslexia* (particularly *developmental dyslexia*).

word identification Term used by some commentators (e.g. Lenneberg) to denote stage in baby's speech development (typically reached at 12–15 months) in which first words are produced, and there are some responses made to simple requests.

Word Intelligibility Picture Identification (WIPI) Test Vocabulary measure, often used to test word identification skills in hearing-impaired children. The subject is told the name of an object, and has to point to the picture of the target from a multiple choice.

working memory (WM) Model of short-term memory, first proposed by Baddeley and Hitch, but subsequently considerably modified. The model essentially consists of a central controller, called the *central executive,* which can itself hold in store a couple of items, but which usually passes on memorization tasks to specialized 'slave systems'. These include a *phonological loop* (in earlier versions of the model, this was called the *articulatory loop*), which memorizes verbal materials (letters, words, and numbers); and a slave system for memorizing visual (what something looks like) and spatial (where items are located relative to each other) materials (the *visuo-spatial scratchpad*). Slave systems have a limited capacity (i.e. they can only remember a limited number of items). The virtue of the working memory model is that it can comfortably account for how information can be held 'in mind' while other mental processes take place (e.g. 'carrying over' numbers in mental arithmetic).

WPPSI *Wechsler Preschool and Primary Scale of Intelligence.*

WRAT *Wide Range Achievement Test.*

writing readiness Possession of skills and knowledge necessary to learn to write. See *reading readiness.*

wug test Test assessing children's knowledge of *morphology* (word structure). Named after an item on the test. The child sees a picture of an imaginary animal called a 'wug'. S/he is then shown a picture of two of these animals and is asked what they are called. A correct answer ('wugs') indicates that the child understands the principle of how to alter the structure of words, since s/he had never encountered the word 'wug' before, and thus cannot simply be answering from memory.

WV *Watts Vernon (WV) Test.*

X

XYY syndrome In males, possession of an extra Y *chromosome*. Can result in *mental retardation* and/or an unusually high level of aggression.

Y

Yerkes-Dodson law The phenomenon whereby the more complex the item to be learnt, the lower the optimal level of motivation/arousal. In other words, complex tasks are best performed when a person has a low level of arousal, whilst the reverse applies for simple tasks. This has been debated.

young elderly The most common definition is the age group between 60 and 75 years (though some leeway in these boundaries is not unknown). See *old elderly*.

young–old plot Plotting on a graph the performance of young subjects on one axis versus the performance of older subjects on the same task on the other axis. The slope of the line gives an indication of how disadvantaged older people are relative to the young.

Z

zeitgeist Spirit of the (historical) age.

Zimmer frame A walking aid for those of restricted walking ability (particularly older people). Consists of a stable four-footed metal frame which is held by the walker in front of him/her and which is leant on for support.

zone of proximal development See *Vygotsky's theory of development.*